Memory, Psychology and Second Language Learning

Mick Randall

British University in Dubai

John Benjamins Publishing Company

Amsterdam / Philadelphia

^{TM} The paper used in this publication meets the minimum requirements of American National Standard for Information Sciences – Permanence of Paper for Printed Library Materials, ANSI z39.48-1984.

Library of Congress Cataloging-in-Publication Data

Randall, Mick, 1946-
   Memory, psychology, and second language learning / Mick Randall.
      p.   cm. (Language Learning & Language Teaching, ISSN 1569-9471 ; v. 19)
   Includes bibliographical references and index.
   1. Second language acquisition. 2. Psycholinguistics. 3. Memory. I. Title.
P118.2.R363   2007

418--dc22   2007018286
ISBN 978 90 272 1977 0 (Hb; alk. paper)
ISBN 978 90 272 1978 7 (Pb; alk. paper)

John Benjamins Publishing Co. · P.O. Box 36224 · 1020 ME Amsterdam · The Netherlands
John Benjamins North America · P.O. Box 27519 · Philadelphia PA 19118-0519 · USA

Table of contents

Preface

This book aims to review the work done in psychology and linguistics on language processing and to relate it to the learning of a second language. It is aimed at the student language teacher who will also be studying aspects of linguistics such as phonology alongside psychological theories and theories of language learning. It is an attempt to pull together the two disciplines with a specific focus on the second language learner. It will also be of interest to postgraduate students in offering them a wide variety of sources for further research. It is also, I hope, an aid for the experienced teacher who is interested in putting current theories of language learning and teaching into a new perspective. In particular, the inclusion of the neuropsychical evidence for established psycholinguistic models provides a interesting perspective for the more general reader who is interested in language processing.

Much of the material on psychology will be familiar to the psychologist and likewise, to the linguist, many of the observations about the structure of languages will be well known. To the purist in either discipline, the ideas may seem overly simplified and some may disagree with the interpretations offered in this book. However, the views in this book are from the perspective of the language teacher and it represents an interpretation of the ideas from both disciplines as they have become incorporated in methods of teaching. In terms of content, the book does not set out to be ground-breaking, but it sets out to provide an interpretation of the field of language processing for an applied audience. By examining the theories and theoretical models from the point of view of the second language learner this book provides a platform of theory on which the student and teacher can evaluate different learning approaches and the learning processes of students. What is different about the book is not the information that it contains *per se*, but the way that information is juxtaposed and the interpretations drawn. It is written by someone who cut his educational teeth on audio-lingualism, but has spent most of his professional career in a communicative language teaching environment. The ideas provided from within the communicative paradigm are certainly important, and powerfully felt by the writer. But, from my experience as someone who has also viewed second language learning in a wide variety of less well resourced settings, the communicative route to language learning can only offer part of the answer. The reliance of many classrooms worldwide on more traditional forms of learning attests to the power of these forms of learning in many minds and this book hopefully shows that there is considerable psychological evidence from learning theory to support these more traditional approaches to teaching. Such traditional approaches are often employed more in elementary and intermediate contexts – again contexts which are probably the most common in the world. This book concentrates on learners in such contexts rather than more advanced learners.

In a similar way, the changes in methodological approaches, from drilling and practice to communication, are underpinned by movements in psychology, from a behaviourist to a cognitive psychological paradigm. The early attempts of the behaviourists to concentrate solely on the matching of external stimuli with observable behaviour and the lack of attention paid to the internal operation of the mind seemed disappointing to me as a young prospective psychology undergraduate in the early sixties. Yet my experience as a teacher of English as a second language, and my own introspection as a struggling second language learner, has made me aware of the fundamental importance of many of the concepts involved in basic associative learning procedures.

Central to all, it seems to me, is memory, and this is the starting point of this book. As set out above, it is not designed as an exhaustive review of either psychology or linguistics – that would be well beyond the scope of this book. It is a selection of, what are to me, key ideas in both fields and their application to second language teaching and learning.

Mick Randall
May 2007

Copyright acknowledgement

The author and publisher tried to obtain permission for reproduction of the figures whenever possible and received permission for the following: the diagram of the multi-component model of working memory from Baddeley, A.D. 2000. The episodic buffer: A new concept of working memory? *Trends in Cognitive Sciences. Volume* \4(11): 417–423, published by Elsevier Health; the balloon cartoon from Bransford, J. & Johnson, M. 1972. Contextual pre-requisites for Understanding: some Investigations of Comprehension and Recall. *Journal of Verbal Learning and Verbal Behavior Volume 11*, 717–726, published by Elsevier Health; the diagram of the holistic/analytical continuum for different scripts from Wydell T.N. & Kondo T. 2003. Phonological deficit and the reliance on orthographic approximation for reading: A follow–up study on an English–Japanese bilingual with monolingual dyslexia. *Journal of Research in Reading* 26(1): 33–48, permission granted by UKLA; the Bock and Levelt network model from Bock, K. & Levelt, W. 1994. Language production, grammatical encoding. In *Handbook of Psycholinguistics*, M.A. Gernsbacher (ed.). San Diego CA: Academic Press, permission granted by Elsevier Health; the general diagram of the connectionist model from Rumelhart, D.E. & J.L. McClelland. 1986. On learning the past tenses of English verbs. In *Parallel Distributed Processing*, Vol. 2, J.C. McClelland & D.E. Rumelhart (eds), 216–271. Cambridge MA., published by the MIT Press; a fragment of an interactive-activation network from McClelland, J.L. & Rumelhart, D.E. 1981. An interactive activation model of context effects in letter perception. Part 1. An account of the basic findings. *Psychological Review* 88: 375–407, published by the American Psychological Association; and a spreading activation model from Collins, A.M. & Loftus, E.F. 1975. A spreading activation of semantic processing. *Psychological Review* 82: 407–428, published by the American Psychological Association.

Acknowledgements

I would like, first of all, to thank Jan Hulstjin for his encouragement and support throughout this project and for the comments that he and Nina Spada have provided on the text. I would also like to thank the many observations made by an anonymous reviewer who pointed out many inaccuracies and offered suggestions on the draft. However, any inaccuracies which remain are my own. I would also like to thank my wife, Lynn Randall, for careful editing and feedback on early versions, a number of my students at the British University in Dubai who read earlier chapters and offered very valuable comments and to Kees Vaes and the team at John Benjamins for their work in bringing the final manuscript to print. Finally, my thanks to the students who I have taught over the years and who have helped me to develop the exercises which are included in the workbook.

Introduction

Background

Language is uniquely human. No other animal has the ability to communicate with anything like the complexity that humans do. The size[1] and complexity of the brain is also a major distinguishing feature of human beings. No other species has the billions of neurons and interconnections of the cerebral cortex. Indeed, palaeontologists classified and differentiated early hominid species by the evolving size of the cranium. Although other animal species have been shown to have systems of communication, none has anything remotely comparable in complexity to that of human beings. The size and complexity of the brain has allowed human beings to engage in reasoning and conceptualising way beyond that of other animal species. As a consequence of this, humans have been remarkably successful as a species in their ability to alter their environment through the capability of thinking and reasoning. Thinking and language are closely connected and any study of the uniqueness of human beings should involve the connection between the remarkable organ which produces thought, the brain, and the artefact that is produced, language.

This book is essentially about the connection between language and the processes which produce it. Traditionally, the study of language is the province of linguistics and the study of mental processes is the province of psychology. This book is about the contributions that both of these disciplines can make to our understanding of the way that languages are processed and from that, how first languages are acquired and how second languages are learnt.[2] It will provide an introduction to important ideas and theories which

---

1. The dolphin brain is similar in size to the human brain and has a larger temporal lobe, but this is probably dedicated to the processing of echo-location signals.

2. The terms 'acquired' and 'learnt' will be used throughout this book to describe the processes by which people go about gaining some sort of mastery of a language. The book will say that a language is 'acquired' when the processes involved are not conscious, when the processes are largely 'implicit' rather than 'explicit'. This is obviously true of the early stages of gaining first language mastery (although during schooling, first language speakers will also be 'taught' features of the language). Learning, however, involves conscious attention to the process. This is the process which is used to a large degree in instructed second language learning – where second languages are learnt in a classroom situation (R. Ellis, 1990), although it is not suggested that processes of acquisition do not also take place in instructed language contexts. Thus the terms 'acquired' and 'leant' are basically related to the processes undertaken, but they also have a close relationship to the learning contexts.

have shaped thinking in psychology and linguistics through the perspective of second language learning and teaching. This examination will concentrate on bottom-up processes of decoding, both of the spoken and written word, and will use this focus to examine different approaches and methodologies for teaching second languages, particularly ESL.

Both psychology and linguistics have undergone profound changes in the last half of the twentieth century. They have both moved from a 'descriptive' approach which dealt with the measurement and description of external behaviour to a more speculative approach based on using behaviour to build models of cognitive processing. The different approaches to psychology and linguistics have influenced second language learning and teaching. From the audio-lingual methods, which drew their inspiration from the work of the behaviourist psychologists and structural linguists, through to communicative language teaching (CLT) methods, which derive their theoretical underpinning from cognitive psychologists, generative linguists and sociolinguistics, findings from psychology, linguistics and psycholinguistics have had a strong influence on second language teaching methodologies. What these methods have drawn from psychology and linguistics is a concern with, on the one hand, the structure and operation of the human mind, and, on the other, models of language. The aim of this book is to provide an overview of the contributions of the two disciplines, psychology and linguistics, to our understanding of how languages work and in particular how this knowledge may be applied to the teaching and learning of second languages.

In addition, the later half of the twentieth century saw the arrival of new technologies which provide detailed images of the internal workings of the brain. This, along with studies of patients with different language impairments, saw a growth in interest in the discipline of neuropsychology, which again concentrates on the internal workings of the brain. This is in contrast to the study of external manifestations of behaviour, which had been the concern of the first half of the twentieth century. This book, then, will also look at neuropsychological evidence to see how it can be used to substantiate the processes derived from psychology and linguistics.

The structure of the book

The book is divided into two sections. Section one provides an overview of the field, examining the different aspects of language processing and learning. It is designed as an introduction and discussion of the topic and is aimed at teachers, students studying second language teaching, and those with an interest in second language learning. Section 2 is a Workbook. It provides a number of exercises/examples of the issues discussed in Section 1. These examples can be used by the individual reader to exemplify the theories and models discussed in the first section, but they can also be used by tutors in group sessions with students to provide a basis for discussion in more formal learning situations.

Section 1

Chapter 1 provides a discussion of the sort of evidence that can be gained from the different disciplines associated with language processing and learning and discusses the shift from behaviourist to cognitive psychology. It introduces the main information processing model of language comprehension and the major cognitive structures implied by this model. It specifically discusses the concepts of neural networking, connectionism, and back-propagation which are central to cognitive models of language processing and looks at the evidence that exists for such concepts, particularly the contribution that is being made by neuropsychological evidence from brain imaging techniques.

Chapter 2 examines the way that the brain deals with perception, pays attention to significant features of language and works on the incoming information to make sense of the sounds we hear. It discusses the role of the Sensory Register and Working Memory in these processes and the way that psychological evidence supports linguistic theory in providing a working model of language perception. It describes the contribution that phonology has made to our understanding of decoding sounds, and discusses the different ways this can be accommodated using serial and parallel processing approaches. It also identifies the problems faced by the second language speaker and specifically the adult second language learner in using such a system for extracting the significant features of the second language from the information provided by the senses.

Chapter 3 then examines the way that written language is processed through the use of the information processing model. It further explores the feature detection theories and the application of connectionist thinking about language processing, paying particular attention to word recognition. It looks at the two ways we can recognise words (as whole words or as a sequence of letters) as they apply to English and discusses them in relation to other languages. It looks at word recognition in different scripts and the way that these scriptal systems may effect the way that words are recognised.

Chapter 4 then discusses the role that top-down processes work on both speech and writing. It looks at the role that knowledge of syntax and language form play in the comprehension of language. It also examines the part that knowledge of the wider world – cultural schema and personal knowledge – plays in understanding and interpreting text. This is discussed initially from the point of view of the fluent L1 speaker and the implications of this approach are then discussed with regard to the second language learner.

Chapter 5 continues with an examination of the way that language is stored in Long Term Memory. It reviews the different models of the mental lexicon, its structure and the form that words might take, again drawing evidence from both linguistics and psychology. The models describe the way that native speakers store vocabulary and this architecture is again questioned from the perspective of the second language learner. It also examines the issue of the use of L1 in the storage and retrieval of words in the L2.

Chapters 2 to 5 examine the role that memory plays in language comprehension. Chapter 6 turns its attention to the role that memory plays in learning a language. It examines different learning theories as applied to language. It also critically examines relevance to second language learning of approaches which emphasise acquisition and explores the concepts of implicit and explicit learning within the context of second languages and general psychological models of learning.

Chapter 7 then applies the ideas generated in the book to classroom methods. It reviews currently accepted general communicative language teaching approaches, and discusses these in the light of ideas which have been developed of cognitive processes involved in second language learning. It also examines some more 'traditional' techniques used in many low-resourced classrooms from the same standpoint. It specifically examines those methodologies associated with so-called 'Confucian' societies, and tries to draw some conclusions concerning their usefulness, again in the light of the psychological theories that the book develops.

Section 2

This section, the Workbook, contains a series of exercises which complement the discussion in the first section. Whilst the first section acts as an explanation of the major theories and the evidence for them, the second section provides the opportunity for the reader or for a class of learners to explore for themselves the ideas presented in the first half. Attention is drawn in Section 1 to exercises in the workbook which illustrate the ideas being discussed. The workbook section can either be used in tutorials and seminars for students to work on in pairs or groups to either exemplify the psychological/linguistic points being made in the main text, or transfer the ideas to a specific language learning/teaching situation. The same activities can be also be used by the individual reader to further explore the areas for themselves.

Chapter 1

Looking critically at the Field

What sort of evidence do psychology and linguistics provide about SLL?

As stated in the introduction modern ideas about how languages are processed and learnt have drawn heavily on the disciplines of psychology and linguistics. Both disciplines have undergone major shifts in thinking in the second half of the last century and this chapter will provide a background to these shifts and evaluate the insights gained from psychology and linguistics into the way that languages are processed and learnt. It will also discuss the evidence that can be supplied from cognitive neuroscience. This includes evidence from language impairment following brain damage and the evidence from imaging technologies allowing us to look inside the brain and view its activity. It will examine the type of evidence each approach provides and will answer the following questions:

1. What is the difference between behaviourist and cognitive psychology?
2. How did psycholinguistics change the view of language learning?
3. What is the evidence for a language-specific module in the brain?
4. What are the cognitive structures thought to be involved in processing information?
5. How does connectionism contribute to our understanding of language processing?
6. What evidence can be supplied from studying the physiology of the brain?

1.1   Behaviourist and cognitive psychology

The Behaviourist psychological tradition was concerned with providing an explanation of human and animal behaviour. It attempted to manipulate conditions and measure behaviour so that general laws could be formed about how external influences, stimuli, affected human and, more often, animal behaviour. One of the central concepts in behaviourist thinking was learning through trial-and-error. This involved non-directed, 'random' behaviour, some aspects of which become reinforced by a positive reward. The basic procedure involved the stimulus, the response and the different conditions in which the two happened, the reinforcement. Positive reinforcement was shown to be a major factor in shaping behaviour, and the more often the response was reinforced, the stronger the response was associated with the particular stimulus and the more rapid it was. The process of tying a response to a particular stimulus is known as associative learning and it still forms a major explanation of how certain aspects of language are learnt. Another of the central conditions for effective language learning is that of making language processing automatic. The tying of a particular stimulus to a response through a process of intensive practice is an obvious mechanism for attaining such automatic processes.

However, there are a number of problems with this view of learning when it comes to language learning. Many of the experiments were carried out with animals (in the famous 'Skinner Box') and the first difficulty concerns the transferability of findings with animals to complex human behaviour, of which language is a prime example. The second concerns the lack of attention paid to the role that the brain plays any part in shaping the behaviour; it is a 'Black box' which is acted on by external factors.

In terms of language learning and use the theory viewed paired associates such as

> "Did you go home?"
> "Yes I did"

as the basis on which languages worked. The surface form of "did" in the past form question and answer become automatically linked to the verb through the association of a stimulus and response. There was no suggestion that the brain is involved in thinking, in deciding to use the past tense, in choosing "did" rather than "do", or in deciding to provide information. Responses are automatic reactions to stimuli.

The behavioural tradition seeks to discover verifiable relationships between observable facts and external behaviour. Indeed, the discipline of neuroscience continues this tradition by trying to establish relationships between behaviour and brain activity through imaging studies. General 'laws' such as the Power Law of Practice state that there is a relationship between the number of times a task has been practiced and the speed with which it is executed (if the two are plotted as log values on a graph, then they generate a straight line). These powerful ideas still underpin much later thinking about learning in general and are obviously applicable to certain aspects of language learning, particularly second language learning. However, the power law relates observable behaviour to factors in the environment, e.g. the frequency and number of repetitions, but in Behaviourist Psychology, there was no explanation in terms of the way that the brain may have been effected by such repetitions, about the concept of memory and storage or of the way that the process of memorisation may have been affected by attentional processes in the brain. The subject/actor was a passive recipient of outside forces and played no significant part in the process. Memory was purely a set of relationships between stimuli and responses.

However, with the arrival of cognitive psychology in the late nineteen fifties, psychologists turned their attention to the mind and mental representations leading to the role of cognition and volition in shaping behaviour. Psychologists continued to use the evidence from behaviour, but they began to use behaviour to hypothesise about the mechanisms which might create the behaviour, to build models of how the brain might operate based on observations of behaviour. Thus, the famous series of experiments which discovered that roughly seven (plus or minus one or two), but not more, bits of information could be repeated back immediately (Miller, 1956), provided evidence for the long-held hypothesis (see James, 1890, primary and secondary memory) that there exists within the brain different types of memory a short term memory (STM) store with a restricted capacity which is different from a long-term memory (LTM). Similarly, Sperling's work with briefly presented arrays of letters (Sperling, 1960) led to the conclusion that there exists a temporary perceptual store where incoming material is held for a brief time before being passed to the STM for further processing. Evidence such as this led to the information-processing models of Atkinson & Shiffrin (1968) which we shall use as the central framework for our examination of how the mind works (see this chapter, p 14 and for a description of the cognitive revolution, and Anderson, 2000).

This extension of the range of psychological thinking from the external to the internal is an important paradigm change and forms the background to much of the discussion in this book. However, there are two important points of caution that need to be stated before we look at the major models of cognitive processing which evolved in the fifties and sixties.

1.   The first is that constructs such as short term memory, working memory and long term memory are only models, not physical realities.

2.   Secondly, cognitive psychologists build their models on the observation of individuals working on tasks, often in laboratory settings. For example, much of the work on learning concerned relatively simple and certainly highly artificial tasks such as the learning of lists of words under different conditions. Such tasks (which have a long history in psychology going back to the 19th century) are a far cry from the complex tasks involved in natural language processing and learning.

However, there is a branch of cognitive psychology which emerged in the late nineteen fifties which combined psychology and linguistics: psycholinguistics. The psycholinguists also use behaviour to derive cognitive models, but the behaviour they concentrate on is language itself. Their explanation of the way that languages are used and processed are based on models supplied from linguistics. The behaviour they observed is language in a naturalistic setting, most notably the way that first languages are acquired.

1.2   Psycholinguistics, acquisition and modularity

Eysenck and Keane (1995: 1) describe a meeting at MIT in 1956 when, among others, Miller presented a paper on the magic number 7 in short-term memory and Chomsky gave a preliminary paper on his theory of language. 1956 also saw the foundation of AI (artificial intelligence) and, whilst we shall not be concerned with AI as such, the use of computational models to understand language processing is important in the development of connectionism which has become highly influential in thinking about language learning.

We have already alluded to the use of Miller's observation of behaviour to postulate the existence of a short-term memory store and we shall further investigate the processing implications of the short term memory later in this chapter, but here we shall examine the effect that Chomsky has had on thinking about language and about language acquisition.

The most problematic aspect of Behaviourist thinking on language is the attempt to explain all learning in terms of stimulus-response chains. It was this aspect for which Skinner was critically taken to task by Chomsky in his famous review of Skinner's Verbal Behaviour (Skinner, 1957) in the journal *Language* (Chomsky, 1959). The dramatic change in thinking about language learning which was ushered in by Chomsky's review and the subsequent criticism of Behaviourist approaches to language led to a completely different way of looking at language. Behaviourists had seen language as in no way different from other forms of activity. Languages were learnt by specific stimulus-response connections in the way that a pigeon could be trained to produce certain actions in response to certain rewards and these could be linked together, step by step, to form more complicated actions by a process of chaining. More complex behaviours could be explained as a succession of learned S-R steps. Language knowledge was accommodated through the notion of 'verbal associations' (see the description of Gagné's (1985) hierarchy of learning in Chapter 6 of this book) and a notion of grammar was accommodated by a process known as 'analogy', but the process was essentially driven by primary associations between stimuli and responses. Chomsky's contribution was to point out that there are an infinite number of sentences which can theoretically be produced in any language and the ability of humans to understand and produce quite novel utterances which had never been encountered before. Such factors are difficult to explain through simple learnt stimulus-response mechanisms. His response was to suggest that:

- ❑   Language is a unique human attribute;
- ❑   Language is an autonomous cognitive ability;
- ❑   Language acquisition is an innate ability hard-wired into the human brain, and that all children will learn a language given the necessary environment.

Furthermore, the suggestion was that, through the study of language, we could understand human cognition (Chomsky, 1972). That the study of language structure would, by itself, shed light on the operation of the mind.

The three consequences of this approach which we wish to consider here, and which have had a powerful influence on the last fifty years of thinking about language learning are:

1. Languages are acquired naturally; language acquisition is innate. There is a specific module in the brain which processes language, the Language Acquisition Device (LAD) and that this device is 'hard-wired' into the human brain.

2. This device works on a series of 'principles' and 'parameters'. Principles are common to all languages and the parameters are set by each different language. These basic principles are defined by a Universal Grammar (UG) but realised in different languages by different switches or parameters. Children apply principles to learn a language.

3. That speakers have an underlying abstract knowledge of the language ('competence') which is separate from the actual language produced ('performance'). It is the language 'competence' which enables speakers to understand and produce the infinite number of actual sentences which can be produced in any language. This competence refers to an idealized, internal, mental representation (Chomsky refers to 'I-language') of a set of generative rules which can be used to construct the actual language produced (Chomsky's 'E-language') (for a discussion, see Lyons, 1996).

These four consequences lead to three important approaches to language comprehension and use; the modular, the symbolist and nativist approaches.

The Modular approach to language processing. The first of Chomsky's constructs, the LAD, has had a profound influence on thinking about language processing. One approach, which we shall describe in the next section, is to suggest that there are common information processing systems for all types of information; they are not language specific. Such a notion is central to Macwhinney's Competition Mode (Macwhinney, 1987) and to connectionist thinking about language. The Chomskian approach, however, suggests that there exists a separate, dedicated device for learning language which is an innate characteristic of all humans. The idea is a powerful one and rests on evidence from cross-cultural studies of first language acquisition. In particular, it attempts to explain the non-linear development in language acquisition where child language develops through phases based on developing sets of internal 'rules'. These rules are not the rules of the mature language, but are formulated by the child from the exposure to data. For example, the child learning the irregular past tense in English would typically go through the following stages:

1.	The verb "go" and a past tense marker	*"I go yesterday"*
2.	The verb "went" in set phrases	*"I went yesterday"*
3.	An attempt to use the regular past tense rule with go, "goed"	*"I goed yesterday"*
4.	Finally, the correct irregular form of "go" in all circumstances	*"I went yesterday"*

This universal tendency for children to develop their own internal rule systems and to generate[1] "incorrect" sentences like 3 above, which they can never have heard, is obviously, a strong argument against the simple behaviourist view that language is learnt by pure imitation (for a powerful exposition of the modular and nativist approach, see Pinker, 1994 and for the evidence of the cross-cultural universality of L1 language development, see Slobin, 1985). Evidence such as this led to the suggestion that there exists an innate mechanism for analysing and generating language, different from a simple associative learning mechanism.

The suggestion that there exists a separate language processing mechanism has led to a debate within psychology as to the existence of such a system which is separate from normal cognitive processes (the 'modularity' debate). It has also had a profound influence on thinking about second language acquisition (see Chapter 6), although its applicability to second language learning (i.e. a second language learnt in classroom settings) is not without controversy and is an area to which we shall return many times. In particular we shall examine the following questions:

❑   To what extent does the 'modular' approach to language processing provide a good model for explaining how languages are processed?
❑   What role would an LAD play in instructed second language learning situations?

The Symbolist Approach. Closely associated with the existence of an innate processing system is the concept of Universal Grammar. The UG concept is based on the premise that all languages use a limited number of symbolic systems to communicate.

❑   All languages are able to use rules to generate a possible infinite number of sentences e.g. 'the cat sat on the mat, that was close to the door which was in the house which ......' This is known as the principle of recursiveness or recursion.
❑   All spoken languages use a restricted number of phonetic signs, combined in different ways to achieve meaning.
❑   All languages use syntactic devices to express basic syntactic relations between word classes (nouns and verbs, for example).
❑   All languages conform to general principles such as the uniqueness principle, the late closure principle and the principle of minimal attachment (Aitchison, 1998).[2]
❑   All languages have means of expressing basic meaning contrasts (such as singular, plural).

---

1.   The term 'generate' in linguistics and in UG/TGG (Transformation Generative Grammar) has a specific meaning which relates to the use of abstract rules to transform one linguistic form into another and so to generate and comprehend an infinite number of sentences. It does not refer to the production of sentences. Unless otherwise stated, this book will use the term 'generate' in its more general sense.

2.   The search for such principles has been the aim of much UG research. The aim was to find a restricted set of principles which could be used by Transformational Grammars to construct all languages. Such principles could also be used to define language as separate from other cognitive processing systems and animal communication. Recently, Chomsky has adopted a minimalist position which suggests that the recursive principle is the essential feature of human language (see Hauser et al (2002) and the discussion between Fitch et al (2005) and Jackendoff & Pinker (2005)).

Each language uses different mechanisms for achieving these ends and the goal of UG researchers has been to search for basic linguistic universals which are then realised in different languages by turning on different 'parameters'. Examples of such parameters are the pro-drop parameter, Binding Theory and the head-direction parameter (Cook, 1993). It is fair to say that the search for such universals in syntax has produced little of use for language teachers (although see the discussion of SL and UG in Cook, 1993). However, although related primarily to syntax, the concept of parameters is a useful one and is particularly relevant in the production and perception of sounds (See Chapter 2).

Following on from such an approach, one of the powerful concepts is that grammar is essentially generative, i.e. that the person's knowledge of the language is used to generate language. From such a perspective, the general notion of using grammar to generate rather than describe language is a powerful one. Chomsky (1964) outlines the following 'mentalist' as against behaviourist approaches to language acquisition,

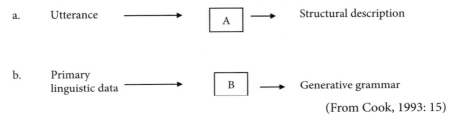

a.   Utterance ⟶ | A | ⟶ Structural description

b.   Primary linguistic data ⟶ | B | ⟶ Generative grammar

(From Cook, 1993: 15)

In (a) the heard utterance works on the surface structure to produce patterns of words in order to be able to put the patterns into use. However, in (b) the language input is used to construct a 'generative grammar' out of the input it receives. The device 'B', generates 'deep structure rules' which it can then use to create novel utterances. This forms the linguistic competence, the I-language, of the speaker. The box 'B' is the LAD and it indicates how people learn languages. The aim of the linguist is to understand the operation of this box. This box clearly operates on linguistic principles. "We can think of general linguistic theory as an attempt to specify the character of the device B" (Chomsky, 1964: 26 cited in Cook, 1993). Thus, to Chomsky, the operating principles for the LAD are essentially linguistic, symbolic in nature. In a UG approach, the underlying principles are syntactic, linked to phonological and lexical (semantic) systems. Universal grammarians have spent much energy searching for universal principles, largely at the level of syntax but it is fair to say that the actual tool used by Chomsky, Transformational Generative Grammar (TGG or TG) has had little practical application in language teaching. However, in a broader sense, the idea that evidence from language structure can be used to model mental processes has been a powerful concept in developing ideas about the operations involved in language processing and the LAD has had a strong influence on ways of thinking about approaches to second language learning. In the semantic field symbolic linguistic approaches have contributed to concepts of lexical storage and retrieval (see Chapter 4 where concepts of semantic distance, drawn from theoretical linguistics, can be verified under experimental conditions) and in terms of decoding oral language, the linguistic insights of phonetics are central to our understanding of the way that language is processed (see Chapter 2).

The contribution that phonology and semantics have made to the study of the way that sounds and words are processed indicates the influence that linguistics has made to our understanding of mental processing. Linguistics explains the way that language symbols provide meaning. The nature and form of language itself generates the cognitive models which are necessary for explaining language production and processing. The evidence is thus drawn from the study of language structure which is often highly abstract and does not primarily draw its data from language in use. It employs essentially introspective judgments about grammaticality rather than examining raw data. From this theoretical study of language form (linguistics), inferences are made about how language is processed which can then be tested in more controlled situations. As an example, MacWhinney's investigation of his Competition Model (MacWhinney, 2001) sets out to establish whether speakers of different languages are sensitive to different salient features such as word order and morphology. Linguistic analysis of different languages suggests that in some languages (e.g. English) word order is the most salient feature to decide actor/recipient relationships in clauses, whereas in other languages (e.g. Spanish) inflections will be more important. These two factors are typical of UG 'parameters'. This theoretical analysis of languages then leads to suggestions of mental processes which can be tested by presenting speakers of different languages with sentence contexts in which word order and morphology are manipulated. The speed with which speakers of the different languages respond to either word order or morphology will indicate which appears more salient to the speaker.

The Nativist Argument. The other major consequence of the psycholinguistic movement initiated in the sixties is the emphasis on studies which concentrate on learning or acquiring languages in naturalistic contexts. Much of the evidence from psychological studies has been based on highly artificial controlled experimentation. We have already mentioned the validity of transferring hypotheses drawn from highly controlled learning tasks from the experimental tradition on to more complex human activity. The approach established in acquisition studies has been quite different. Although conditions may be controlled to some extent, this tradition seeks to study language learning in a more naturalistic environment. Whilst this clearly relates to studies of first language acquisition, it has also had an effect on second language learning studies, where the data is often gathered from classroom interaction and observation of learning rather than experimental studies. This has led to a whole research tradition, Second Language Acquisition (SLA) (for further discussion see R. Ellis, 1990, 1994 and Chapter 7). One of the essential questions which will reappear throughout this book is:

❑   To what extent is second language learning different from first language acquisition?

1.2.1   The Critical Age hypothesis

One influential theory, initially proposed by Lenneberg (1967), is that there exists a period, usually extending up to puberty, when the brain is especially receptive to learning languages and that, beyond this point, the ability to learn a language decreases. It may even be impossible to achieve full competence in a language after this age. These observations were based on the evidence from certain children who failed to learn their first language in early childhood. Most famously, this included studies of *enfants sauvages* – rare cases of children who for one reason or another were isolated from normal human conduct until their early teens. Such children never achieved full fluency in language. The arguments for the critical age hypothesis usually rest on two factors; the decrease in plasticity of the brain as children get older and the availability of the LAD later in life. Lenneberg suggested that the neurological basis for a critical period may lie in the plasticity of the brain which decreases with age. He suggested that both changes in neural connections and lateralisation are complete by early puberty. Both of these arguments have since been modified. Whilst changes in neurological connections do continue after this period, lateralisation is largely complete by the age of six and the neurological connections for speech production, for example, have been shown to be complete by the same age.

In addition, studies of pathological cases of first language children may not be relevant to second language learners, although the concept of a critical period has been the subject of considerable debate in SLA studies. In particular, the concept of age of onset is one that has been considerably researched and is an important concept in bilingualism (see Hamer and Blanc, 2000). The decreasing plasticity of the brain is possibly best supported in second language learning in the area of phonology. The ability to pronounce sounds accurately relies very strongly on establishing automatic motor-neural pathways in the brain which entails the ability to perceive different patterns in the second as compared to the first language (see Chapter 2). A number of studies have indicated that late bilinguals are much more likely to retain a foreign accent than early bilinguals. Typical of such studies is that carried out by Oyama (1976) who studied 60 Italian male ESL students in the USA. The results indicated that the strongest effect on accent was age of arrival. This effect was much stronger than the length of exposure. However, in many other aspects, second language learners seem to outperform first language learners and there are many factors involved in second language learning (for a review of the factors effecting phonology, for example, see Moyer, 2004).

Whilst the strong version of the critical age hypothesis (i.e. there is a definite cut-off point beyond which it is impossible to acquire languages naturally) is no longer maintained, in its weak form it is still relevant, especially as it relates to the applicability of psycholinguistic thinking to second language learning. It is perhaps better to think of the situation as one of a sensitive period in which the adaptability of the brain allows for ease of language learning, a sensitivity which gradually decreases with age (Aitchison, 1998).

The psycholinguistic movement which we have been describing above represents one of the powerful movements within cognitive psychology. However, there is another powerful strand within cognitive psychology which examines general cognitive processes rather than the language-specific modular approach of the psycholinguistic movement. The central framework used within such studies is that of information processing and its associated cognitive architecture. It is this which we shall examine next.

1.3   The information processing framework

The principal concept which has dominated thinking about cognitive processing for the last fifty years is that of information processing which operates by means of a series of memory stores. The one which is generally adopted is that of Atkinson and Shiffrin, 1968, with its three types of memory, the Sensory Register, the Working or Short Term Memory and the Long Term Memory. These three stores represent different stages of processing information from the outside world.

The outline of the general framework of information processing is as follows:

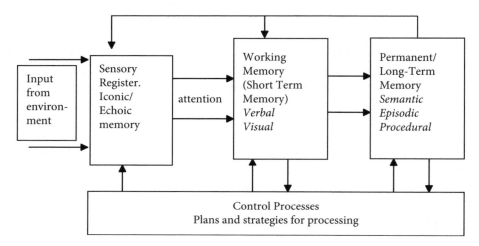

Figure 1.1. A diagrammatic representation of information processing (adapted from Atkinson and Shiffrin, 1968)

The model is seen as a flow of information from the stimuli in the environment, through a short-lived sensory register (where essential information is extracted from the mass of stimuli coming into the brain), into the working memory (where the material which has been selected as important is further processed). The filtered message is then passed on to a long term permanent store. This Permanent/Long Term Memory (LTM) contains information about the world, from our experiences about language and shapes (the Semantic Memory), the cumulative experiences which we have had in life (the Episodic Memory) and the automatic procedures involved in skilled behaviours (the Procedural Memory).

Making sense of the world is seen as a two-way process, with data being passed up the line from the senses to the longer term processing mechanisms whilst being worked on and made sense of by the knowledge contained in the long term store. At each stage in the process the raw data is being 'interpreted' in the light of our previous experience and thus 'packaged' into shapes/concepts which make sense and which thus form themselves into more manageable chunks.

Coupled to these three stages of processing is the concept of restricted capacity. Incoming information is selected and filtered by the Sensory Register and the Working Memory. The system, including the STM/WM has a limited capacity, and this is a crucial concept for our understanding of second language processing. It is the operation of this central store, the WM, which underpins much of the discussion about how languages are processed. The general characteristics of STM/WM are thus important to understand.

1.4   Short Term versus Working Memory

It may seem odd that a concept which is so crucial to this book and to the understanding of how language is processed can have two different terms. The two terms derive from two different characteristics of the memory. The first, short term memory, refers to the temporary **nature** of the store and is associated more with a serial model of language processing. Sounds/words/phrases come into the STM/WM and are held for a short time whilst new information is heard/read. This then assumes that language is received and assembled in a serial fashion, sound by sound, word by word or phrase by phrase. The second term, working memory, refers more to the **function** of the memory store, and is the more recent. It is more associated with parallel processing models of language comprehension. Sounds, words and phrases are taken in and combined with other information (e.g. the wider context, knowledge of grammar and so on). Both aspects are important to our understanding of the way that we process language. This book will tend to use the term Working Memory (WM) as we are principally interested in function rather than temporal characteristics, but both will be used, from time to time, depending on what aspect is being discussed.

1.4.1   Limited capacity

We mentioned above that limited capacity was one of the central concepts in the information-processing framework. Research has shown that our working memories can hold about as much information as we can recite in about 1.5 to 2 seconds and we have already alluded Miller's discovery that on average we can store 7 ± 2 bits of information at any one time (Miller, 1956). This can be demonstrated by repeating a list of random letters or numbers (see Wkbk 2.2). Look at each list of letters without repeating them, then close your eyes and try to say them. As the list increases in length this becomes increasingly difficult until it finally becomes impossible for most people when the list reaches eight or nine items. Storage capacity can be increased by chunking information (in the case of lists, by putting numbers and letters into groups) demonstrating that the WM can hold 7 ± 2 'chunks'[3] of information. Thus the integration of individual sounds into larger linguistic units greatly facilitates the amount of material which can be temporarily stored and used to make sense of the message.

The sensory stores act as the guardians to our minds by selecting and filtering information, thus avoiding us being inundated with too much information. They pass the selected information on to WM which is the central site for the receipt and interpretation of this data. This is the place where thinking and analysis take place. It is often equated with consciousness and, in language terms, it can be described as where 'meaning' is extracted. Although top-down processes operate on the Sensory Register, (the LTM will supply routines for recognising sounds, letters etc), it is in the WM where the linguistic symbols from the Sensory Register are assembled into meaningful units. To do this, incoming symbols are stored long enough to be compared and integrated with subsequent input. It is the place where the incoming language is constructed into longer stretches of meaningful text and where contextual information such as cultural schema can be brought to bear on the message. Once the message has been fully understood and interpreted it can then be passed on to LTM for long-term storage. WM in terms of information processing can be described as a scratch-pad on which incoming data can be noted down, joined with previous information and interpreted in the light of what we know about the world. All conscious processing takes place in the WM, but conscious processing uses space in the WM (rather like programmes take up space in a computer's RAM). As the WM has a limited capacity this fact is crucial to understanding the problems faced by second language learners in comprehending language.

1.4.2   Working Memory

The major model of WM which underpins thinking about memory derives from the work of Baddeley and Hitch (1974) and culminates in Baddeley's three component model (Baddeley, 1986) which is still the most commonly accepted model in cognitive psychology.

The concept of STM was initially incorporated into the information processing framework as an explanation of the concept of limited capacity. Initially, the emphasis was on two aspects of the store, its limited capacity and its temporary nature. Although also temporary in nature and limited in capacity, the concept of the WM in the Baddeley model is widened to include both storage and processing. The model, drawing on analogies from computer processing, postulates a central executive (or supervisory attentional system, SAS),

---

3.   Miller, in his 1956 paper uses bits in a technical sense as it is used in information theory and discusses the difference between 'bits' and 'chunks'. However, the concept of chunking has become an important concept in language processing so we shall use this term in its more general sense as it has come to be used in language processing rather than the technical term 'bits' as used in information theory.

linked to two slave systems, a phonological buffer (or phonological loop) and a visuo-spatial sketchpad. What is important for language processing is that the phonological loop takes in verbal material and holds it in memory by a process of repetition/rehearsal.

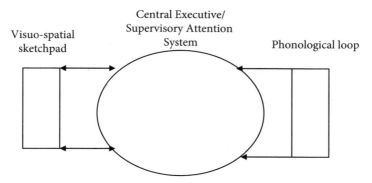

Figure 1.2. The components of Working Memory adapted from Baddeley and Hitch (1974)

The architecture suggested by Baddeley includes both storage and processing functions and is designed to respond to a range of effects found from experiments involving recall of lists:

1.   The phonological similarity effect where similar sounding words interfere with recall supports the idea that part of WM, the phonological loop, is speech-based;

2.   The word length effect which shows that memory is better for short words than long words, thus arguing for a restricted capacity in a phonological memory and;

3.   Articulatory suppression where the repetition of words/syllables restricts verbal memory but not visual memory argues for the separation of the memory into two stores, the visual and phonological stores.

(For a review of evidence, see Andrale, 2001 and Cowen, 1995)

Although there are a series of different models of WM (see Miyake and Shah, 1999), there is consensus among researchers that WM "is those mechanisms that are involved in the control, regulation and active maintenance of task-relevant information in the service of complex cognition." (Miyake and Shah, 1999: 450). It is the place where information is analysed and meaning extracted.

There are arguments put forward for a more integrated model of STM/WM and LTM (for a critique of the WM, see Cowen, 1995 and Ward, 2001). The criticisms point out that some of the frequency and serial effects previously associated with WM alone can also be seen to operate in LTM under certain conditions. Of particular interest for language processing is a recent model (Baddeley, 2000) which suggests that a section of the episodic LTM may also act as a temporary store for material expressed in a symbolic form (i.e. as language or visual semantics), and this will be further discussed in Chapter 6.

In addition to the general information processing framework and the specific memory structures it subsumes, there is also another set of ideas which have emerged from cognitive psychology which have been very influential in guiding thought about language processing; connectionism and parallel distributed processing (PDP). They deal with the way that connections are formed within the brain and the way that material is processed.

1.5   Neural networking, connectionism and parallel distributed processing

1.5.1   Serial and parallel processing

Before looking at connectionst models *per se*, there is another issue which has concerned psychologists, that of serial or parallel processing. To what extent should the processing of language be characterised as a serial process (first identify sounds, combine them into words and then into sentences) or to what extent should it be seen as a number of different processes acting at the same time and at different levels?

The information processing model described above, although not stating it explicitly, suggests a serial processing approach; information is taken in via the senses and then various features extracted through a series of memory stores. The symbolicist approach (following from linguistic descriptions which are hierarchical in nature) also suggests serial processing of language input. From this perspective, syntactical processing precedes semantic processing. The brain first of all decodes the input from a rule-governed syntactical viewpoint which then accesses a semantic representation (for language comprehension). The brain uses a similar reverse path for language production; the semantics generate the syntax which then produces output (for a discussion of symbolism and mental representation, see O'Halloran, 2003 and Chapter 5 in this book).

However, serial processing models have been challenged by parallel processing models. Based on what we know about the structure and function of the brain, a simple serial model would seem to be inadequate (although there will be times that a serial approach will provide good explanations of how language can be interpreted). The brain contains a vast number of neurons connected into neural networks which carry out myriad simultaneous and complex operations. This neural architecture has led to a general theory of language processing and storage known as connectionism (also known as "parallel distributed processing", "interactive activation" or "spreading activation"). These theories postulate that the brain is able to carry out multiple levels of activity simultaneously and thus several processes can take place at the same time and not in a serial order, spreading activation through many parts of the brain through a highly complex system of neural networks.

Let us take an example from general cognition. Let us say that we know someone such as Lynn Brown. There are all sorts of facts we know about her. We know her name, her age (about 35), what she looks like, her job, her personality, and we remember the times we have met her and what we did. These are all connected together in a web of information, or a neural network. Accessing any one of these pieces of information will activate all the other pieces of information to some degree or other. These activations will obviously depend on the strength of the information held (we may not know her very well, we may not have met her very often) but they will all be activated simultaneously, for example, on being shown a photograph or hearing her name.

In the same way, parallel distributed processing envisages different processes being carried out in different parts of the brain simultaneously. The difference between serial and parallel distributed processes working on sounds can be represented as:

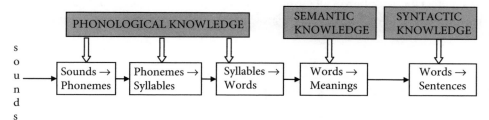

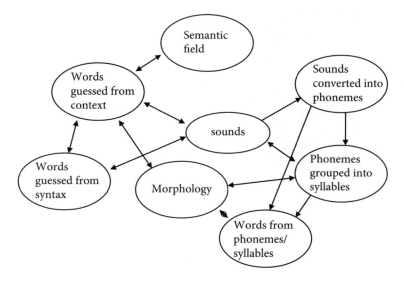

Figure 1.3. The different processes involved in serial and parallel distributed models of understanding language

Parallel distributed processing and connectionism rest on the strength of the connections between different language features (such as words) and present a very different picture of language processing than is assumed by symbolist approaches (for discussion of the symbolist/connectionism distinction, see Hulstijn, 2002).

1.5.2   Connectionist models of language

One of the earliest connectionist models was McClelland and Rumulhart's "interactive activation model" (1981) designed to explain how individual letter features can be seen to produce word recognition (see Chapter 3 for a more detailed description). Connectionist approaches set out to explain how language can be decoded through the operation of simple processes whereby large numbers of neurons co-operate to process information. The process is described in more detail in Chapter 3, but it involves the simultaneous activation of internal 'nodes' within the brain. These nodes also interconnect to either inhibit or suppress the activation of all the other nodes involved until a threshold point has been reached. A simplified diagrammatic representation of the process is given in Figure 1.4.

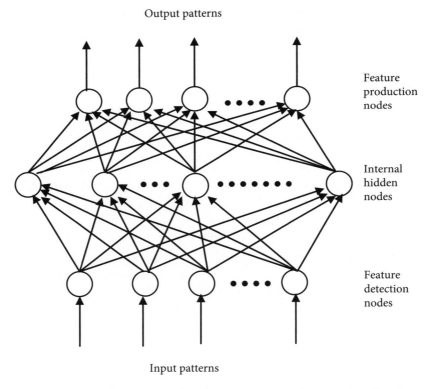

Figure 1.4. A general diagram of the connectionist model adapted from Rumelhart and McClelland 1986

Nodes are assumed to be numerical processors and the information passed between them is numerical rather than symbolic. The output from a node is assumed to be the numerical sum of its inputs. The strength of connections between the nodes can be given a numerical value representing the probability that one node will co-exist with another. Through this process the interconnectivity in the brain reflects the probabilistic relations between features in the language. The input from the language data will 'train' the network. Thus, the brain 'learns' a language from the input. Language rules 'emerge' from the input as a series of probabilities of the co-occurrence of certain features not as symbolic representations such as grammar rules.

Thus, the simple sentence "*It is running*" would be seen as a correct piece of language and * "*They is run*" as incorrect due to the fact that

1.   the verb form "is" is highly frequent after "it" and not after "they"
2.   a verb in the "-ing" form frequently follows "is", but not a verb in its base form.

The input node "it" would activate a node for "is" which would then activate nodes for "-ing". A symbolic representation, however, would describe the situation in terms of grammatical features, such as subject-verb agreement, the auxiliary verb "to be" and a present participle, the present continuous tense form. The counetonist model relies on basic associative learning principles as did behaviourist principles, but with the associative learning connected into associative networks.

Evidence for the validity of such systems involve the degree to which artificial systems can be set up to mirror actual human learning. For typical examples of the process see Rumelhart and MacClelland (1986) who produced a computer model to replicate the learning of the irregular past tense in English that we have described above or Van Heuven's evaluation of how second language scripts are processed (Van Heuven, 2005).

Although the evidence from such investigations is highly computational, reflecting, as it does, the close connection of PDP with artificial intelligence, the theory is a powerful metaphor for understanding possible mechanisms for language learning and language processing. It has instigated a number of interesting lines of research. For example, in the study cited above, MacWhiney (2001) demonstrated that the salience of different language features across languages is reflected in different patterns of noticing by the native speakers of those languages. MacWhinney suggests that such evidence demonstrates the psychological validity in language processing of the frequency of surface features within a language.

Connectionism offers an explanation of the micro-processes though which language structure (grammar and semantics) is implemented based on a highly plausible model of neural activity. Connectionism is designed as a complete explanation of language processing, but only a few areas of language activity have, as yet, been investigated, such as letter recognition and past tense acquisition (cite above). However, it can be seen as a promising alternative explanation of language processing, combining language performance with neurological mechanisms. It is also possible to suggest that language processing "can be described at two levels: at the psychological level, in terms of symbol processing; and at the implementation level, in neuroscientific terms (to which connectionism approximates)" (Chater & Christiansen, 1999: 236). At times the symbolic level may appear to be most applicable (for example in designing a language programme) at others the connectionist model may be more applicable (for example in designing the types of activity). It is precisely these two levels which we shall be investigating in this book and in the next sections we shall look at language activity in the brain from neuroscientifc perspectives.

1.6   Cognitive neuropsychology

One of the most important areas of information about brain function in general and language processing in particular comes from cognitive neuropsychology. Cognitive neuropsychology involves studies of individuals who have sustained some sort of neurological damage which has led to a specific impairment of cognitive processing, including impairment of language functions. Most of these individuals have suffered strokes which led to different forms of aphasias (for example, acquired dyslexias). Prior to their strokes they all had normal language functions, but after the stroke, lesions in one area of the brain left them without the ability to perform certain language functions. Studies of such individuals have a long history. In the late nineteenth century two scientists, Broca and Wernicke investigated different forms of aphasia. Broca investigated an individual who had almost totally lost the ability to speak, although he retained some ability to understand language. A post mortem on the brain of this person revealed a large lesion in the area in the left frontal lobe, an area which has come to be known as *Broca's area*. Wernicke discovered that similar damage to another area in the left hemisphere of the brain, the superior temporal lobe, led to an inability to process language input, and this area is known as *Wernicke's area*.

However, neuropsychological evidence is not restricted to the anatomical investigation of the functional anatomy of the brain, it is also used in its own rights to suggest models of brain functions which are not specifically located in any particular area. For example, the existence of separate short-term and long-term memory stores is supported by cases of amnesic patients who have extremely poor long term memory but virtually normal short-term memory as evidenced by memory span for free-recall of digits (Baddeley & Warrington, 1970). Shallice & Warrington (1970) describe a patient who had the reverse problem: a relatively intact long term memory, but a digit span of only two or three items, well below the norm of seven plus or minus two (Miller, 1956). The separate WM functions of storage and rehearsal have also been shown to possibly have discrete anatomical locations by a study of two patients with brain lesions in different places. One patient was able to store phonological information but was less able to rehearse. The other showed symptoms of impaired storage but the ability to rehearse was intact (Vallar et al, 1997). There is also considerable neuropsychological evidence for other aspects of WM; for the separation of the phonological loop and the visuo-spatial sketchpad, for separate neural systems for object and spatial WM and for the difference between verbal storage and retrieval (see Henson, 2001, for a review).

In language processing, studies of patients with aphasia have suggested two broad categories of reading impairment, phonological and surface dyslexia. In the former, patients have lost the ability to retrieve words from sounds. They can read real words (including irregularly spelt words) but have problems with reading non-words. In the surface dyslexic, irregularly spelt words will cause problems but they can read aloud invented nonwords using letter-sound correspondences. These findings have led support to the Dual Route theories of lexical access (Coltheart et al, 2001) and these models will be discussed in detail in Chapter 3.

In both of the above examples, neuropsychological evidence has been used to support cognitive models of brain function. The argument is that if a specific function has been lost in a particular individual after a brain trauma of some description, then this is evidence that there exists within the brain a specific system to perform that function. The evidence would seem to support the model of short- and long-term memory in terms of general cognition and the dual route theory of lexical access in word recognition. The early studies of Broca and Wernicke can also be used to support the modular concept of language processing; there clearly exist specific areas of the brain which support language processing. However, although such studies are persuasive, they are often based on single case studies, and, although the findings of Broca and Wernicke seem quite robust, there are differences between individuals in the degree of impairment. In the case of phonological and surface dyslexics, rarely are the routes completely impaired. The inability to read different types of word are partial rather than total, suggesting a much more complex set of structures within the brain for processing written words.

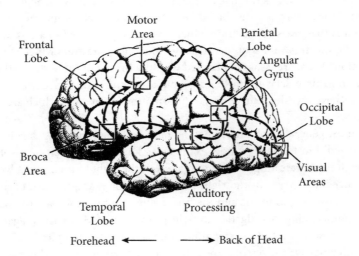

Figure 1.5. The left side of the brain and areas associated with various language tasks (from Byrnes, 2001, p. 132)

1.7   Brain imaging and cognitive neuroscience

This chapter began with a discussion of the behaviourist approaches to psychology and the unwillingness to speculate beyond observable data. The mind was a 'black box'.

The chapter has traced the movement of cognitive psychology in its endeavour to open this black box and to speculate about the processes and representations which may be within it. In the information processing framework, different models of memory have been constructed and tested against behaviour. However, all these models have been inferences built on observations of behaviour. Apart from the anatomical work discussed in the last section, none of these brain functions have been physiologically located. In the last twenty years, new advances in scanning technology have allowed us to peel away the final wrapping of the black box and look directly at the mind at work through the examination of such factors as metabolic activity, blood flow, and magnetic fields. It is the description of the processes by which the pictures of the mind at work are taken and critical examination of the information provided by such pictures which form the basis of this last section.

Along with ERP (event-related potential) which measures electrical potential of parts of the brain from surface electrodes, the two technologies which have provided the most stunning images of the brain at work are positron emission tomography (PET) and functional magnetic resonance imaging (fMRI). Although the two types of scan use different techniques, both work by taking images of slices through the brain showing areas which have increased blood flow at any given moment (PET measures blood flow through the monitoring of a weak radioactive dye and fMRI measures the flow through the magnetic properties of components of water, blood and several chemical compounds in the brain). The argument is that areas of the brain which are actively engaged in a task will have increased blood flow. Thus, 'hot spots' with greater blood flow are areas which are processing the information. There are issues concerned with the timing of these slices (the slices are taken after a short time delay in fMRI scans), but the pictures that have been produced by these methods have revealed a great deal of information about areas which are involved in different tasks.

On the most general level, brain imaging has confirmed that language processing is highly lateralized. Most language tasks excite areas located in the left hemisphere of the brain, although it is interesting to note that areas in the right brain are involved in some aspects of processing. Areas in the right hemisphere, for example, have been shown to activated when listening to music and the processing of intonation patterns will thus use such areas. An interesting investigation into the processing of Mandarin as against English indicated that, in addition to the activation of areas in the left temporal lobe universally associated with language processing, areas in the right temporal lobe where also activated when listening to Mandarin (Scott et al, 2003). It was suggested that this could be due to the necessity to process tones in Mandarin.

One of the first observations about brain activity is its complexity. Even with the simplest of tasks many areas are activated. This lends a great deal of support to the neural networking models which underlie connectionist thinking about language. In order to be able to isolate the significant areas involved in any particular process (such as reading a word aloud) experimental techniques have been evolved which compare the brain activation patterns under different task conditions and then subtract one image from the other. For example, in a typical task a subject is asked to look at a simple fixed point. A scan is taken of the activated areas under this condition to act as a 'base line' to compare with activated areas on other tasks. The subject could then be asked to read a word silently and a second scan taken. Then the subject could be asked to read the word aloud and finally asked to generate a verb from the noun. At each stage an image is generated and by subtracting the original image (the 'base line, fixation image') from the image generated under the different tasks a picture can be built up of the areas involved in silently reading, in reading aloud and in generating a new word.

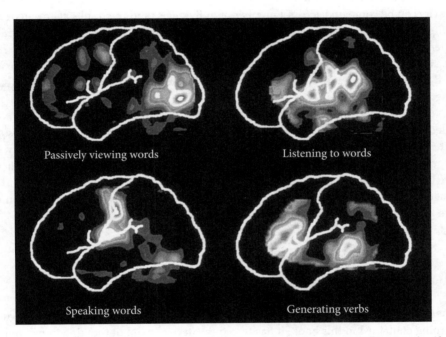

Figure 1.6. Examples of PET scans of the left side of the brain during different tasks (from Posner & Raichle, 1994: 115)

Such techniques have already begun to confirm many ideas about the working of the brain. On a macro level, in addition to the localisation of language activities in the left hemisphere, the importance of special language processing areas such as Broca's and Wernicke's have been confirmed both in normal subjects and in subjects with brain lesions. However, imaging techniques have also shown that many other areas are also actively involved in the comprehension and production of language, including areas in the right hemisphere. Brain imaging has also shown that functions predicted by the WM model discussed, such as the differentiation between the maintenance of visual and phonological material, between storage and rehearsal functions and executive functions, such as monitoring, do appear to have different patterns of activity in the brain (see Henson, 2001). In particular, there is strong evidence that certain areas are heavily involved in executive tasks. One, called the *anteria cingulate gyrus* seems to be activated in tasks which require some sort of target detection or manipulation, suggesting that this area is involved in directing attention (see Byrnes, 2001 and Henson, 2001). This area is closely connected to structures involved in WM and Semantic Memory and would seem to validate the existence of a Supervisory Attention System as part of WM.

Information about brain activity can thus be built up by varying the tasks set. Brain activity can be compared across a number of individuals (and the results aggregated) and comparisons can be made between different groups of subjects. For example, readers of different languages can be compared to see if the processing systems for the different scripts are similar (e.g. ideographic versus alphabetic scripts). Dyslexic readers can be compared with normal readers and bilingual subjects can be compared working in their different languages.

Although imaging techniques, especially fMRI, are able to provide much more de-tailed information than previously, such pictures are still fairly coarse-grained. It is still rather like a satellite picture of the earth at night – areas of habitation show up clearly, but to draw detailed inferences about social organization from such images is very difficult. The brain images can provide broad confirmation that macro-processes involved in lan-guage do seem to be taking place in certain areas as predicted by theory, but are often not fine-grained enough to tell us about differences on the micro-level.

1.8   Summary

This chapter has sketched the background for the later discussions of second language learning contained in this book. It has traced the development of thinking in psychology and to some extent linguistics over the last half a century and introduced the main frame-works within which the discussion of second language learning will be located. Starting from the Behaviourist ideas which established the importance of associative learning with-out any speculation about the mechanisms that brought this about, the chapter has exam-ined the movement from the concentration on behaviour *per se* to a closer examination of the internal workings of the brain, concluding with the even more detailed views of brain activity provided by brain imaging.

One of the reasons for carrying out this examination of the different approaches was to evaluate the reliability of the different sources of evidence provided by each approach.

The approaches, the sources of evidence and their strengths and weaknesses is summarized in the table on pp. 28–29.

The first break away from Behaviourist models of language was provided by the 'psycholinguistic' movement which argued that the complexity of language and its ability to generate and understand new utterances made it difficult to describe language learning in purely stimulus-response terms. It introduced the possibility that there exists a separate module for processing language, but as shall be pointed out later in the book, provided no explanation of how this might work. In some ways the 'black box' of the behaviourists was recreated in a different form. As against this modular approach, the chapter outlined the common cognitive framework of information processing with its constructs of different types of memory store, and in particular, the importance of WM within this process. It is this framework which will be adopted and examined in this book. It will be argued that the WM model provides a very useful concept in examining second language learning as against ideas of first or second language acquisition. In fact, the concept of the WM is central to connectionist ideas about how natural languages may be learnt. Connectionist thinking has returned to simple associative learning concepts to explain language learning and this approach provides a plausible explanation of the way that a specialized language module might operate. This argues against the modular theory if language processes can be described in general cognitive processing terms. The WM and the central executive within it, with its emphasis on language related features such as phonology, may well encompass the function of the language acquisition device. It is not impossible to speculate that the development of such a sophisticated device as the WM in humans is primarily related to language processing. Whether this is so, or whether in evolutionary terms humans have developed this sophisticated device to handle language does not concern us here. What is important is that it is a central metaphor for helping us to consider how second languages are learnt.

Finally, the chapter examined the emerging physiological evidence for the models of memory which have been outlined. It found that, in general terms, there is good evidence from brain imaging to substantiate these general models, although the possibility of locating something such as WM in any one place is not possible. There are areas of the brain which are implicated along with others in certain tasks, but none of these areas can be exclusively allocated to any one specific task. The picture emerging is that of combinations of areas working cooperatively in any given task, much as assumed by the connectionist approach. Evidence from brain imaging and neuropsychology will be presented where appropriate throughout the book to highlight the degree to which the ideas presented in the discussion of language processing and learning have been substantiated by these approaches.

In the next chapter, we shall examine the way that the information processing approach can be used to explain the comprehension of spoken language and the implications for the second language learner.

Table 1.1. A comparison of the approaches to language processing and their evidential bases

Approach	Sources of evidence	Leads to hypotheses	Strengths	Weaknesses
Cognitive psychology	Observation of behaviour in controlled conditions People can only repeat 7 digits accurately	There exists a part of the brain which can hold up to 7 bits of information	The hypothesis is in one sense 'scientific' in that it rests on observable behaviour.	The tasks set are usually highly artificial and run under laboratory conditions. The models of the cognitive structure are speculative. There is no direct evidence that they exist. The models describe *functions* of the brain, not anatomical structures.
Linguistics	Analysis of language patterns Phonemes are significant language symbols. Changing one small component of a sound changes its significance	There must be a mechanism in the brain which knows the significant characteristics of the phonemes and is able to recognise them	Languages are rule-governed and an understanding of the rules will give insights into how languages are processed. There is a lot of careful research into the rules used by languages and such rules have been used successfully in teaching.	The study of linguistics has its own criteria which may not be the same as used by the brain. For example, simplicity of explanation (parsimony) is important in linguistics, but may not be important in terms of cognition.
Connectionism	Analysis of frequency patterns and the building of computer models to replicate language behaviour e.g. The frequency of occurrence of irregular verbs is built into a computer programme to generate outcomes. These outcomes mirror the way children produce irregular verbs.	Such models describe the way that neural networks are built.	If a process can be modelled on a computer, then it indicates how language can be processed by simple computation. It suggests how experience can shape brain structures.	In a similar way to behavioural evidence, the computer models only deal with fairly simple language processes. There is no essential reason to believe that the brain processes language like a computer. Indeed, computers still have great difficulties in dealing with language compared to the brain.

Cognitive neuropsychology	Analysis of impairments following brain traumas (e.g. strokes) e.g. Before a stroke a person could read irregularly spelt words easily. After a stroke they made many mistakes reading irregularly spelt words.	There is a specific area of the brain concerned with the processing of 'sight' vocabulary.	Such evidence has a high degree of 'face' validity and there is a lot of evidence over a considerable period which is linked to anatomical and brain imaging studies to suggest that this is a fairly robust way of investigating language processes.	The main problems are that most of the studies are linked to individual cases. The results often vary, even conflict. It is also rare to find a complete loss of faculties, thus suggesting that there are multiple ways of performing the same task.
Brain imaging	Observation of blood flow Certain areas have increased blood flow when listening to sounds but not when reading silently.	These areas are involved in processing sounds.	This is perhaps the most 'direct' way of looking at brain function and allows speculations about brain function to be tested.	As with other methods of 'scientific' investigation the tasks are highly artificial and the experimental designs allow for only certain types of task. The results indicate the complexity of the processes involved and the interpretation of the results is highly complicated.

Further Reading

Andrew Ellis and Andrew Young (1995). *Human Cognitive Neuropsychology: A Textbook with Readings*. Hove: Psychology Press.
Contains a series of articles concerning issues such as memory and dyslexia with original articles exemplifying the neuropsychological approach to cognition.

Michael Posner and Marcus Riachle (1994). *Images of Mind*. New York NY: Scientific American Library. Although written some time ago and only dealing with PET imaging, this is a fascinating read and a very clear and accessible account of the different functions of parts of the brain. It contains really good, clear images with good explanations in relatively plain English.

Jackie Andrade (ed.) (2001). *Working Memory in Perspective*. Hove: Psychology Press.
A good collection of articles on different aspects of Working Memory with a good introduction surveying the main issues.

Ruth Lesser and Lesley Milroy (1993). *Linguistics and Aphasia: Psycholinguistics and Pragmatic Aspects of Intervention*. London: Longman.
Provides a very interesting discussion of the use of psycholinguistics in aphasia with good examples of actual aphasic patients and the way data is interpreted.

Chapter 2

Taking in and sorting out the information

Extracting features from the spoken message

In the previous chapter we examined various issues concerned with language processing. We introduced the idea of a general information processing system and its component parts. We also looked at issues connected with a separate language module and the degree to which languages can be considered innate, or the degree to which they can be seen as learnt. In this chapter we are going to consider the implications of these broad approaches for the perception and processing of spoken language. The questions which we shall be asking are:

- How do we get from a series of sounds to meaningful language symbols?
- How do the different components of the information processing system provide a model for the perception and analysis of these sounds and their interpretation as language symbols?
- What are the important (salient) features of sounds which enable us to interpret them as language symbols?
- What evidence is there for the fact that the processes of noticing such features are innate in first language acquisition?
- What are the implications of this for the second language learner?

In essence, we shall be looking in detail at the micro-processes involved in listening comprehension from the bottom-up, in the decoding of spoken input. The chapter will concentrate on the processing of what Hulstijn (2002) calls the 'lowest end' of the linguistic domain, discussing its integration with the higher ends of the domain and the interaction between bottom up and top down processes.

To examine the first stage in this process, this discussion will commence with a brief discussion of general recognition processes used by the brain and how visual data is interpreted. Although this does not deal with language as such, the operation of many general principles can be more clearly seen in visual pattern detection.

2.1   Perception and attention

The brain receives information from the senses. The raw information is received in the form of physical properties. In the case of visual information it is in terms of colour, patterns of light and dark, movement and edge detectors. In the case of touch it is in the form of pressure, in taste and smell, through various chemical compounds and in hearing through sounds at different frequencies and intensities. Most processing of input from the senses is carried out unconsciously and rapidly, and we are usually unaware of the actual physical properties of the input; we 'perceive' the world as meaningful concepts. Perception is not a photographic process, but the result of an information processing system which is constantly interpreting incoming information in the light of previous experience.

For example, let's examine the following simple illusion:

At first glance this would appear to be two silhouetted heads looking at each other. In fact, what is hitting the retina is two solid black blocks and this information is being transferred through the optic nerves to an area in the brain which deals with the processing of optical information (an area at the back of the cerebral cortex, the occipital lobe). However, as well as the physical information coming in from the eyes (the bottom-up information) there is information being fed back from the long-term memory as to the interpretation of this physical data and the extraction of significant features from it. The information used to interpret the physical data is stored in long term memory which has been built up through our experience with the world. Typical of such information (or 'schema') is the fact that we generally see dark shapes as foreground on a white background. Thus, the two 'heads' are usually seen first as the brain automatically tries to make sense of what it considers is the most salient information, and assigns this to the foreground. The 'heads' are highly stylised and are far removed from any real head which may have been actually experienced physically. Again, drawing on schema stored in long term memory, certain salient 'features' are extracted from the physical image. The profile of the nose, forehead and chin and their relationship to each other are extracted as significant features and constructed by the brain into the concept of a face in silhouette. These stylised features are not real noses, chins or foreheads, they are symbolic representations. They represent noses, chins and foreheads through some sort of extraction of significant features from a whole range of individual noses, chins and foreheads which have been experienced.

It may also be that our brains are 'hard wired' to extract face-like features from visual input. It has been shown that neonates from a very early age actively respond to caricatures of faces, suggesting that there is an innate capacity for processing images which resemble faces. Thus, there can be argued to be a specific mechanism in the brain for recognising faces in the same way as there is an argument for a specific module to process language. Further support for specific modules in the brain for processing faces comes from patients with *prosopagnoisia*, a neurological disorder in which sufferers are quite able to recognize common objects, but have lost the ability to recognize faces. Studies of patients with brain lesions have shown damage to the organisation of the *extrastriate visual cortex* (in the occipital lobe). This, in humans, is a common factor in this condition, and the use of these areas for processing facial features is a factor we share with nonhuman primates.

However, although certain facial characteristics may be 'hard wired' in the sense that our brains are pre-tuned to notice face-like features, the specific features in the above illusion are not free from cultural factors (the silhouettes are clearly not African, for example). Cultural experience can be seen to play an even more important role when we examine the second image which is involved in the illusion; that of the candlestick. If the first interpretation of the illusion is usually two faces due to experience with foregrounds and backgrounds, then the second interpretation involves the suppression of this general assumption and the viewing of the white area between the two dark shapes as the foreground – as a candlestick or vase. The ability to 'see' this will clearly be very heavily determined by cultural experience with such objects – not all cultures have such artifacts. But the 'seeing' of this interpretation of the illusion illustrates another of the automatic interpretative functions of the perceptual process – the ability to see things as wholes, to delineate objects, making connections where none actually exist. Thus, when we see the candlestick, the brain 'draws' imaginary horizontal lines at the top and bottom of the white space to connect up the candlestick into an object. This ability to impose order on to incoming shapes and to form closure was extensively studied by Gestaldt psychologists.

The final point to note about the illusion is the way that it is quite difficult to see both interpretations at once. Our attention can be switched from the faces to the candlestick, indicating conscious control over attention. Certain 'sets' of features would appear to be supplied automatically from long term memory, but which set of features are called up seems to be under more conscious control.

We thus have the following process taking place when interpreting incoming visual information:

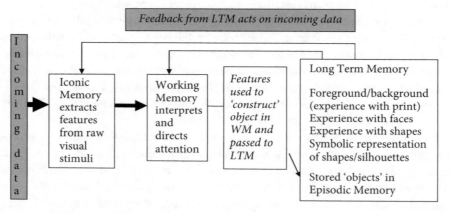

Figure 2.1. Interpretation of visual images by the brain

Further examples of visual illusions are provided in Workbook 2.1. So powerful are the judgments that we make due to our prior experiences and established concepts, that it is often quite difficult to 'unlock' the straight jacket imposed by the permanent memory and allow us to see the stimuli in another light. Figure 1 shows how different features can be highlighted to give different versions of the picture. Figure 2 illustrates the difficulty of changing foreground and background decisions and Figures 3 and 4 the order which the brain imposes on simple linear sketches. Examples of the sort of order that is imposed on our perception from our long term experience is the inability to see the two vertical lines as equal (Figure 3) and the long-established 'gestalt' effects, where processes such as 'closure' (Figure 4) enable us to see a head rather than a series of lines. Closure shows the brain's predilection for making sense of visual input and relating lines and shapes to some established schema. This ability to create meaningful images from partial information as demonstrated by the closure effect is centrally important in language processing, especially when listening to the flow of speech in the difficult environments that characterize most oral interaction. It may be that such an automatic cognitive tendency to construct order is 'hard-wired' into the brain. It may be this which is an innate ability, not specifically a language module (N. Ellis, 2001).

2.2   Sorting out the important information from the background

In the above discussion we showed how we could direct attention to certain aspects of the data and how attention could be consciously directed. Such an ability probably resides in the Supervisory Attention System (see Chapter 1), and has obvious importance for second language listening where attention will need to be paid to different sets of features involved in the second as against the first language. However, there is another aspect of attention which needs to be considered; that of the routine, usually unconscious filtering of incoming information.

Our senses are bombarded with an amazing amount of information, yet we are actually consciously aware of only a small portion of this as little is actually passed on beyond the sensory store. On an aural level this can be demonstrated by the 'cocktail party phenomenon' (Wood and Cowan, 1995). In such situations we routinely block out much of the surrounding noise and concentrate on what our neighbour is saying. However, should our name be mentioned, it is likely that our attention will immediately be diverted, thus indicating that the surrounding noises, although mentally blocked out most of the time, are being monitored and are available for attention if required. Similarly if we are briefly presented with a picture we are able to take it in, recognize it again, but unable to recall all the details.

The nature of the mechanism by which such brief images are stored was investigated by Sperling (1960). When subjects are presented with stimuli for very brief periods (up to 50 milliseconds), they are not consciously aware of what has been presented, but are able to accurately report 4 or 5 characters from 12. This would indicate the presence of a brief sensory store (which he called the Iconic Memory) which has a capacity of 4 or 5 characters. This, in itself, would not necessarily indicate anything unusual; the senses could just be acting as a narrow conduit for information, only allowing a severely limited amount through. However, Sperling presented the subjects with 12 letters displayed in three rows with four letters in each row. Immediately after exposing the subjects to the visual displays, they were asked to report the top row of letters if a high-pitched bell was rung, the middle row of letters in response to a middle-pitched bell, and the bottom row for a low-pitched bell. He found that under these conditions the subjects were able to report up to three out of four from the designated rows. As they had no idea which row was going to be chosen when they were exposed to the letters, it therefore followed that they had all three rows available for them to extract information from. From the investigation of the length of time that such information was available to the subjects, it appeared that the facility only lasted for about one second after the bell was played; after this period the recall of the letters became no better than chance.

A similar sensory register (the Echoic Memory) has been found to exist for sounds but here, interestingly, the duration of the advantage seems to be something like 4 seconds (Darwin, Turvey and Crowder, 1972). This longer storage is probably crucial in our perception and processing of speech sounds. Visual images usually exist permanently outside us and can be inspected for a longer period. In speech, the sounds are entirely transitory and thus extracting features from the flow of speech will need the mental record to exist longer in the brain. The sounds, unlike the pictures, are not physically available for re-inspection.

These experiments suggest a short-term sensory store in which visual and auditory information is briefly stored, features extracted and then the resulting information passed on to the Working Memory for further processing. As we saw in the discussion of the visual illusion, the criteria on which such selection is made will be supplied from the LTM.

2.3   Deciding what is salient in speech

We shall now look at the raw data for spoken language and examine how the information processing system, and particularly the sensory register could work on this data to extract meaning from what is, essentially, a set of sound waves.

What is speech? It is a series of sound waves at different frequencies. The following is a speech spectrogram of someone saying "And he cleaned the car again this morning".

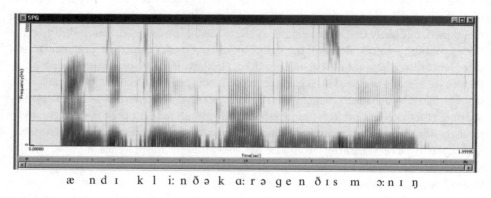

æ n d ɪ   k l iː n ð ə k ɑː r ə g e n ð ɪ s   m   ɔː n ɪ ŋ

Figure 2.2. A voice spectrogram of "And he cleaned the car again this morning"

The pitch frequencies are shown on the vertical axis and the time is shown on the horizontal axis. The dark bands on the spectrogram indicate the pitch frequencies which are being sounded at any particular time. The darker the bands, the more intensive the pitch at any given frequency. Under the spectrogram are the representations of the English phonemes which are involved in the utterance. The symbols represent the **sounds**[1] of the language. What we are going to examine is the sort of information which needs to

---

1.   The symbols used here are the phonemic symbols used to describe the *significant* sound symbols used in English. Phoneticians differentiate between the actual sounds (called 'phones') and the abstract symbols (called 'phonemes'). This is analogous to writing where there are any representations of a letter, such as 'a' *'a'*, 'A' etc., but they all represent the same general letter in the alphabet. Phones are represented within square brackets [ ] and phonemes within slashes / /. For the sake of simplicity this book will refer to phones as 'sounds' and will generally transcribe spoken data using phonemic script.

be retrieved from the LTM to be able to make sense of these bands of sound at different frequencies; to turn raw sounds into language symbols.

2.4   Evidence from linguistic theory: The phoneme

The concept of the phoneme is central to all linguistic analyses of spoken language. Each language has a limited set of phonemes which are sounds which have *contrastive signifi- cance*; which make a significant difference to the word if changed. Thus, the two sounds [p] and [b] represent a phonemic contrast in English because the substitution of one for the other in words means that the meaning of the word changes (e.g. 'pad' and 'bad' are dif- ferent words). Both sounds are made by the lips and are thus called 'bilabial' consonants. Both sounds are produced by stopping the flow of air with the lips and then opening them producing a release of air and are thus called 'stop' or 'plosive' consonants. Yet they are heard as different by English speakers. The simplest description of the difference between /p/ and /b/ is that one is 'voiced' (/b/) and one is 'voiceless' (/p/); with /b/ the vocal cords are vibrating while the sound is produced and with /p/ they are not. Voicing can then be seen as a *distinctive feature* for distinguishing between consonant phonemes.

Every language in the world uses a restricted set of features to make sounds and linguists have shown that every language has a set of around 40 phonemes with which it com- municates. This restricted set of features and the fact that all languages can be shown to use these features in similar ways is a powerful argument in favour of a *universalist approach* to language processing associated with the ideas of Chomsky, Halle and the 'psycholinguistic' movement of the 1960s and 1970s. All languages, for example, use the voiced/voiceless distinction, but the implementation of this feature will vary from language to language, and thus each language has a different set of phonemes.

However, closer acoustic analysis of the difference between the two shows that it is not that one lacks voice completely, but that, in a word in which /p/ and /b/ are followed by a vowel, /b/ the voicing starts very quickly after the beginning of the sound whereas in /p/ the voicing starts later. This distinction is known as voice onset time (VOT) and it has received a lot of attention in terms of trying to understand the way that sounds are decoded. The delay in voicing for voiceless phonemes can be clearly seen in the white band (silence) following the /k/ consonant in the above spectrogram, but not after the /g/ consonant (a voiced phoneme). Thus, in terms of extracting features from incoming speech, one of the basic procedures would be to scan the raw data making distinctions between consonant sounds in English based on the amount of delay between the beginning of the consonant and the start of the voicing. The sounds would be temporarily held in the Sensory Register while the differences in VOT between voiced and voiceless consonants in English will be retrieved from the models stored in LTM and 'downloaded' to work on the sounds in the Sensory Register and decoded into linguistic symbols or phonemes.

The actual realisations of VOT will vary from language to language and a specific value of this distinguishing feature will be 'set' within any particular language. One way of understanding this approach to speech comprehension is to borrow the concept of *parameter setting* from Universal Grammar. We can consider these features such as voicing as 'parameters' which are turned 'on' or 'off' or activated in different ways in different languages.

For example, in English the voicing feature is set to 'on' for the contrast between /p/ and /b/ and the critical time for hearing the voicing is 25 milliseconds. A bilabial plosive will be heard as a /p/ if the listener detects no voicing before 25 milliseconds, or a /b/ if voicing is detected before then. In Arabic, for example, this feature is turned 'off' for the bilabial plosive; there is no /p/, /b/ distinction in Arabic. However, the [p] **sound** does exist in Arabic. The standard spoken dialect does 'devoice' the /b/ before another voiceless consonant. The word for dam, /hibs/ is pronounced [hips], but this change from a [b] sound to a [p] sound is not significant to the listener in Arabic, but would be in English. This realisation of the phoneme /b/ as [p] is what linguistics call an '*allophone*'.

Arabic also has a set of 'emphatic' (or velarised) consonants (consonants in which the back of the tongue is raised, producing a sound similar to the [t] sound in the English word "Tom"). Thus, for an Arabic speaker the [t] sound in Tom would be perceived as a different phoneme from the [t] sound in "tin". For an English speaker the two sounds, although *phonetically* different, are part of the same *phoneme*; they are allophones of /t/. The distinctive feature of 'emphasis' is not significant in English but it is in Arabic.

Let's take another example, from India. In Bengali there are four alveolar plosive consonants, the voiced/voiceless distinction between /t/ and /d/ as made in English, plus a difference between an unaspirated /t/ and an aspirated /tʰ/ (a t-sound which is followed by a puff of air as English speakers produce normally at the beginning of a word like "tea"). Similarly, Bengali has an unaspirated /d/ and an aspirated /dʰ/. Thus the aspiration feature is significant for phonemic discrimination in Bengali, but not in English.

The following Table illustrates the three languages we have been talking about and the way that each sees different features of the input as 'significant' and represents them as different 'letters' in their orthographies.

Table 2.1. The different choices made by English, Arabic and Bengali on the significant features for alveolar plosive consonants in the 3 languages

ENGLISH		ARABIC		BENGALI	
1 phoneme (1 letter)		**4 phonemes (4 letters)**		**4 phonemes (4 letters)**	
Feature	Letter	Feature	Letter	Feature	Letter
[– voice]	**t**	[– voice] [+ velar]	ط	[– voice] [+ aspiration]	ঠ
		[– voice] [– velar]	ت	[– voice] [– aspiration]	ত
[+ voice]	**d**	[+ voice] [+ velar]	ض	[+ voice] [+ aspiration]	ঢ
		[+ voice] [– velar]	د	[+ voice] [– aspiration]	দ

If we accept this view of the perception of language, these *distinctive features* will play an extremely important role in the initial filtering of speech sounds in the sensory register (an inventory of such features is provided by Chomsky and Halle, 1968). The use of such evidence for explaining how languages are processed is essentially 'symbolist' in its approach – it sees language as a set of symbols which are determined by a set of characteristics. For the first language these search characteristics will be set through long term constant exposure. Speech sounds will come to be processed automatically in the Sensory Register, using established routines stored in the LTM. For second language learners without such large amounts of exposure, however, such routines will need to be learnt. The features will need to be 'reset' for the new language. It is likely that the 'distance' between the target language and the first language in terms of the overlap or separation of features will influence the ease with which the second language is learnt and thus a Contrastive Analysis (CA) of the first and target language is likely to prove useful in determining the areas to be taught in the second language. Although the CA approach has proven disappointing in terms of predicting grammar errors of second language learners, it has proved extremely valuable in predicting segmental phonetic problems. This difficulty which second language learners have with phonemes suggests the psychological relevance of the symbolic/linguistic framework we have been discussing.

The phoneme is not a physical reality – it does not correspond to any particular waveform – it is an abstract concept, a symbol which exists in the mind of the speakers. Just as the nose in the visual illusion above cannot be absolutely defined as one set of lines, a phoneme cannot be defined as a unique set of physical characteristics. It is a mental construct which exists in the mind of the speaker/listener. The central challenge of psychology and linguistics is to provide an understanding of the way that the physical reality of raw data can be transferred into the abstract symbolic representations of language.

2.5   Modularity and attention

From the above, we can see that the ability to make immediate sense of incoming language stimuli depends on

a.   the attention to data which is specific to language and the rejection of other data; and
b.   the extraction of salient information from this specific data to create language 'symbols' from the raw physical input.

How are these salient features learnt? One argument would be that they are learnt by exposure to language. However, there is a strong argument that our ability to differentiate and pay attention to certain features is not simply learnt, but is an innate feature of the human brain. There is evidence that there are certain features of incoming language data for which the brain is physiologically adapted. For example, there is a lot of evidence that certain time delays for the onset of voicing in the voiced/voiceless consonant distinctions (e.g. /p/; /b/, /f/; /v/ etc.) of 20 and 40 milliseconds are used by many languages in the world (see below for further discussion of voice onset time research). There is also evidence that similar differences are recognised by other mammals such as the chinchilla (Kuhl and Miller, 1978), thus leading to the speculation that attention may be governed, at least in part, by the physiological construction of the ear and its connection with the nervous system. This would position the voicing distinction as part of an evolutionary legacy. Thus, there would seem to be some support on a neurological/physiological level for the observations made by language universalists that all natural languages make use of a very restricted range of physical cues to create the highly diverse languages which exist.

However, in addition to the common neurological/physiological constraints which may play a part in explaining how sounds are processed, the much more important debate is on the way that the brain acts on the incoming data, and there are also strong arguments as we have seen for the existence of a separate set of processes in the brain which are specific to language; the modular approach.

The existence of specific structures involved in language processing owes much to the writing and thinking of Chomsky (1972) and, in particular, to his hypothesis that our brains are 'hard-wired' to acquire language. This suggests that we all possess an innate capacity to make sense of and learn languages. In the way that our interpretation of visual features is largely unconscious, we are largely unaware of the way that we process languages. Pinker describes the effortless and automatic way that we perceive language; "phonetic perception is like a sixth sense. When we listen to speech the actual sounds go in one ear and out the other; what we perceive is speech." (Pinker, 1994: 159). The implications which can be drawn from this approach in terms of learning will be discussed in further detail in later chapters when we examine language acquisition and learning, but here we are concerned with the grounds for believing that there are specific cognitive structures which exist for processing language. The difference between Unitary and Modular approaches for language processing are illustrated in Figure 2.3.

In the previous chapter we have seen that the neurological evidence from brain scanning experiments and from neurological damage following traumas lead us to believe that there are functionally different areas within the brain for dealing with verbal/linguistic material or visual/spatial material. Amongst these studies, there are also fMRI studies which have examined the existence of specific areas associated with phonological, syntactic and semantic processing. Whether these constitute completely separate routes or separate components within a general processing structure remains to be seen. However, from the point of view of trying to understand language processing in general, and second language processing in particular, evidence will be used from both to try to provide the best explanation that we can of the facts about language learning. At times a unitary view will provide a better explanation, while at others the concepts derived from the modular approach will supply better metaphors with which to explain the processes which we observe.

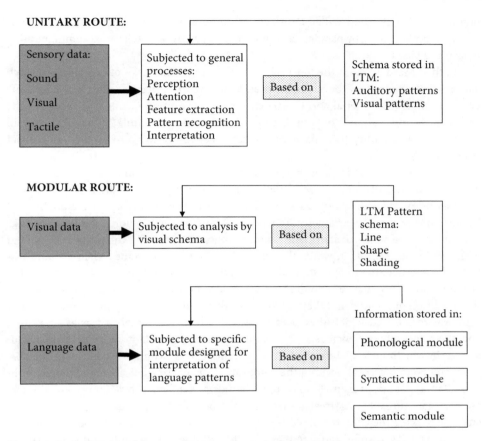

Figure 2.3. A diagram of data processing using a modular or unitary route

2.6   Nativism vs. Learning: Discrimination in infants

One of the ways to examine the degree of 'hard-wiring' in the brain is to look at studies which deal with extremely young children and neonates. If it can be seen that very young babies possess certain processing capacities, then it can be argued that such processing systems are "innate". In terms of general perception, neonates have been shown to be particularly attentive to certain shapes. Abstract shapes which approximate to faces or checkered surfaces, the boundaries between light and dark shapes (Fantz, 1963) and particular faces, such as that of the mother (Walton et al, 1992), have been shown to capture the attention. All of these show that the infant brain is not a *tabula rasa* but is predisposed to pay attention to certain features of the visual input.

However, more germane to this enquiry are the studies which attest to the sensitivity of neonates to language features. Young babies have been found to synchronise their movements to the prosodic features of speech, only making movements in between syllable boundaries (Condon and Sadler, 1974). Other studies have shown the intricate synchronization of mother and baby paralinguistic gestures as a precursor to full verbal communication (Clark and Clark, 1977).

In this regard, perhaps the most significant finding is the series of experiments which suggest that children are born predisposed to differentiate between different phonemic characteristics (Eimas et al, 1971). The classic demonstration of this was shown in the ability of 1- and 4-month olds to distinguish between the sounds /p/ and /b/, and, in particular, their ability to make a categorical decision based on varying voice onset times (VOT).

As discussed above, in English, the distinction between a /p/ and a /b/ is described as a voiced/voiceless distinction (with the former being voiceless and the latter voiced). In auditory terms, this can be expressed as different voice onset times for each sound. Normal English-speakers will hear any sound where the voicing starts before 25 milliseconds as a /b/ and any sound which starts later than 25 milliseconds as a /p/. Infants were presented with continuous sounds in which the onset of voicing was constant. When a sound was initially presented, the infants showed a lot of interest. This interest was measured by the rate on which they sucked on a dummy. Gradually, however, they became habituated to the repetition of a sound and their sucking rate declined. If a sound with a different onset time was introduced which they perceived as different, their interest was again roused and their sucking rate increased. In this experiment, the infants were presented with sounds in which the VOT was either 0 or 20 milliseconds (within the adult range for /b/) or 40 and 60 milliseconds (within the adult range for /p/). If the VOT was changed from 0 to 20 milliseconds or from 40 to 60 milliseconds, the infants showed no renewed interest, i.e. suggesting that they treated them as the same sound. However, when the VOT was changed to cross the adult threshold (e.g. from 20 to 30 milliseconds), the infants showed extra interest. This would indicate that they 'heard' the latter sounds as different (those which crossed the threshold) but the former (i.e. those which did not) as the same.

It could be argued that the children had had experience of speech sounds in the womb corresponding to the VOT of English. However, studies with Guatemalan infants born into Spanish-speaking environments (Lasky et al, 1975) found this not to be the case. These infants were sensitive to distinctions which were not made in their language. They were exposed to the English VOT distinction and a prevoiced/voiced distinction which is phonemic in Thai, but not Spanish or English. Similarly, the Thai distinction was also 'noticed' by infants born into English-speaking environments (Aslin et al, 1981). However, the ability to hear these phonemic distinctions from other languages than their own appears to decline quite rapidly. Studies by Werker et al (1981) and Werker and Tees (1984) demonstrated that this ability disappears sometime between the age of 6 months to a year as the infants experience more of the language in which they live. This would argue that children start with an "open channel" which is predisposed to look for voicing distinctions and are naturally interested in such differences, be they those made by their own or other languages. As they gain more experience with their own language, they lose the ability to notice the distinctions made by other languages. Such findings are supported by studies of brain plasticity which show that the plasticity of the brain (i.e. its ability to adapt different areas for different functions) decreases with age (for a discussion see Greenfield, 1997). It would also lend some support to the critical age hypothesis (Lenneberg, 1982) which, as we have seen, argues that there is an age at which languages are naturally acquired and an age (often identified at about 13 years) beyond which it is difficult to acquire language.

Whilst discrimination between features used in the native language and similar features used in another language declines with experience, it has been shown that the ability to distinguish completely strange features such as Zulu click consonants does not decline (Best et al, 1988). This ability to continue to discriminate between these highly 'marked' sounds (i.e. sound distinctions which are used by very few languages) supports cognitive theories of attention which suggest that the degree of attention is affected by the distinctiveness of the target feature (see Eysenck & Keane, 1995).

The predisposition of infants to notice, apparently innately, voicing in language which becomes honed in on their own native language features is an example of a language learning instinct which rapidly gets adjusted to one language. 'Noticing' as a mechanism for first and second learning is becoming an increasingly central issue in language learning and the degree to which such noticing happens unconsciously (implicit learning) or needs to be directed (explicit learning) is keenly debated. It would seem from the above evidence, that, at least on the lowest level of sound discrimination, the innate ability to notice features in strange (i.e. non-native) languages is one which rapidly declines, but that exposure to highly marked situations will still be noticed. The noticing of marked features may best be explained in general cognitive terms of directed attention to highly unusual features rather than innate processes of language acquisition.

2.7   Distinctive features and language parameters

Thus, it would appear from the evidence, that young children are born with a pre-determined, hard-wired, 'scanner' which is designed to pay attention to a range of sound features used by all languages in the world (universal features). This is attested by their interest when such features are changed. If we use the universal grammar analogy, these features, such as voicing/devoicing, VOT, and aspiration will, initially, be set to a default value and then set to "off" or "on" depending on the way they are used in the native language. Babies then have to 'calibrate' their scanners to the way that these features are realised in their own language. The parameter-setting metaphor for the recognition of phonemes provides an ideal mechanism for explaining how the Sensory Register might go about the business of filtering incoming sounds, converting them into linguistic symbols and passing them on to the next stage of the information processing system, the Working Memory.

However, the superficial attraction of such a model of phoneme recognition is somewhat complicated by the variation that exists between the acoustic footprints (the actual sound features) of the phonemes when they appear in different environments. This is often called the *problem of invariance* and we shall consider this in the next section.

2.8   The problem with distinctive features

The distinctive feature of voiced and voiceless has traditionally been one of the most obvious features for distinguishing between pairs of stop consonants (/p/ v. /b/, /t/ v. /d/, /k/ v. /g/). Consequently the psychological reality of VOT has received a lot of attention from experimental studies. Several experiments have shown that adults are able to separate speech sounds into two categories, either voiced or voiceless and that these judgments happen across very narrow VOT boundaries. The crossover value for /p/ and /b/, as we have mentioned, is 25 msecs. (Abramson & Lisker, 1970). However, the voice onset time for plosive consonants produced at different places in the mouth vary. For the /t/ /d/ pair (produced at the back of the teeth, on the alveolar ridge), VOT is 35 msecs, and for the /k/ /g/ pair (produced at the back of the tongue, on the velum), VOT is 45 msecs. Thus, there is no single measure of VOT which can be used to identify the voiced/voiceless feature.

However, there is a high degree of redundancy in the speech signal. The [± voice] feature is not the only feature which differentiates between the plosive consonants. They also differ in the presence of aspiration. In initial positions in English voiceless plosive consonants are aspirated whereas voiced ones are not. Listeners thus have a choice between which features to use to distinguish between consonants such as /p/, /b/; / t/, /d/ and /k/, /g/. There is evidence in experiments with /k/ and /g/ of a trade-off in the types of cues used to distinguish between the two sounds (Summerfield and Haggart, 1977). If one feature is more indicative of /k/ (for example, VOT), then it can offset the information from another feature (for example, the pitch characteristics, formant frequency) which would indicate a /g/. The point is that people will categorise quite different sounds as a /k/, depending on a combination of features, not just a single feature.

The challenge from the linguists is to provide a description of workable distinctive features which can be shown to be salient from a perceptual point of view. Traditional phonetic descriptions have concentrated on the way we produce sounds using articulatory terms such as 'bilabial', 'alveolar' (indicating where the sound is produced) and 'stop', 'plosive' (indicating how the sound is produced) or impressionistic-phonetic terms such as 'fricative', 'voiced'. Such terms are not purely perceptive and attempts to use purely perceptual descriptions have not been very successful. The challenge for the psychologist is to provide a mechanism which can respond to these features, particularly as we shall see below that there is a great deal of variability in the features associated with any one phoneme. However, before considering the variability problem, there is one theory which suggests that articulation is important in perception and can perhaps provide a solution at both levels.

2.9   The motor theory of speech perception

Carroll (1999) suggests that one of the answers to the problems of variance in categorical perception (i.e. the difficulty of recognizing phonemes which are produced in very different ways in different phonetic environments) lies in a theory of speech perception deriving from Liberman (Liberman et al, 1967). This suggests that the perception of speech relies on the activation of similar neural processes which are involved in speech production. Thus, instead of there being separate modules for reception and production of sounds, both production and perception share the same modules. Deriving evidence from studies which show the importance of visual features such as lip movements and position in speech perception (MacDonald and McGurk, 1978), Liberman developed a theory of phonetic 'gestures'.

This is an idea which is also supported by Halle in his later work (Halle, 2002). One of the arguments used by Halle to support the use of articulatory features to describe phonemes rather than using perceptual terms is that such a description is more parsimonious, it is more efficient. To a linguist, an explanation which is the most straightforward is the most acceptable. This exposes one of the problems of using linguistic, symbolist approaches to give insights to psychological processes. Linguists are primarily interested in deriving consistent and economic systems for describing language structure, but the brain may not operate in the same way (for further discussion see Lessor and Milroy, 1993, Chapter 3).

However, although the motor theory of speech perception is far from being universally accepted and remains controversial, there is evidence from brain imaging (Fadiga & Craighero, 2003, St Heim et al, 2005) that perception and production of sounds activate common areas in the brain. In particular, areas associated with speech production (in the central motor area), are activated when listening to words. From another perspective, it also offers an explanation as to how a second language learner may implicitly learn distinctive phonological features of a second language by practice of that language. Traditional drill activities provide intensive practice of sounds and lay down motor neural pathways which then get utilized for perception.

2.10   Listening to sounds in context: The variability problem

In addition to describing the distinctive features of a consonant in isolation, when we examine the perception of consonants in real word environments, the subtlety and complexity of the operations that the processing mechanism has to undertake are awesome. Consonant phonemes change their acoustic properties depending on their place in a word. The /t/ in tar, /tɑː/, is very different for the same sound in train, /treɪn/, (the former will have strong aspiration, the latter may even be realized as /tʃ/). It is quite different from the same sound in Tom /tom/ (where the sound is velarised – as we saw, a phonemic feature in Arabic, but not in English). Another contrast will be provided with the /t/ at the end of a word like 'cut' /kʌt/ (where aspiration will be less). As we have discussed, these different realisations are described as 'allophones'. Any speech perception process must provide an explanation of how these different sounds are recognised as one phoneme. In the final position, the consonant may not be released at all and the strongest indicator of its presence will be the fact that it considerably shortens the /ʌ/ sound before it, in contrast to the longer /ʌ/ before a /d/ as in cud, /kʌd/. Therefore, a simple serial processing system which compares incoming sounds one by one with a "phoneme template" constructed of a set of distinctive features will not suffice. The system will need to contain a large number of different templates to account for the large variation of actual sounds that constitute one phoneme. In addition the system will need to be sensitive to the position of the sound in a word in order to select the correct template for each environment. It thus needs to be iterative and to consider the incoming sounds in relation to other sounds in the environment.

Thus, even on a basic template comparison level, any model devised must be able to take account of the position of the sounds as well as their acoustic features. It will need to take account of subsequent sounds as well as the current sounds, and thus will require some feedback mechanism, a backward as well as a forward pass, which, in operation, can be characterised as a feedback loop or 'back-propagation' (Harley, 2001). By examining in detail the processes which need to be involved in such a recognition system a number of micro-procedures which are central to current thinking about language processes will become obvious.

Let us take as an example the four words cut, cart, cud and card. Table 2.2 shows the traditional linguistic explanation of the difference between the words.

Table 2.2. The phonemic distinctions between 'cut', 'cart', 'cud' and 'card'[2]

cut	cart	cud	card
/k/ + /ʌ/ + /t/	/k/ + /ɑː/ + /t/	/k/ + /ʌ/ + /d/	/k/ + /ɑː/ + /d/
consonant + short vowel + unvoiced consonant	consonant + long vowel + unvoiced consonant	consonant + short vowel + voiced consonant	consonant + long vowel + voiced consonant

Phonemic theory suggests that these four words are distinguished in RP by the different phonemes in each word. Each word differs from the next by a single phoneme (they are minimal pairs). Thus, the words are differentiated by the vowel (importantly the length of vowel – either short or long) and/or the final consonant (either voiced or voiceless). However, this symbolic description does not match the actual realisation of the sounds. We have already mentioned that the final consonant may not be fully released and that the main clue to the final consonant may be the effect it has on the preceding vowel. Thus the /t/ at the end of 'cart' will shorten the /ɑː/ sound so that it may be of the same duration or even shorter than the short vowel /ʌ/ in 'cud'.

---

2.   Note that the pronunciation illustrated here is that of an RP (Received Pronunciation) speaker. With speakers of 'rhotic' dialects (e.g. Scottish and GA) 'cart' and 'card' may also be differentiated by the addition of a weak [r] sound after the vowel.

In a serial model of processing the following would be the way of accessing the word:

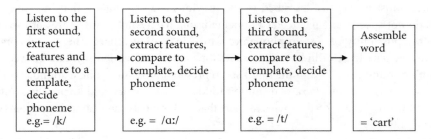

Figure 2.4. A serial model of processing the word 'cart'

The problem with such a model, as we have seen, is that there does not exist a single, simple template which can be used in all cases for phonemes in all positions. A serial template model would need to store multiple sets of features for the phonemes in their different environments. The length of the vowel phoneme, which is one of the crucial features in deciding between "cut" and "cart", is not absolute, but relative to the following consonant. There thus needs to be a way of adjusting the decision as to which vowel is heard based on the information from the rest of the word, a back-propagation.

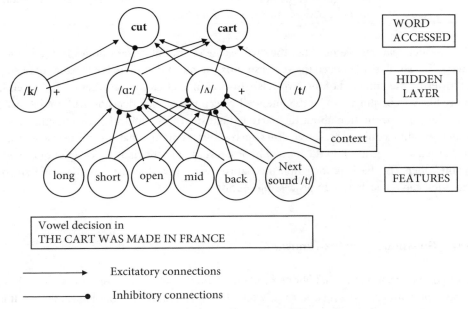

Figure 2.5. Diagram showing the way that a connectionist model would deal with the distinction between the vowels in 'cut' and 'cart' based on the McCelland and Rumelhart (1981) interactive activation model of visual word recognition

2.10.1 Connectionist models

Connectionist models as described in the previous chapter suggest that incoming features do not specify any particular phoneme immediately, but that features of the input raise the possibility of certain phonemes whilst inhibiting others. The models suggest an intermediate level of hidden representations or 'nodes', which mediate between the incoming sound features and the linguistic representations. Subsequent sounds (and the wider context) will equally raise or inhibit hidden nodes, which will, themselves, inhibit different words. Figure 2.5 illustrates the way that such models can deal with such on-going adjustments.

At the bottom level of the diagram is a simplified representation of the features of the incoming sound. The distinctive features of the sounds are described as:

Length	Whether the vowel is a long or short vowel is one of the most basic criteria for vowel recognition in English according to phonological theory
Quality	The degree of openness of the mouth affects the size of the resonating oral cavity and thus the pitch of the vowel. Here the vowels are described as 'open' or 'close' (produced at the top or bottom of the mouth)
	The position of the tongue in the mouth will also change the pitch of the vowel. The phonological descriptors for vowels describe whether the tip of the tongue is at the front, in the middle or at the back. Here the distinction would be between the middle or the back.

As such features are detected they will excite or inhibit certain nodes in the hidden layers. The similarity between the vowel sounds will mean that there is a mixture of raising or lowering the potential of the 2 vowels. This will mean that one or other of the vowels is more likely to be judged to be the intended vowel. However, a decision will not be made until further information about the narrow linguistic (phonological environment) or the wider semantic context is received. These extra sources of information will also send positive or negative feedback to the hidden nodes, resulting in the final selection of one vowel or the other. This back-propagation mechanism is proposed as the way that the issue of variation can be dealt with in processing sounds.

2.11   Guessing rather than knowing

From the above, it is clear that phoneme identification is not a simple one-to-one matching of a sound with pre-existing criteria as would be suggested from phonological theory. It is suggested that the brain is making a series of 'guesses' about what is heard. Identification of a sound is thus not absolute, but the acceptance of the most likely possibility. Another way of looking at this process is given in Figure 2.6.

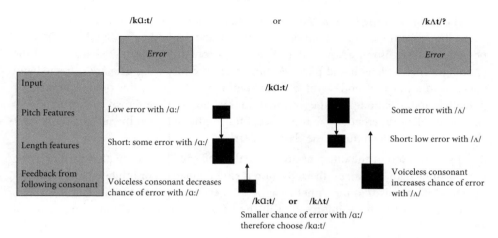

Figure 2.6.   Making as guess about the vowel sound in 'cart'. Estimating the chances of getting it correct.

In the same way, the incoming word is shown as consisting of three sounds, an initial consonant, /k/, a long back vowel /ɑː/ and a final /t/. On the left are two critical distinctive features which are used (as above) to decide between the two vowels (/ʌ/ and /ɑː/); pitch features (the physical properties of quality) and length features. In this model, the brain is characterized as making a series of progressive estimates as to the correct vowel based on the incoming data. The vowel selection is based on the choice which has the least chance of error. There are two sources of information on which the decision can be made, quality or length, thus leading to a trade-off decision. In terms of pitch information (quality), if the listener decides to assign the sound as /ɑː/ there will be a smaller chance of error than if the choice is /ʌ/. However, information from the length feature may lead to the opposite conclusion; there will be more chance of error with the /ɑː/ choice than with the /ʌ/ choice as in this situation the length of the /ɑː/ vowel is reduced by the final /t/ sound. Therefore, at this point the chance of error is about even using the information from the pitch and length formants.

However, if we then add in the information that the next sound is a /t/, a voiceless plosive consonant, it changes the balance of probabilities in assigning the vowel to either the /ɑː/ or /ʌ/ phonemes. The knowledge that voiceless plosive consonants decrease the preceding vowel length and voiced plosive consonants increase it provides more chance of error with the choice of /ʌ/. This tips the balance of probabilities in favour of /ɑː/. This choice of /kɑːt/ as the incoming word which is heard will then be passed on up the processing system. The combined sounds will be compared with memories of words stored in the lexicon and compared with other information from the particular context in which the word appears.

This discussion highlights two important features which are central to connectionist models of language processing.

1.   The first is that the incoming data is not immediately assigned to one representation alone. The system subsumes a number of "nodes" corresponding to the different vowel phonemes in English. It assumes that these nodes contain the distinctive features of the phonemes such as length and pitch. Features from the incoming data are extracted and matched to a range of nodes which share common features. At this point a number of potential candidate nodes will be activated (in this case we have shown two, /ɑː/ and /ʌ/) and these will be differentially activated according to the chance of them being the correct choice (we have shown this as the chance of error).

2.   The activation of the different nodes are then effected by information further along the incoming data stream, i.e. the activation is either enhanced or inhibited by later information. This means that the sampling process is essentially 'iterative' in that it involves constant re-assessment of information in the light of new information being activated and received.

2.12   Neuroscientific evidence

The evidence for a separate language module rests to a degree on the studies, especially aphasic studies mentioned in Chapter 1, which identify Broca's and Wernicke's areas as being centrally involved in all language processing. Studies of acquired language disabilities have also indicated different areas of the brain which deal with specific language tasks. Phonological processing seems to be associated with the superior temporal lobes and the angular gyrus (Byrnes, 2001), and studies of dyslexia indicate that it is a disorder within the phonological processing system as separate from other subcomponents of the language system (Shaywitz & Shaywitz, 2005). However, there are studies which have shown activation of motor production areas as we have noted in the discussion of the Motor Theory Speech of Perception, above. These areas which deal with phonological processing are quite separate from those which deal with orthographical processing, which includes visual processing as well. The areas associated with orthographical processing are centred in the visual area and an area just outside the occipital lobe, the extrastriate area. Semantic processing is associated with Broca's area in the frontal lobe and areas in the medial temporal lobe. These studies would seem to confirm that there are separate areas which deal with phonological processing as distinct from other aspects of language such as orthography and semantics.

Interestingly, although we have discussed the changes that a second language learner will need to make to the L1 'parameters', the processing pathways would seem to be the same in both languages. An fMRI study of bilinguals performing a number of different tasks in both their L1 and L2 by Klein et al (1995) shows that the neural pathways activated by bilinguals are identical in both languages. They were asked to repeat words in the L2, provide synonyms in L1 or L2 or translate words from L1 to L2. Each of these tasks was compared to a simple repetition task in either the L1 or L2 and the brain images in the simpler tasks subtracted from the more complex tasks. Although the degree of activation in the tasks varied (again, according to task complexity with more complex tasks producing greater levels of activity), the same left frontal area (Broca's area) was found to be involved in both L1 and L2 activities. This not only reinforces the argument for neural pathways which are common to language processing, but that both these areas are used in first and second languages.

2.13 Summary

This chapter has looked in detail at the key processes involved in decoding spoken messages. It examined the mechanisms which would need to be used by the brain in paying attention to significant features of the message and selecting what is passed up the line. The general framework used to examine these processes was that of information processing as put forward by Atkinson and Shiffrin, 1968, and a parallel was drawn between visual and verbal information processing.

The chapter examined the nature of the features involved in the assignment of symbols (phonemes) to incoming sounds as seen by linguists as an example of the symbolist approach to verbal processing. All languages use a restricted number of articulatory mechanisms and acoustic features to communicate. However, the combination of these features differs from language to language and the first job of the second language learner is to adjust to the new combination of features used in the second language. At birth it seems that the child is hard-wired to notice these features and to learn them implicitly, but it seems that this ability to notice significant sounds from other languages quickly disappears. The ability to respond to language features at a very early age, it was suggested, provides evidence for the theory that there exists a language-specific modular route for language learning, certainly as far as first language acquisition/learning is concerned.

It was also seen that an approach which relies heavily on linguistic theory to determine significant features of messages would be consistent with the idea that within a language module there may also be separate modules for handling separate components such as phonology, semantics etc. It would seem from neurolinguistic evidence that this may be the case.

The feature recognition process is controlled in first language speakers by fully automatic procedures from the Long Term Memory. For second language learners, however, such **procedures** will be automatic (all languages use similar distinctive features such as voicing) but the **features** will be calibrated for their first not the second language. The implications for this are twofold:

a. the second language learner will need to re-calibrate the feature detection system for the new language, and that this system will need to become highly automatic;
b. until second language learners achieve automaticty in this area, they will need to be more consciously aware of such features and this will have problems for the locus of attention that they can bring to bear on interpreting the message; they will need to spend more processing capacity on formal, bottom-up features than on contextual, top-down features.

However, the more mature second language learner may have lost the ability to unconsciously notice differences. The degree to which such unconscious acquisition procedures may operate in second language learning is a major area of debate within the field. However, at the very least, given the linguistic analysis of how languages work phonologically, the second language learner will need a structured environment to be able to hear the difference between the significant features in the second language. From the point of view of noticing differences, exercises such as minimal pairs, exercises which have long been criticised as lacking in communicative purpose, may well be essential for second language learning.

In the discussion of the mechanisms which need to be involved in the conversion of raw data into linguistic units, in this case phonemes, it was shown that a basic feed-back process is necessary to understand at even the simplest feature level how language recognition takes place. Given the complexity of identifying the different forms by which phonemes can be represented, it was suggested that simple serial processing models would not suffice, neither would static template models based on distinctive features. Any model devised would need to be highly iterative – it would need to take account of incoming data and initially assign such data to symbols but be ready to alter this initial decision in the light of the environment in which the sounds appeared. Thus, it needs to be iterative, using information from the linguistic context along with incoming information to make an estimate of the sound heard. It was suggested that connectionist models would offer a mechanism by which such a process could happen. However, such a process places an extremely heavy cognitive load on working memory; a load which is considerably increased in the case on the second language learner who lacks the automatic procedures of the first language speaker.

Having looked at the way that the brain deals with the extraction of specific language features from the incoming stream of spoken data, in the next chapter we shall consider the way that the brain may deal with information in the written mode.

Further Reading

Trevor Harley (2001). *The Psychology of Language: From Data to Theory (2nd Edn)*. Hove: Psychology Press. Chapter 2 offers a good overview of the recognition of spoken words.

Peter Roach (2000). *English Phonetics and Phonology (3rd Edn)*. Cambridge: Cambridge University Press. This is an extremely thorough guide to English phonetic and phonology for those who want an accessible description of the way that the sound system in English works.

Katrina Hayward (2000). *Experimental Phonetics*. Harlow: Pearson Education.
Chapter 5 provides a more detailed account of the experimental evidence which exists for models of speech perception.

Maurice Halle (2002). *From Memory to Speech and Back: Papers on Phonetics and Phonology 1954–2002*. Berlin: Mouton de Gruyter.
The introduction provides an overview of the development of thinking about phonology from a more theoretical point of view.

Chapter 3

Decoding print
Processes of word recognition
in a second language

In the previous chapter we considered the role different types of memory played in the intake and decoding of sounds. We considered the implications that current information processing models might have when operating in a second language as seen from the viewpoint of the spoken language. In this chapter we wish to turn our attention to the other central process involved in language comprehension, that of decoding print.

In this chapter we shall be setting ourselves similar questions to those we used in Chapter 2:

- How do we get from arbitrary marks on a page to meaningful linguistic symbols?
- Does this process simply involve the conversion of these marks into sounds and then into words?
- Is this the same for all languages?
- What are the implications of different language scripts on the processes involved in word recognition?
- What are the implications of the above on the second language learner reading in the second language?

Processes of word recognition and especially the way that features are extracted from letters and words has received considerable attention within the psychological literature, but relatively little attention in the methodology of language learning; the latter preferring to concentrate on more macro, top-down, processes of the use of context in understanding the printed word. Indeed, proponents of the new literacy approach, such as Street (1984) and the 'London Group', have pointed out the inadequacies of relying on 'autonomous literacy' as the only approach to literacy. The implications of this methodological view in second language learning will be discussed in Chapter 7. However, in our examination of the mental processes involved in language comprehension, we shall begin by considering the difficulties involved in the decoding of print.

Within this examination there are two broad strands which will inform our discussion. The first concerns what is known about word recognition in English and the second is to examine these theoretical models in the light of other languages and the second language learner of English.

3.1   Word recognition and reading

We shall begin our examination of the reading process by examining the way that features are extracted from the incoming visual stimulus and converted into meaningful units – words – in the same way that we examined the incoming sounds and their conversion into words. We saw in the last chapter that the mind actively works on and interprets the incoming stimuli according to previous experience possibly driven by innate mechanisms. We noted the way that the mind imposes order on the incoming visual information. The interpretation of most visual images relies on recognising the picture from the features on the page based on our experience of the world. The images are not 'arbitrary'. They have a one-to-one relationship with the things that they represent. The stimuli examined were generally pictorial, but if we look at the way that the word "LET" in Workbook 2.1, Figure 2, becomes a powerful template for interpreting the image once it is seen, it is clear that letters/words can also have a powerful effect on perception. "LET" is different in that the shapes/marks are arbitrary. There is nothing inherent in either the whole word or the individual letters to indicate what they represent. They are only given significance by reference to a language system, in the same way that sounds and words do not have any meaning in themselves, except as part of a language system. It is the arbitrary nature of language which many psycholinguists claim is a very important rationale for a symbolic approach to language processing and learning (see Aitchison, 1998). In this chapter we shall be examining the mental processes in interpreting these linguistic symbols.

The process for word recognition thus implies a serial process in which the Iconic Memory extracts features from the visual image, constructs these into meaningful linguistic units which are then combined into longer chunks in the Working Memory (see Figure 3.1): As we shall see, as with a simple serial information processing approach to speech recognition, such a model is probably too simplistic, but it is within this general framework that much of the thinking about word and letter recognition has taken place.

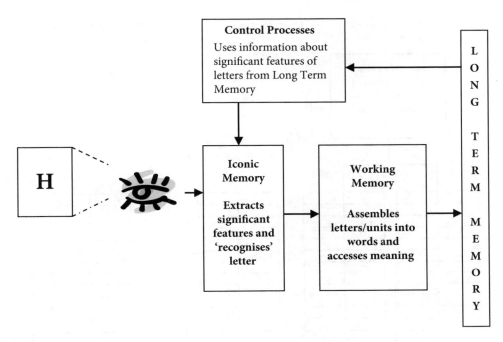

Figure 3.1. A simple serial processing model of letter recognition

There have been two broad approaches to the mechanisms involved in word recognition and lexical access in English which are closely related to the symbolic and connectionist concepts of language processing. The symbolicist approach is best encapsulated in Forster's search model (Forster, 1976, 1979 and 1994) and the connectionist approach in McClelland and Rumulhart's interactive activation model (McClelland and Rumulhart, 1981). The latter relies on a series of models deriving from Morton's Logogen model (Morton, 1979). As these concepts are so powerful in thinking about visual word access and about the processes involved in moving from visual features to meaningful word recognition, it is worth examining them in some depth.

3.1.1   The search models

Forster's autonomous serial search model envisages that words are stored in the mental lexicon in a master file which is accessed via a series of 'bins' or access files, the orthographic, phonological and syntactic/semantic access files (see, Figure 3.2). This reflects the 'modular approach' to language processing which was discussed in the last chapter; with different modules for processing the different aspects of language, orthography, phonology and syntax.

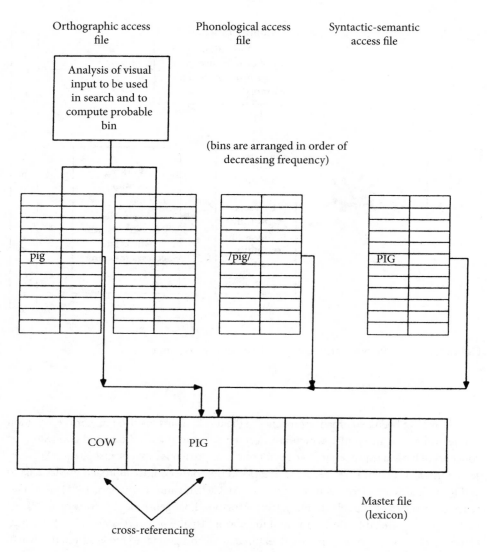

Figure 3.2. Forster's serial search model of lexical access (based on Foster, 1976, taken from Harley, 2001)

Within each access file, words are stored in decreasing order of frequency and a search is initiated by searching though each file from top to bottom. When a match is found between the incoming stimulus and an entry in the file the entry provides a pointer to the master file (lexicon) which contains all the information concerning the word. The syntactic/semantic access file is then used to confirm the final selection in the mental lexicon by a process of cross-referencing.

Although the model is intuitively simple and it accounts for the frequency effect on word recognition (we recognise common words more quickly than less common words),[1] one of the main criticisms of the model is that it is essentially a serial search process and would seem to be inherently slow (although Forster, 1994 has adapted the model to allow for parallel processing). The model rests on a dictionary analogy and does not have the multiple interconnectivity of the connectionist models. The model does not allow easily for the interaction between elements such as context in word recognition. However, another important difference is that words are represented symbolically (as words themselves) within the store, not as potentials, as in the Logogen models, which will be considered next.

3.1.2 The Logogen Model

The alternative model initially proposed by Morton (1969) is the Logogen Model. The logogen concept has underpinned much of the thinking behind connectionist approaches. The logogen models are characterised as 'direct-access' models. Unlike search models, the features of the word access the semantic store by directly comparing an individual word with a single complete entry of that word in the memory. Central to all these models is the concept of the logogen, which is an 'information-gathering' device (Coltheart et al, 2001).

According to the logogen model, each word in the lexicon has its own individual entry, the logogen, which contains all the information necessary for the word to be recognized. As with the search models, there are separate input, output, visual and auditory logogens. Lexical access is achieved by a particular input logogen becoming activated above a certain threshold level. Incoming data which matches the stored information in the logogen increases the level of activation within that specific logogen until a predetermined threshold level is reached, the logogen is 'fired', and lexical access occurs. Each logogen has a 'resting' threshold level, depending on factors such word frequency. Thus a high frequency word has a much lower threshold than a low frequency word and less activation will be needed to 'fire' and thus access this word see Figure 3.3. In this way the model accounts for the frequency effects of words in a different way, by using the activation and raising of potentials within different words.

The logogen is analogous to a stored word 'template' which is activated when enough information is received to identify the word. As with the Foster search model, Morton sees his logogen model as working for both visual and auditory input. (Morton, 1979). In postulating words as independent 'nodes', the logogen concept provides a useful base mechanism which is incorporated into interactive processing and connectionist models of lexical access, for example Bock and Levelt's (1994) 'lemma' model (see Chapter 5).

---

1. For a review of word frequency research, see Harley, 2001.

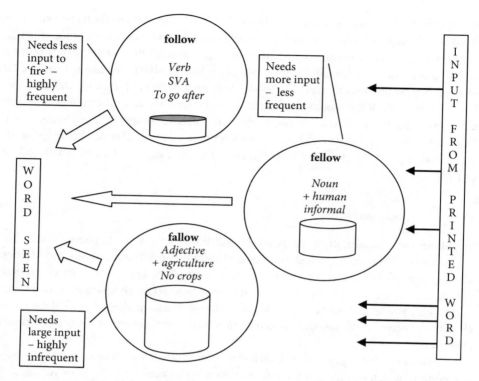

Figure 3.3. Diagrammatic representation of 3 logogens for the words 'follow', 'fellow', and 'fallow'

3.1.3   The Interactive Activation and Competition (IAC) Model

In fact, although we considered connectionist models when talking about spoken language in the last chapter, the earliest connectionist model was based on written word recognition, not on spoken language. McClelland and Rumelhart's interactive activation and competition (IAC) model (1981) was designed to show how individual letter features could be used in combination to recognise a word. The ideas which they introduced have, in one form or another, underpinned approaches to word recognition for the last twenty years.

They introduced two additions to the basic logogen idea, which are common to all connectionist models of language processing. Firstly they suggested that there exists a series of hidden units (nodes) which take part in the processing of language (see Figure 1.5). These turn 'raw' features into symbols. The second major idea is that these processing units can have either an excitatory effect or an inhibitory effect on other nodes in the system.

Their original model envisaged three levels involved in word recognition, a feature level, a letter level and a word level. Incoming information (e.g. letter features such as horizontal lines, vertical lines, diagonal lines, curves etc.) will tend to increase the activation of letters at the letter level containing such features (see Figure 3.4). This is a partial network

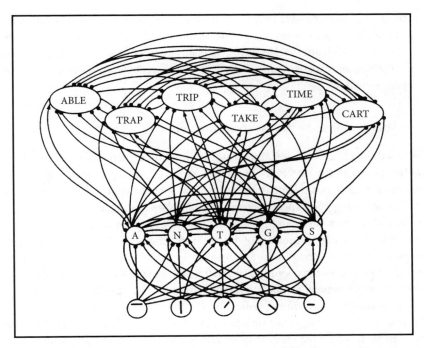

Figure 3.4. A fragment of an interactive-activation network. McClelland and Rumelhart, 1981

for looking at the word TAKE. Looking at the first letter, a high horizontal line will excite T, G and S, but inhibit A and N. These letter nodes are the hidden nodes. A vertical line in the centre will excite T but inhibit all the others until a letter is recognised (in this case T). This will raise the potential of a whole set of words beginning with T (TRAP, TRIP, TAKE, TIME) but inhibit other words (ABLE, CART). Once the second letter is recognised, then other words within the cohort will be inhibited, but in turn will activate words containing the activated letters. The innovatory approach with this model is that each node at each level will produce inhibitory as well as excitatory connections. Thus the model allows for new information to either raise or lower the activity of other nodes at the same level, at the level above or at the level below. The process is therefore iterative and interactive; it makes on-going approximations as the information evolves and feeds back information once new information is received. (for an example of how immediate contexts can effect letter recognition, see Workbook exercise 3.1).

Such models, as discussed earlier, provide an intuitively powerful way of thinking about how raw features are converted into abstract symbols of language. The strength of the excitatory and inhibitory connections between the nodes will depend on the frequency with which such connections exist in the language. By using mathematical models of probability it should be possible to model the way that language features are recognised.

Connectionist researchers have spent much time trying to 'prove' such relationships by altering the weightings between nodes and seeing if computer simulations match what happens in reality. Such approaches have also been extended to second languages (see Van Heuven, 2005 for an investigation into how interactive activation models can be applied in bilingual contexts).

3.1.4   Letters in context – the variability problem

We discussed the difficulty that simple feature extraction explanations and serial processing models have with the variability in pronunciation of phonemes in real speech and the recognition of writing poses similar problems. That such difficulties exist is attested by the difficulty of designing good speech recognition software in unrestricted environments, or that the postal services have had in designing machines to read addresses.

On one level, there is the problem of different fonts and of the different forms of letters. In tachiscopic experiments, changing the font from upper case to lower case in one of the cues has surprisingly little effect on recognition times. It would seem that (for readers of the Roman Alphabet) there is a general symbolic representation of a "a", be it "A", "a" or "ɑ" and that making comparisons works on symbolic, not a feature, level.

On another level, there is the variability and ambiguity which can be clearly seen in handwritten text, where the context is necessary to disambiguate the symbol. Consider these two sentences:

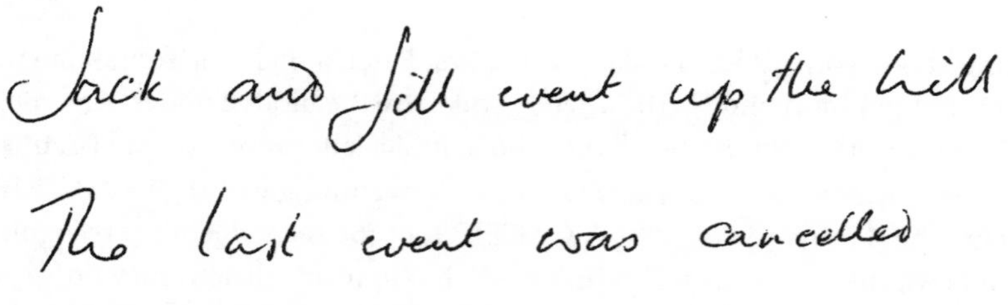

Figure 3.5. The same word shape in different contexts

We have no difficulty in assigning the features of the same graphic image, "went/event" in one context to 'went', and in the other to 'event'. One way to account for this variability is to propose some sort of 'back propagation' mechanism in the processing memory which assigns not one, but multiple, readings of the word which are subsequently enhanced or inhibited by the surrounding context. This is just such a mechanism which is suggested by the connectionist models in which a particular word is activated on the basis of probability and this probability changes as more information is received. This is sometimes referred to as 'fuzzy logic': make an approximation based on the evidence that you have, but then change your estimation as more information comes in. This is the same process as we saw with assigning phonemes to sounds in Chapter 2 and a probabilistic explanation of recognising "went/event" can be seen in the following:

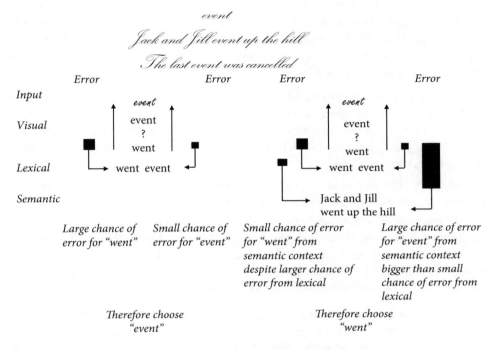

Figure 3.6. A probabilistic explanation of the decisions about event/went

3.1.5   Implications for second language learning

Within the field of psycholinguistics and the associated area of first language acquisition, reading is generally considered to be a secondary, later, learnt skill in relation to oral/aural skills, and there is, by implication, a similar unspoken assumption often made about second language learning; reading rests on oral competence. Such a view is clearly correct as regards first language studies. Oral competence does precede literacy and thus literacy builds on an extensive, though not complete, knowledge of the spoken language. Except for specific impairments, all children learn to speak a language; not all become literate. Thus, literacy can be seen as more of a learnt behaviour whilst speech is more a naturally acquired skill.

However, the situation is not so clear cut when considering literacy in a second language. The second language reader will not necessarily be building on a sound oral competence in the language. The oral competency will often be developing simultaneously with the reading skill. Indeed, as we shall argue, second language acquisition may, in many cases, be mediated through print. For many second and foreign language learners, their exposure to the second language is likely to be largely through the medium of print. This reason alone must make the approaches to reading in a second language different from those of the first language.

The models described above are an attempt to describe and make predictions about highly unconscious, automatic processes involved in the bottom-up processing of print. Much recent thinking in second language reading studies has concentrated on more holistic and top-down language processing as we shall discuss later, and, consequently, less attention has been paid to the implications on such automatic behaviours of different bottom-up processes deriving from different languages. As those interested in second language learning there are three questions we need to ask:

1.   The first question concerns the features involved. Following from the feature-extraction models, what features are salient? On the level of the script, they are likely to differ, certainly between different systems. They differ between logographic and alphabetic systems, and within alphabetic scripts such as the Roman, Cyrillic, Arabic and Hindi (see Birch, 2002 and Cook and Bassetti, 2005).

2.   Given that the features are probably script-specific if not language specific, then are the processes involved in feature extraction different from one scriptal system to another?

3.   If these features are language specific rather than universal, there will clearly be a processing cost in Working Memory for the second language learner in trying to identify the significant features of the L2. In order for fluent reading to take place, base processes like word recognition need to become automatic to reduce the processing cost. The question then becomes, how does one make such processes automatic?

Most approaches to second language reading have assumed that such skills will be automatically transferred from the first language and will not need specific training in the second language context and the acquisition/learning of such skills needs to be taken into account in approaches to second language reading.

McClelland and Rumelhart's interactive activation model discussed above looks at letter-level features and examines how different letter features interact to recognise words. The features used by the model are those associated with the Roman Alphabet, yet it is obvious that other scriptal systems (e.g. Arabic, Hindi, Korean) will use different significant features. For example, Arabic uses base forms with small diacritical additions to differentiate between letters.

Table 3.1. Five Arabic sounds and their graphic representations (NB letters shown in their 'joined up' form[2])

Arabic Letter	ﺒ	ﺒ	ﺜ	ﺘ	ﺜ
Phoneme it represents	/j/	/b/	/θ/	/t/	/n/
base +	2 dots under	1 dot under	3 dots above	2 dots above	1 dot above

---

2.   An Arabic letter has a different form if it is the letter on its own, or a letter which is connected to the next letter; the 'joined up' form. The script contains rules as to which letters can combine to the right or the left thus determining which of the forms of letter to be used in any context.

It is quite possible that the highly detailed feature recognition procedure which is needed to differentiate Arabic letters will require very different processing strategies than the processing of the highly redundant features of the Roman Alphabet. Ibrahim et al (2002) in a study of word identification showed that Arabic first language speakers who had learnt Hebrew as a second language were slower at visual word identification in Arabic (their L1) than in Hebrew (their L2). They suggest that this is due to the complexity of the Arabic orthography as compared to Hebrew (in other respects a highly similar language). Another study by Eviatar and Ibrahim (2004) confirmed the difficulty that Arab readers experience while visually processing Arabic on a CVC (consonant vowel consonant) identification tasks. The extra demands of extracting small detail from the orthography was also indicated in an Egyptian study which showed that dyslexic children were less able to discriminate fine detail as compared to normal reader (Farrag et al, 2002).

There is evidence that general perceptual systems may be affected by exposure to different language systems. In cross-cultural comparisons, it has been noted that Arab subjects pay close attention to small detail in visually presented ink blots (Bleuler & Bleuler, 1935). In an aesthetic judgment task, Heath et al (2005) compared English subjects with Arabic systems and found a difference in preferences between the two groups with the readers of a right-to-left script (the Arabs) scanning pictures the opposite way from the readers of the left-to-right script (the English).

It has also been shown that languages do affect automatic processing strategies in array-scanning experiments (Green & Meara, 1987, Randall & Meara, 1988) and that such automatic, unconscious processing is highly stable (Randall, 1989). Array scanning experiments present subjects with a target shape or character on a computer screen which is then removed. This is then followed by five shapes or characters in a horizontal array. The array may contain the target shape or character or it may not. The position of this character when it is present can appear in any of the positions in the array. The subjects are asked to indicate if the shape or character is present in the array and their reaction time to its presence in different positions is then measured.

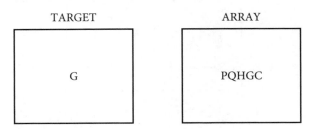

TARGET   ARRAY

G   PQHGC

Native speakers of English scanning arrays consisting of five shapes produce characteristic U-shaped search curves in Figure 3.7b. The middle shapes are seen more rapidly than the outer shapes. However, when the target stimuli are changed to either letters or digits, native English speakers produce a very different, yet highly stable search pattern where the ends of the arrays are also seen very quickly as in Figure 3.7a.

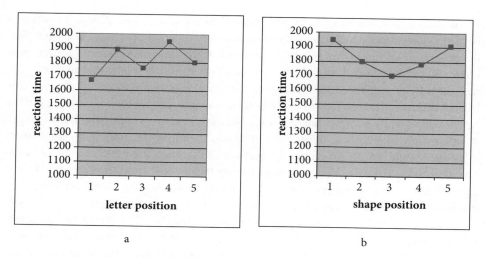

Figure 3.7. Typical array search patterns with native English speakers

These search patterns begin to emerge at a very early age (Green et al, 1983). However, with Arab subjects and Arabic letters, digits and with English (both in a longitudinal study over 2 years of learning English in England and with highly trilingual Algerians) the search pattern remained solidly U-shaped (Randall and Meara, 1988).

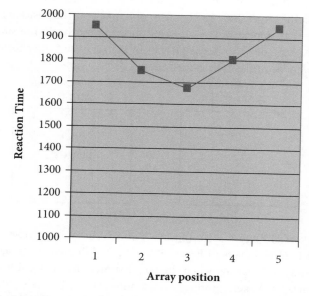

Figure 3.8. Typical search patterns found with Arab subjects and arrays

   Work such as this would clearly indicate the sensitivity of psychological studies to language backgrounds. Very often the psychological literature does not discuss the influence that the language of native English speaking subjects may have on the results of the experiments. This is especially important in the field of language processing where so much of the psychological experiments have been carried out with native English speakers. For example, the reason for such differences in search strategies between shapes and linguistic material in the native English speaker subjects shown above could be due to the well established initial-final-medial letter saliency effects in English (the so-called 'bathtub' effect, Aitchison, 1989). In English it has been clearly established that we pay most attention to initial letter sequences, next we pay attention to final letters and medial letters least of all. Perhaps these saliency effects are peculiar to English and are part of the dual route process of word recognition (see below).

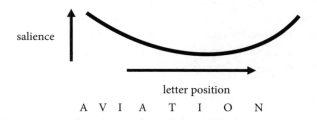

Figure 3.9. The 'bathtub' effect

Leaving aside the issue of whether it is possible to alter such highly unconscious, automatic processes, there is clearly the issue of which features need attention in the different scriptal systems. At the early stages of learning to read in a new script, learners will need to consciously pay attention to these features in the new script, leading to a processing cost in Working Memory.

3.2   Whole words or spelling it out; holistic versus analytic word recognition

The above considerations of which features are salient are similar to the phonological "parameter" argument which we presented in Chapter 2. Just as the aural perceptual system needs to be retuned to pay attention to the new parameters of the SL, so, too does the visual system. However, there are other factors involved in word recognition which have more to do with the way that languages combine individual letters into large units such as syllables and words. Word recognition can either be 'holistic' or 'analytic' or a combination of the two. There is a continuum whereby words can be mainly accessed through whole images (logographic systems), through syllables (syllabic systems) or through letters (phonetic systems). Clearly, logographic systems such as Chinese are very different from alphabetic systems. Some writing systems (e.g. Japanese) contain scripts which use both logographic and syllabic/phonetic systems. Japanese has Kanji, which is logographic and Kana, which is syllabic/phonetic. It also has Hirakana which is alphabetic and reserved for imported "Western" terms.

However, there are large differences within alphabetic languages. Spanish, Italian, German, Greek and Bahasa Malaysia are very regular languages and can be understood by giving each letter a sound. English is not the same. Its orthography is often regarded as highly irregular. It is certainly very complex. It is suggested that languages such as English cannot be accessed simply by a conversion of letters into sounds, but need to be read either as whole words, syllables or ONSET + RIME (the onset is the sound which starts the syllable and the rime is rest of the syllable). Such differences between alphabetic scripts have been characterised by Goswani et al (1998, 2003) as 'psycholinguistic grain size' and it has been shown that young readers of English are sensitive to larger units within words than are young readers of Greek or German (Goswani et al, 1997, 2001). It is argued that this difference is due to the transparency of Greek and German orthography (where letters and sounds have a very regular relationship) as against English, which is less transparent. It is also clear that in English we use both a 'whole word' method to read as well as a 'sound it out' method (for an exercise illustrating whole word recognition, see Workbook 3.2).

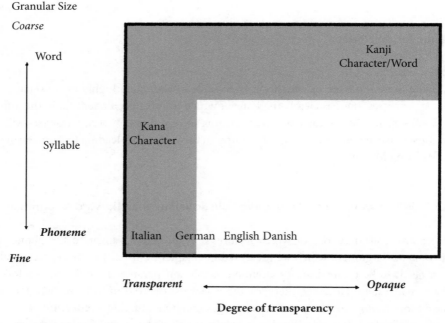

Note: The shaded area on the 'transparency' dimension represents almost 100% transparency.

Figure 3.10. The holistic/analytic continuum for different scripts (from Wydell & Kondo, 2003, p. 38)

Thus, not only will the significant features of the scripts vary from language to language, but there may also be large differences in the more macro aspects of word recognition, such as the size of the primary unit which is used to access meaning. In terms of the general information processing framework used in this book, there will be a need for any control processes to 'learn' new procedures for recognising words in the second language. This will involve not just the individual letter features, but also where to look inside the word; initial and final letters, syllables, morphemes and whole words. In many ways, English with a highly 'opaque' orthography, differs from many other alphabetic languages. This factor may well be the reason for the apparent necessity for using dual routes to word recognition both whole word and phonetic assembly approaches.

3.2.1   Dual Route Theory of word recognition in English

This extremely influential model of word production and recognition for English (and its final form, the Dual Route Cascaded model, Coltheart et al, 2001) proposes that there are broadly two separate routes for being able to recognise a word in English and say it out loud, a whole word (lexical route) and a phonological assembly (non-lexical) route. The latter is considered non- or sub-lexical as it is possible to convert the letters (graphemes) into sounds (phonemes) without necessarily understanding the word. This is very much like the phase of 'barking at print' which English children go though when learning to read. It is also highly pertinent when considering reading aloud in the second language classroom as a technique or the memory implications for the second language learner who does not already possess a sound oral command of the SL.

The model proposes a number of stores which can work to produce a spoken word from a printed image.

- A grapheme to phoneme store which contains the rules for converting letters into sounds.
- An orthographic lexicon, which contains individual word logogens, i.e. representations of the written form of words.
- A phonological lexicon which, like the orthographic store, contains representations of words, but represented as sounds, not letters.
- A semantic store which contains the meanings of words. This store is accessed from either the orthographic lexicon (in the case of reading a printed word) or the phonological lexicon (in the case of writing words from dictation).

Although not explicitly stated, these stores will form part of the Long Term Memory of the speaker.

The model in Figure 3.11 represents the process involved in reading a word aloud. The model proposes the following routes:

1. One is a called a 'sub-lexical' phonological assembly route (the grapheme-phoneme conversion (GPC) route). This involves assembling words from the individual letters/graphemes,

assigning a sound to each one. It is called sub-lexical because it does not rely on the shape of the whole word for access. In the representation of the model given here, this process involves both a serial letter-to-phoneme conversion process, and/or the assembly of the phonological shape of the word from the initial letter/grapheme (onset) plus the 'rime' – all the letters completing the syllable.

2.   Another is a direct, lexical route which involves recognising the word as a complete unit (i.e. its shape), and then recognising its meaning in the semantic store and then outputting the spoken word.

.

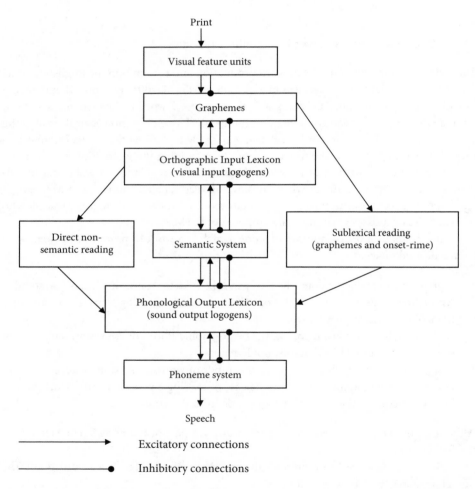

Figure 3.11. The Dual Route Cascaded model of reading (adapted from Coltheart et al, 2001).

3.   Finally, the model proposes a direct non-semantic route in which the complete word logogen in the orthographic lexicon connects directly to a complete word phonological logogen in the phonological lexicon which then produces the word

The design of this model incorporates elements of the logogen models as proposed by Morton (1969) and much of its architecture is based on cognitive neuropsychological evidence from aphasia as we have suggested. For example the two routes to word naming accounts for surface and phonological dyslexias by providing routes to word production which account for such disorders. It also incorporates interactive activation by allowing for the different elements to either excite or inhibit other elements at the different levels. In the model the semantic system plays a part in determining the actual logogen which is activated in the orthographic lexicon, either by raising the activation of logogens which fit the existing context or inhibiting logogens which might be emerging as candidates from the feature-driven system but which do not match the context. Although shown here as mutually exclusive routes, it is also quite possible to theorise that the different routes will be acting in parallel and interchanging information with each other.

The metaphor of two pathways for word recognition is a powerful one and one which has played an important role in thinking about print decoding in English for the following reasons:

- It has a degree of intuitive soundness derived from teaching initial reading. Phonics versus Look and Say have been hotly debated as methods of teaching initial literacy in English and clearly relate to the two pathways.
- It provides an explanation for common types of dyslexia.
- It fits well with the highly complex orthography of English whereby many words are difficult to access through simple sounding out of letters.
- Its operation is supported by the separate visual and phonological processing structures in the brain.

However, there are two issues which should be raised in connection with the above:

1.   Although there is considerable evidence that both routes are necessary for effective reading in English, are they equally necessary in all languages?

2.   Again, English native speaking readers with deficits in either route seem to have problems with fully effective reading in English, but does that mean that it is **impossible** to use other strategies for word recognition (i.e. a purely whole word method which might be used by Chinese learners, for example)?

Although these two issues need to be born in mind, in view of the importance of the dual route model, we shall use the framework to explore the way that word recognition may work from a second language learner's perspective.

3.2.2   The Dual Route model and second language learners; what is significant?

We shall discuss the implications of lexical access for the second language learner in relation to the different levels of the model.

Level	Significant features	Implications for learners	Evidence
Visual features	The recognition of these are highly automatic for L1 readers and probably operate in the Iconic Memory stage. McClelland & Rumulhart identify 8 font features for the Roman Alphabet and their model uses 8 basic font features. Other alphabetic scripts will have quite different features (c.f. Arabic). Logographic languages will have yet again different features which need to be extracted from the printed image.	At initial stages learners will need to consciously analyse each visual unit to extract the significant features. Thus, the processing of these features will have a processing cost in WM, reducing the capacity available for storage of other information.	Personal experience with Arabic where the presence of a small dot will change the letter, and observation of young Arab learners of English copying all the features of a typewritten font regardless of their significance. Many studies have found processing speeds dependant on fluency and familiarity with orthography (see Bernhardt, 1991).
Graphemes	The combination of visual features into graphemes in English is highly complicated. Different letter combinations form single graphemes (e.g. <th>, <ch>, <igh> etc.) and many graphemes have different phonological representations, especially the vowels.	Again, these combinations will need to be learnt by the L2 reader and, more importantly for L2 readers of languages with alphabetic scripts, the L1 values will need to unlearnt. This will also lead to processing costs in WM.	Studies with L1 and L2 Lexical Decision Tasks using 'orthographic neighbours' (words which are close orthographically) indicate that such effects are present in L1 but not in L2 (see van Heuven, 2005, for a discussion).

Sublexical reading: grapheme-phoneme conversion (GPC)	Although this route is probably less favoured by fluent L1 readers, it is available for use with unfamiliar words. Such information is, however, stored and available for use (see Workbook exercise 3.2). For readers with non-alphabetic scriptal systems, this route to lexical recognition may well be less developed. For readers with highly regular orthographies, this route may well produce many false lexical entries.	Often condemned by some L1 reading theorists as a 'slow' and cumbersome method for decoding print (Smith, 1978, calculates that there are more than 200 GPC rules), but it is one of the principal methods by which an L2 reader will have access to the language. Again, this will have large processing costs in WM.	Several studies have found L2 readers attend to graphemic features which override attention to meaning. Support for phonological processing in L2 word recognition found in a number of studies (Bernhardt, 1991). Koda (1989) found differences in logographic/phonological processing in Japanese. Bialystock et al. (2003) found differential phoneme awareness across different literacy languages, with Chinese children performing worse on phoneme segmentation tasks.
Sublexical reading: onset + rime	There is increasing awareness of the importance of the syllable structure in English and its importance in word recognition/reading. Initial and final letter saliency may also reflect the need to read syllabically in English. There is also a lot of evidence that initial and final letter sequences are highly salient in English.	Automatic syllable processing strategies used by different languages, even those using the alphabetic systems may impede efficient word recognition reading. Syllable structure in CV languages (the most common syllable structure used by languages in general) will be reflected in the L1 orthography and thus important inflectional information carried by the end of the syllable in English will not be attended to by the L2 reader (see also discussion of aural perception of syllable in Chapter 2).	Goswani et al (1998, 2001) have demonstrated differences in phonological awareness between L1 Greek and German (low grain size) and L1 English (high grain size) readers reading English depending on psycholonguistic grain size. Meara (1984) demonstrated difference between L1 English and L1 Spanish readers in initial and final letter saliency.

Direct non-semantic reading	This route to word recognition exists within the model to account for certain dyslexics who are able to read words aloud in English without knowing their meaning, but who are also unable to read aloud non-words, thus suggesting that they have an impaired GPC system. Whilst rare in L1 English readers, such a route may provide an explanation for the way that readers whose L1 is logographic, (e.g. Chinese students), may go about word recognition.	Such a route may not play an important role in most approaches to reading comprehension, except that it may become an unintended consequence of a "Look and Say" pedagogic procedure. With Chinese learners it may be a problem in trying to attach phonological shape to recognised words and to access the meaning of the words.	The evidence derives from English speaking dyslexics and little work has been done on its implications for L2 processing. The necessity for such a processing route is a good example of the reliance in modeling word recognition processes of evidence from one language group (i.e. English L1 readers, see discussion below), although studies are emerging of cross-scriptal neurological impairments in other language and English (Wydel et al, 1999).
Semantic System	In terms of fluent reading and comprehension, the role of this system is crucial. For the L2 reader the semantic store will be automatically set to the L1 syntactic and word association systems. Thus, such effects as word priming (one of the lexical roles that the semantic system provides in terms of reading) will probably work through L1 mediation.	For the L2 reader, the syntactic and conceptual frameworks of the L2 are unlikely to have been fully automatised and thus will have to be retrieved from the LTM and consciously applied to the reading task. This will have a high processing cost in WM. Knowledge of vocabulary/conceptual knowledge is important in the semantic processing. Another contributing factor will be the topic knowledge of the reader (see top-down processes in the next chapter). Concepts and topics are likely to be mediated through the L1, and this will also have processing costs, restricting the amount of information which can be held in WM.	Studies have shown that vocabulary knowledge is a key factor in increasing reading comprehension, but syntactic complexity of the passage has not been shown to effect comprehension. However, syntactic knowledge of the reader *per se* has not been investigated except that increasing proficiency has been shown to correlate with increasing comprehension (for a discussion see Bernhardt, 1991).

Phonological output logogens	In the Dual Route Cascaded model which Coltheart et al, 2001, use for computation there are assumed to be 7131 logogens, each corresponding to monosyllabic words available in English. These correspond to a comparable number of orthographic logogens, less homophones. Thus, the model assumes 'grapheme chunks' which correspond to 'phoneme chunks' and uses frequency information about these chunks for computation.	The model uses monosyllabic words as its base which is clearly quite restricting. However, if the syllable is used as the basic unit, then the system would have more power to explain more than monosyllabic word recognition/reading. However, the task for the L2 reader is to access phonological representations from such 'orthographic chunks'. Such associations will be automatic in L1, but not in L2. The L2 reader will also not have the developed phonological lexicon in the L2 to which to relate the orthographic chunks.	Psycholinguistic grain size experiments (Goswani et al, 2001, 2003) and the effect of syllable structure on spelling in English (Randall, 2005).
Phonemes	The placing of final output shape is seen within the DRC model as organised into 8 units, within each of these units the 43 phonemes of English.	As discussed in the previous chapter, the automatic phoneme inventory for the L2 reader is that of the L1 and there will be WM processing cost in applying the L2 parameters. There may also be considerable processing space taken up by conscious control of the motor execution programmes to produce the sounds until they become proceduralised (see Chapter 5, below).	

What emerges from this examination of the bottom-up processes involved in feature processing and word recognition is that the L2 reader will need to devote considerable processing capacity to the mechanical recognition of words. This devotion of a significant proportion of WM capacity to this task will compromise the reader's ability to attend to wider features of text or to wider aspects of topic knowledge or general schema. This theoretical perspective of the task faced by the L2 reader matches with the findings from very many studies which show that L2 readers do not pay sufficient attention to wider context, are 'word bound', and concentrate on form not meaning (see Workbook 3.3 for illustration of the differential attention paid to function and content words). This has largely been interpreted within SL/FL reading methodology as the necessity to 'instruct' the L2 reader in the use of the wider context and meaning to improve L2 reading proficiency. What our theoretical perspective suggests is that it is probably impossible for the L2 reader to devote sufficient processing capacity to this wider perspective, until such basic feature recognition processes have become automatic. As the majority of L2 readers have already gained literacy in their first language before learning their second language, much second language instruction has assumed that the micro-skills involved in reading have already been acquired in the L1 and are readily transferable to the L2. Our analysis above indicates that such an assumption may not be correct, and there is emerging evidence that the basic processes in reading are not universal, but may be quite language specific.

In the next section, we wish to take this further by looking at the general assumptions which underpin the models of word recognition which we have described and question the degree to which such models and the cognitive architecture which they describe will work as truly universal models, or the degree to which they are 'linguicentric'; they have been devised in response to English and are highly coloured by the orthographic nature of English.

3.3   Phonological representation, orthography and semantics

Word recognition procedures, and, indeed the Dual Route model we have been examining, are based on the assumption that there is an interaction between three types of 'code' the orthographic, the phonological and the semantic. They are linked into what has been dubbed the "triangle model". (Seidenberg & McClelland, 1989).

The assumption is that the three sources of information, print, sounds and context are the primary sources of information needed for successfully pronouncing and writing a word. Norris (1994) argues that the Seidenberg and McClelland model does not account for the ability of readers to shift strategically between lexical and non-lexical routes to word naming, and we wish to extend this to suggest that readers of other scripts and orthographies may well employ the different routes to different degrees.

For example, Malay has a highly consistent consonant vowel (CV) syllable structure. In such a highly regular CV orthography such as Malay, readers may well prioritise the phonological-orthographical pathway to the virtual exclusion of the phonological-semantic-orthographic pathway. As Meara (1985) points out with regard to his discussion

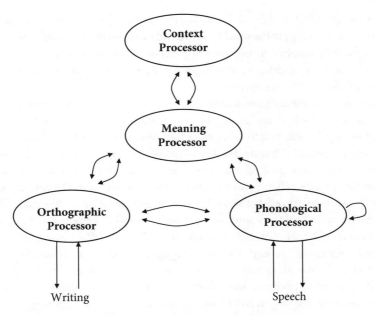

Figure 3.12. The Seidenberg & McClelland (1989) "Triangle Model" of word production and writing (from Adams, 1990)

of a native Spanish speaker who displayed problems with reading in English and Spanish, the problems were less noticeable in Spanish He argues that the use of the phonological-orthographic route would not prove problematic in Spanish with its highly transparent orthography, but would cause problems in English. Another demonstration of the effect of language on reading ability is the case of a bilingual English-Japanese teenager with an Australian father and an English mother who was brought up in Japan (Wydel et al, 1999). At the age of 16 he could read perfectly in Japanese, yet was highly dyslexic in English. This would suggest very different processing strategies in the two languages.

In a discussion of spelling errors for inflected and non-inflected words with Malay speakers, Randall (2005) has suggested that the deletion of the final consonant when it is a past tense morpheme but not when it is part of the root word can be explained by the differences between the phonological systems of the two languages and the processing strategies. Thus, in response to the target word PLANNED, most of the students wrote PLAN. In response to the target word LAND (which ends in the same phonological structure), there were far fewer errors, and those that there were consisted of vowel misspelling e.g. LEND or putting the wrong consonant at the end e.g. LANT. In terms of the phonology the differing syllable structure will mean that the last consonant will not be perceived (see Chapter 2 for a discussion of this). However, when the last consonant is part of the root word it is supplied by the listener and written down. In an identical phonological environment, when it is a morpheme, it is deleted. Given the lack of perceptual evidence available to the reader the only way to supply the morpheme would be through the use of context. Contextual evidence will be supplied from a context processor. The failure to use such a processor as a principal route for reading/word recognition would explain the failure to supply the final consonant when it is a morpheme.

The situation is quite different when we consider the word recognition procedures of ESL students who have had initial literacy in logographic scripts. There has been a considerable amount of research into users of logographic scripts and the spelling of English real words and non-words. A wide number of studies have shown that Chinese readers do not in general make more spelling mistakes on real, known English words, but make considerably more mistakes when presented with pseudo-words (for a review see Wang and Geva, 2003). This is interpreted as the Chinese subjects using direct, lexical rather than a phonological encoding route to word recognition fostered in response to basic processes transferred from the L1 literacy studies. Similarly Koda (1989) demonstrated that Japanese ESL students with initial literacy in Kanji (a logographic script borrowed from Chinese) showed better use of visual processing skills on lists of unpronounceable letter strings but were less able to use of phonological information on pronounceable letter strings. Most studies have been carried out on adult learners whose intial literacy training was in a logographic script, but a study by Wang and Geva (2003) demonstrated that Chinese subjects spelt English words better using a holistic word strategy. This was true even in L1 Chinese ESL students who had not had an intensive school-based exposure to the Chinese script.

Rather than seeing all language word recognition processes as the same, it is probably better to think of different languages making differential uses of analytic/holistic processes as exemplified in Figure 3.13.

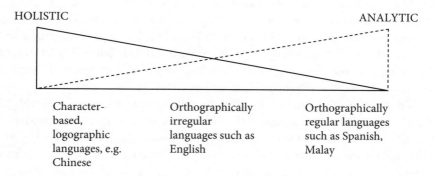

Figure 3.13. Use of holistic/analytical approaches to word recognition

The use of holistic, visual recognition approaches by Chinese readers on ideographs may well effect the cognitive strategies employed. It has often been commented that readers of logographic scripts are, in some senses, reading in 'concepts'. A Chinese listener, when presented with a spoken word, will have a number of alternative characters, the correct one depending on the meaning of the word. As an illustration,

> 文 the hanzi (*character*) represents the morpheme 'written language', whose spoken form is /wən/. Many morphemes share the same pronunciation /wən/, but each has a different written form: when /wən/ means 'to hear' it is written as 闻; when it means 'mosquito' as 蚊; when it means 'line' as 纹. Meaning-based systems can be read by people who do not know the phonology of the language or who indeed speak different languages: 文 means 'written language' regardless of whether it is said /wən/, as in Standard Chinese, or /mîn/, as in Cantonese. Indeed a Japanese who would read 文 as /buŋ/ would still understand it as 'writing, literature', as would a Korean who would say it as /mun/. (Cook & Bassetti, 2005: 5)

Thus, it would appear to be mandatory for the Chinese listener to access the meaning of the word in order to decide on its form. In writing down a single word from dictation, it is not possible to work through a simple phoneme-grapheme conversion. In reading Chinese the favoured route may well employ the meaning processor to a greater extent than the GPC processor. It is quite likely that this process will be transferred to the reading of the second language. In this situation, the triangle model may well become a 'hub-and-spoke' model (Wen & Weekes, 2003) for Chinese readers, where the Meaning Processor in Figure 3.12 has strong links to the Context Processor, the Phonological Processor and the Orthographic Processor, but there are weak links between the Phonological Processor and the Orthographic Processor.

In the reading of Bahasa Malaysia, however, with its extremely transparent orthography, a serial GPC approach for both writing from dictation and reading aloud from print will produce access to meaning via the oral word and thus there is little cognitive advantage to be gained by involving context in the process.

Finally, if we consider Arabic, we have yet another situation. Although often described as having a highly transparent orthography, in standard written form, it does not represent unstressed vowels. In writing words from dictation, a serial GPC approach will work well as unstressed vowels will be provided from the spoken word and present no problems. Thus, we might expect a route like that used by Malay speakers. However, in reading aloud words, a series of 3 written consonants (the base form of the Arabic word) can have a variety of meanings, depending on the context. Thus the full phonological representation of the word can only be accessed via the context.

Table 3.2. The three possible realisations of the letters ن + ك + س in Arabic

Written form	Possible spoken forms	Meanings
سكن	/sakana/	he lived
	/sʊkina/	he was dormant
	/sakan/	residence

Following from this, it is possible that Arabic may use more of a hub-and-spoke model for reading aloud, although given the highly regular correspondence between the consonants and their phonological representation, aspects of the GPC route may also be involved. Fender (2003), found in a comparison between native Arabic- and Japanese-native speaking ESL learners that the Arabic native speakers were significantly better at integrating words into larger phrase and clause structures and then using this for comprehension than were the Japanese. This would suggest that the Arabic ESL learners were, in fact, using the context more than the Japanese ESL learners who were using a more direct word recognition procedure.

In another study of the different uses of phonological and orthographical processes, Arab-Moghaddam and Sénéchal (2001) examined the spelling errors in Persian/English bilingual children. They found that the errors in English were explicable in terms of both orthographic and phonological processes, whereas the Persian errors were predicted by orthography only. This again, indicates the different processes involved in processing print, and provides support for the idea that the dual route theory (i.e. the necessity of using both orthographical and phonological routes) may well be something which is peculiar to English and any other language with a less transparent orthographic system.

The differences between the possible uses of the phonological, orthographic and context processors are represented in Figure 3.14.

A number of points emerge from the description of word recognition models which we have looked at.

1. The models have very much been developed in response to reading aloud single words in English. There is an underlying assumption that the provision of the 'correct' sounds to letter strings is crucial to word recognition. Whilst this may be true of first language word recognition, it is problematic with regards to recognising words in a second language. Second language readers may understand the word but pronounce it wrongly; words may be effectively accessed in terms of their meanings, but be given quite different phonological shapes (for example, depending on first language orthography).

2. The common idea that reading involves accessing the sound of a word (i.e. the prioritisation of phonology for word recognition) is perhaps a derivative of an alphabetic reading system and is not necessarily true of non-alphabetic reading systems.

3. Different orthographies may well use different word recognition strategies and these strategies will be transferred to the second language, in this case, English. Just as the direct non-lexical route in the Dual Route model is a response to explaining specific dyslexic tendencies in English (and thus is perhaps purely a process used in English alone), other orthographies may well use different strategies in different combinations and the overall architecture of word recognition needs more careful research.

We thus need to be careful when using cognitive models which have been devised for English with other languages, but the examination of the mental processes involved in word recognition, especially cross-linguistically, is important in trying to understand the

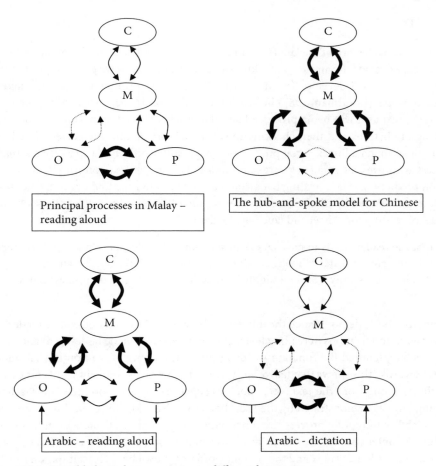

Figure 3.14. Possible lexical access routes in different languages

problems which second language learners face in trying to read in English. It is also clear that there will need to be a mechanism in the brain which is able to direct attention to different salient parts of the printed word and this may not be the same for all languages, but may have language specific components. If this is true, then second language learners will need to 're-learn' such attention mechanisms in the second language.

3.4   Using the immediate context

Throughout the discussion of word recognition, we have referred to the need to use the context as an aid to recognising words. There are two levels at which context works. One is the wider context and schema within which the word and text are based, and this will be considered in the next chapter, but there is also the immediate linguistic context, and this is what we shall examine in this section.

3.4.1   Language form

Since Goodman's work of the late 1960s in L1 reading there has been a lot of interest in the reader's use of syntactic and semantic knowledge to make successive guesses about the way that a sentence will develop. This approach characterised reading as a 'psycholinguistic guessing game' (Goodman, 1967) in which the reader would make successive predictions about the text as it was being processed and the process of reading would become one of making predictions and then checking to see if such predictions are correct. Reading is then not so much a linear, serial process of recognising words, but a successive sampling process with eyes moving backwards and forwards over the text confirming and checking on predictions. Such reading behaviours can be seen in the rapid eye movements and fixation points used by efficient readers (see Bernhardt, 1991). The implications for such a model of reading for the second language reader are:

1.   that the reader needs to have an established knowledge of the syntactical structure of the language in order to make sensible predictions for later confirmation;
2.   that it is necessarily based on highly automatic word recognition processes in the first place.

Bernhardt (1991) demonstrated the differences between native and non-native reader's eye movements and fixations in reading texts. The native speaker made far fewer fixations and, in particular, ignored the function words in the text, pausing instead on the substantive content words. This shows that native speaker readers prioritise content words for extracting the meaning from the text, very much as suggested by the Goodman approaches to reading (and as demonstrated by the Workbook exercise 3.3). However, this process rests on the ability to rapidly process the function words, automatically access syntactic rules and fit the content words into this pattern. Non-native speakers, on the other hand, need to think about both the syntax and the content words, as shown by their fixations on function words. This demonstrates the difficulty that the non-native speaker has in using top-down approaches to reading. Processing capacity will be taken up with the processing of syntax via function words, leaving less capacity for processing the content words which are the core meaning of any text.

Further work with on-line fixation studies of L2 readers has examined the way that L2 readers interpret ambiguous sentences to see if L1 strategies are transferred to reading in the L2. The results of these studies have been somewhat mixed, some showing the transference of L1 preferences, others finding no such effects. Felser et al (2003) found no transfer of parsing preferences by L1 German and L1 Greek to L2 English reading of potentially ambiguous sentences, but both these advanced learners showed different preferences to L1 readers. This suggests that the situation is more complex than a simple transfer from L1 to L2, but it does indicate that even advanced L2 learners do not parse sentences in the same way as L1 readers.

What, then, are the implications of these findings for memory and the non-native speaking reader? The processes involved in interpreting written text are similar to those we discussed earlier in aural comprehension; incoming information must be held in WM for a short time whilst new information is taken in and then compared to the already received information. However, the WM processes in reading are rather different from those of aural comprehension. In listening comprehension the already received information is not available for inspection or re-inspection. In processing written text, this information is available on the page and can be re-inspected by the reader. This leads to the non-linear eye movements observed in reading a text. However, for efficient reading to take place, some textual information must be held in the WM long enough to be worked on and integrated with new information. The longer and greater number of fixations of the non-native speaker are indicative of a lack of storage capacity in WM due to

1. the necessity to pay attention (and thus store) both content and function words;
2. the need to consciously use syntactic rules to continually process the text;
3. the lack of automatic word recognition strategies (the longer fixation times indicating time spent decoding the words).

Thus, native speakers, through their knowledge of the language structure, are able to take in and 'chunk' more information at one time. One way this chunking and information load reduction is realised is through the knowledge of the syntactic structure of the language, but another related mechanism by which this can be achieved is through the knowledge of the associations between words, their collocations and colligations.

3.4.2   Word associations and collocations

Psychologists have long been aware of the power of word associations in priming responses to visually and aurally presented words. A large number of experiments have been carried out using lexical decision tasks. In such experiments, subjects are presented with a 'prime' word, e.g. NURSE, which is then removed, and then asked to make a decision as to whether target word, e.g. DOCTOR is a real word or not (the lexical decision task). The relationship between the prime and the target can then be altered (e.g. they can be related by sound or by orthography, targets can be words or pseudowords) and the speed of response used to indicate the strength of the priming effect and, by implication, the associative bond between the words. Many of the models of word storage and retrieval have been based on such experiments (Forster, 1976, Taft, 1981, Taft and Forster, 1975, Morton, 1979).

However, a more radical explanation of language comprehension has begun to emerge based on the highly stable relationships between words in different genres and discourse types deriving from the large number of investigations which have been enabled by the studies of large corpora in linguistics (Hoey, 2003). Such 'associative chunks' provide useful models for trying to understand how language is processed and we shall return to a discussion of these when we consider both lexical storage and semantic networks in Chapter 5 and in the automatisation of basic language skills in Chapter 6. However, it is clear that the native speaker's knowledge of the relationships between words and their immediate neighbours built up though extensive experience with the language, allows them to chunk the incoming text, thus reducing the processing cost in WM.

3.5   Neuroscientific evidence

3.5.1   The dual route model

A lot of attention in brain imaging research has been paid to the attempt to verify physio-logically the presence of such dual routes in the brain. An analysis conducted of 35 neuroimaging studies suggested that word and pseudoword access share common procedures (associated with the Visual Word Form Area – see below) but that grapheme-to-phoneme conversion (the GPC route) seemed to rely on different brain structures than lexico-semantic (the 'whole word' route) processing suggesting "the suitability of the dual route framework to account for activations observed in nonpathological subjects while they read" (Jobard et al, 2003: 693). In another experiment, Joubert et al (2004) found different brain areas were activated at different levels by lexical as against sub-lexical tasks. The lexical tasks involved subjects silently reading high frequency regular words and the sub-lexical tasks in reading nonwords and very low frequency regular words (which would require sound-ing out). Using a similar methodology with regularly and irregularly spelt low frequency words and a spelling task, Norton et al (2007) found activation of different neurological areas with the two types of word. These studies suggest that the results show that lexical and sub-lexical processes in reading activate different regions within a complex network of brain structures and lend support to a dual route model of lexical access.

We have made many references to the way that evidence from aphasics and the dif-ferent forms of reading impairment and dyslexia have lead to the development of the dual route theories of lexical access (for discussion, see Harley, 2001) but one of the points that we made earlier was that subjects with brain lesions do not usually show the complete loss of the ability to either use one route or the other (reading regular words but unable to read irregular words, for example), they merely show impairment of the route, making more mistakes than would be expected. This would suggest that either the neural pathways are only partially damaged or that subjects can compensate for this loss by using other means of accessing the words. This would tend to support the neural networking model of brain function where many systems are involved in language processing. Indeed, as was sug-gested earlier, the processing of language in the brain is a highly complex process involving a large number of different areas working together. An fMRI study using the naming of irregular words, regular words and non-words (Binder et al, 2005) was also unable to find evidence of an 'exclusive' dual route effect and the authors suggest, instead, that a model of 'parallel' access routes is more acceptable.

3.5.2   Modular or unitary pathways

As with cognitive psychology in general, neuroscientists have been very much concerned with the question of whether our processing of language is best characterised as a single general cognitive ability or as a separate set of modules, specifically designed for this task. fMRI studies are providing a lot of evidence to suggest that there are specific areas involved in different tasks and one of these areas has been referred to as the Visual Word Form Area.

As early as 1892 a French neurologist, Déjerine, suggested that damage to a particular area could lead to pure alexia where visual input was separated from optical images of words. This suggestion has been investigated in a number of fMRI studies which have shown the involvement of a small area in the occipital lobe with visual word processing. This area is different from the areas which are involved in other specialist object recognition tasks such as recognising faces, tools, and houses which we mentioned earlier. There was a degree of controversy in the studies as to the degree to which this area, or damage to it, was implicated in causing alexia (for a discussion see Martin, 2006), but a recent careful case study carried out by Gaillard et al (2006) seems to provide evidence that the Visual Word Form Area does play a causal role in disrupting normal reading. In this case study, a patient underwent some highly localised surgical treatment as a cure for epilepsy. Prior to the surgery he was carefully assessed on a wide range of language and other cognitive tasks and brain images were taken. After the surgery, he was reassessed on a similar range of tasks and further brain images were taken. In tasks involving object naming and face recognition the surgery had no effect, and language skills, including writing to dictation, remained normal. However, he complained of difficulty with reading and it was discovered that he could only recognise words slowly though a letter-by-letter combination process and word recognition times lengthened considerably as the word got longer. Subsequent fMRI scans on word recognition tasks showed that the VWFA was not being activated during these tasks. This, the researchers argue, gives credence to the importance of this area in word recognition tasks and thus provides neuropsychological evidence for the importance of whole word recognition in reading and for the existence of language specific modules in the brain.

The findings, then, appear to point to separate areas in the brain, not only for language, and, more specifically, for reading. However, as Martin (2006) points out, they are rather surprising given the relatively recent appearance of literacy as a major human activity. It is only in the last century or so that there has been anything like a mass access to literacy. For such a short period to have resulted in a specific module for word recognition seems rather unlikely in evolutionary terms. The evolution of language specific networks involving a large number of interconnecting brain structures over the last 20,000 to 40,000 years (although relatively short in evolutionary terms) would appear to be feasible (for a discussion of language, the brain and evolution see Wills, 1994), but to suggest that there might be an evolutionary adaptation over such a short time is more difficult to argue. However, McCandliss et al (2003), suggest that the VWFA is an adaptation of an existing mammalian perceptual expertise structure which develops a reading specificity in humans during the process of learning to read. They review evidence of children's sensitivity to word features such as length and their ability to handle pseudowords as evidence of this developing expertise.

3.5.3   Brain imaging in cross-linguistic studies

The above studies attest to the importance of the dual route theory in reading and to the presence of specific structures in the brain which are sensitive to the processing of print. Most of these studies have used alphabetical European languages in their studies. However, we have argued that second language readers of English may use these different pathways in different ways according to the effects of their first language. The most dramatic differences lie between readers of ideographic and alphabetic scripts and it is the investigation of such differences that has received a lot of attention from brain imaging studies.

Just as Binder (2005) above suggested that there is no evidence that there exists an exclusively visual as against GPC route for recognising words in English, Peng et al (2004) showed that in briefly presented words that phonology was automatically generated for low frequency words, even in Chinese. It would thus seem that phonology plays a part in lexical processing even in languages where the orthographic – phonological mapping is highly inconsistent. If differences exist, then they probably exist on the degree to which the different routes are used.

Studies involving examination of differences between logographic and alphabetic scripts have shown conflicting results. Disappointingly, in a series of experiments run at the Neurological Research Laboratory in Singapore which looked at the processing of Chinese characters and alphabetic material by different subjects (bilingual English-Chinese subjects at different levels of proficiency), no substantive differences were observed on the tasks set (Chee et al, 1999a, 1999b). It appeared that the general language processing areas were being utilized under both character and alphabetic conditions. A similar lack of difference using non-fluent Chinese-English bilinguals was found by Xue et al (2004), although the volume of activation in all areas was much greater in the L2 than in the L1. However, Tan et al (2001) found a number of right hemispherical regions activated when reading Chinese relative to reading English which they attribute to the need to analyse the complex visual information associated with the Chinese character. In studies with Koreans, whose script involves both alphabetic Korean words and logographic Chinese characters, Yoon et al (2005) also found that both alphabetic and logographic characters activated the same general language processing areas, but that the logographic characters also activated areas of the right hemisphere associated with higher order visual control.

There is evidence from studies with developmental Chinese dyslexics to show that different pathways are used for reading. Whereas a number of studies across different countries (England, France and Italy) have shown that developmental dyslexics share weak activation in the area of the posterior temporal lobe (an area associated with auditory processing) in a study with Chinese reading impaired children, Siok et al (2004) did not find a disruption in this area, but found weak activation in an area linked to the conversion of orthography to syllable and orthography-to-semantic mapping. This would tend to suggest that the direct mapping of character onto meaning is a route used in fluent Chinese reading, although as we have seen other studies (Peng et al, 2004) have shown that phonological areas are activated in normal readers.

Studies with Hebrew and Arabic users, both of which share similar characteristics (they both write from right to left and are 'consonantal' languages; neither mark short vowels in normal text) with users of alphabetic languages also show differences. A bilingual Hebrew/English acquired aphasic showed alexia in reading Hebrew but none when reading in English, thus suggesting different pathways for the different languages (Leker & Biran, 1999). In a study of native Arabic speakers and native Spanish speakers,

Al-Hamouri et al (2005) found strong activation of the left hemisphere in both groups immediately after a reading task (200 ms), but a difference in the degree of activation between the groups after 500 ms. This would suggest the initial use of common language processing mechanisms across all languages, but with differences emerging later. The dependence on the time selected for imaging could well be an explanation for the sometimes conflicting results as in the Chee studies mentioned above.

These studies would seem to indicate that word recognition is a highly distributed process involving a great deal of overlap, but that there are differences in emphasis depending on differences between scripts.

3.6   Summary

In this chapter we have looked in some detail at the way that print is decoded and how the basic building blocks of reading-word recognition – is thought to proceed in English. We have identified the dual route access model as a central framework for understanding word recognition and examined the importance of this framework for all languages, and, importantly, the necessity of such a route for all languages. There would appear to be a degree of neuropsychological evidence to support different access routes in the brain for the GPC and the whole word processes, although there is evidence that different languages would use these routes to different degrees. The implications for second language learning and structuring of the memory processes are that second language learners will probably need to be re-orientated to, not only the significant letter features of the new scriptal system (if the first and second language scripts are different), but that more strategic control processes, such as the size of unit and the salient letters will also need to be changed. This will also be true of learners who use the Roman alphabet, but with different orthographic frameworks, particularly the degree of orthographic regularity.

We also examined different models for word recognition, and, in particular, connectionist models for decoding print which allow for the use of context in the decoding process. In this chapter and in Chapter 2 we have very much restricted ourselves to the immediate linguistic environment, however, there are many arguments for the role the wider situational context and schema play in understanding the message, and it is this which will form the basis for the next chapter.

Further Reading

Vivian Cook and Benedatta Bassetti (eds) (2005). *Second Language Writing Systems.* Clevedon: Multilingual Matters.
This book contains a lot of useful pieces of research into how second language users of different first language backgrounds read and write in English. The introduction contains a very good overview of different issues concerned with different writing systems.

Barbara Birch (2002). *English L2 Reading: Getting to the Bottom.* London: Lawrence Erlbaum Associates.
This is a very good overview of many of the issues to do with the cognitive processing of English as a second language.

Chapter 4

Using background knowledge to interpret the message

In the previous two chapters we have looked in close detail at the way that the brain works on the incoming raw information, extracts features and recognises the base units, the phonemes and the graphemes. We also discussed how it begins to assemble these basic units into words and meaningful language strings. In the information processing framework which we have adopted this process involves using established procedures and 'rules' which are supplied from the LTM. In terms of letter and sound features it was suggested that these procedures act unconsciously on the sensory stores which filter the information being passed on to the Working Memory. The unconscious operation of these rules depends on the degree to which they have become automatic; not a problem for the fluent first language speaker or reader, but more of a problem for the second language learner.

In this chapter we are going to look at the way that other information stored in the LTM is used to give meaning to the linguistic data supplied from the senses. We are going to answer questions such as:

- What sort of information is used to interpret texts (both oral and written)?
- How does this happen with first language speakers?
- What are the implications for the second language learner?

4.1   Working Memory

As we have discussed earlier, the term Working Memory refers to the specialised brain function involved in putting together units of information and making sense of data. It carries out a function which holds images and ideas temporarily while new images and ideas are added. The process not only involves the addition of incoming language data with that already received, but it also involves the comparison of this language with what is known about the world; the process of giving meaning to language and interpreting the message. Because of this, WM is often equated to consciousness. It acts as the coordinator of different bottom-up and top-down processes. The bottom-up being the language symbols and the top-down being the experience of the world. Figure 4.1 represents the general function of the Working Memory:

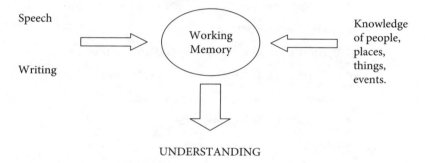

UNDERSTANDING

Figure 4.1. Diagrammatic representation of the role of the Working Memory in comprehension

To examine this role further, we shall first look at the role of the Working Memory in the comprehension of spoken information.

4.2   Listening and the real-time processing of speech

The processes of individual phoneme discrimination have been described in some detail in Chapter 2 in order to illustrate the complexities involved in language processing and also to illustrate the contribution that linguistics can and has made to an understanding of the mental processes involved. Much cognitive modeling has rested on linguistic insights, in particular the phoneme. The construct of the phoneme has been central to thinking about speech decoding for over a century and psychologists have used this concept, both to build models of how languages are processed and to investigate its psychological validity. However, such initial pattern recognition is highly automatic and unconscious in fluent speakers and, as has been suggested, acts within the sensory register with information being supplied from the LTM. However, once the initial decoding has been achieved, the resulting message is then passed on to the WM.

4.3   Assembling the message: Working Memory and Long Term Memory

Chapter 2 examined the way that forward and backward processes can be shown to be acting on the incoming 'raw' sound frequencies to produce linguistic symbols for the working memory to manipulate. These symbols are then passed up the line to the Working Memory. We now intend to examine the processes which are thought to be taking place inside the Working memory by looking at the comprehension of the following simple conversation.

Husband:	I can't believe what's come over him. He's been so helpful recently.
Wife:	Yes, he helped with the washing up and he spent all that time with you in the garden last weekend as well as cleaning the car.
Husband:	And he cleaned the car again this morning.

We shall examine, in particular, the way that the final sentence, "And he cleaned the car again this morning" can be comprehended. The sound frequencies of this sentence were illustrated on a spectrogram earlier, Chapter 2, p 36.

From the general information processing framework which we have adopted, Figure 4.2 represents in abstract terms the symbolic processes and language modules involved in comprehending the sentence. These processes, supplied by the linguistic modules stored in the LTM, act on the data held in the WM. The output is a new understanding, which is then added to the episodic memory.

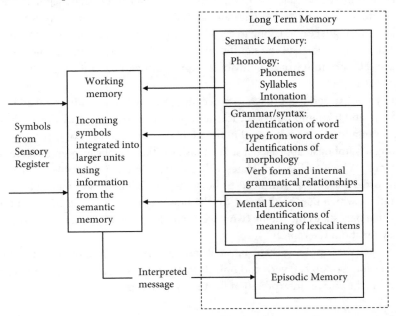

Figure 4.2. The use of language information in the LTM for extracting meaning from a message in the WM

As we have discussed in Chapter 2, the first job of the information processing system will be to convert the frequency bands into the abstract phonological units (the phonemes).

The next task in a serial approach to processing language will be to group the sounds into syllables and the listener will need to think of the boundaries between syllables. The listener will need to decide which of the following is the correct way to chop up the initial phrase, /ændɪkli:n/.

Phonemes		Possible syllables
		/æn/ + /dɪ/ + /kli:n/
/ændɪkli:n/ →	Or	/ænd/ + /ɪ/ + /kli:n/
	Or	/æn/ + /dɪk/ + /li:n/

Figure 4.3. The possible ways of dividing the acoustic phrase into syllables

This processing at one level will depend on the rules of English. All of the above are 'legal' syllables in English. They follow the **phonotactic** rules for English; they can exist phonologically. In this example /æ/ + /ndɪk/ would not be possible in English. It is impossible to begin a syllable with /nd/. We cannot talk about 'a ndick'. Yet it would be possible in several African languages. For the second language speaker the 'legality' of the combinations may need to be consciously thought about in order to begin to segment the stream of sound into separate units. We have all had the experience of initial exposure to a completely foreign language and trying to get a handle on the different 'units' of the message. In addition to trying to sort out the significant sounds, the task of chunking the message into syllables and thence into words, contributes significantly to the difficulties that the second language learner faces.

In a 'symbolist', serial approach to processing, having successfully chunked the sounds into syllables and then into words, the learner will then need to compare the resulting words with representations of words stored in the Mental Lexicon in the Long Term Memory.

Taking a 'symbolist' approach, the next task for the listener is to grammatically parse the sentence. Which of the candidates is the verb? Which is the subject? In UG terms, the word order parameter will need to be set to the English SVO (subject-verb-object) configuration, which may be different for the first language of the learner. In information terms, which part states the theme (what we are talking about)? Which is the rheme (what we are saying about the topic)?

Even once these processes are automatised (i.e. the learner automatically looks in the right places for the subject, verb and object), the listener will still have several candidates for choice. Is the correct interpretation for the subject/verb:

i.   And Dick leaned?
ii.   And he cleaned?
iii. Andy cleaned?

Note that (i) can only be ruled out once the object "car" has been identified, again showing the iterative nature of language processing. These decisions initially derive from the knowledge of the syntactic structure of English (decisions about word order etc.), but they also involve lexico-grammatical rules ('cleaned' can take a direct object but 'leaned' cannot) and semantic knowledge (cars are a set of objects which can be cleaned).

Once the listener has ruled out the first interpretation, the utterance is still ambiguous. Is the correct interpretation that it was Andy who cleaned the car or is it that someone they were talking about, 'he', who cleaned the car? Both are acceptable from the utterance in isolation. In this situation, the correct interpretation is the second, but it can only be arrived at from the surrounding linguistic context, i.e. that the couple are talking about someone they know (their son?). Thus, the ideas contained in the initial exchanges, where they both refer to the change that has come over someone, need to be kept in mind whilst the new utterance is being processed. Reference to 'he' rather than 'Andy' only emerges in the context of what has been said. This reference backwards to what has been said is also confirmed by the fall-rise intonation pattern shown in Figure 4.4.

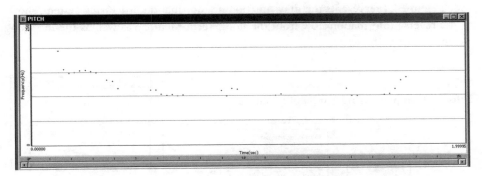

Figure 4.4. A spectrogram showing the intonation patterns for "And he cleaned the car again this morning"

Interpretation (ii), 'And he cleaned', relies partly on the wider context, but this, in turn, needs to be congruent with the information from the linguistic rules for stress and intonation. These involve the contrastive significance of moving the main stress (the tonic syllable) to the conjunction 'and', thus emphasising the fact that the speaker is adding extra information to what has been supplied. Furthermore, fall-rise intonation patterns in English, according to the discourse intonation system (Brazil, 1997), are used when speakers are referring to something which is shared between them. The pattern thus indicates that the speaker is referring back to what has already been said or understood. This combination of matching information from context with that of language decoding is the essential iterative processes working at a 'higher' level. However, it is very demanding in the use of cognitive resources (for a consideration of how these issues relate to second language learners, see Workbook 4.1).

Other powerful cues in the interpretation of this message will also come from the episodic memory of the two speakers. This memory relates to all of the events which have happened in a person's life. These two speakers obviously share memories of a particular person and his characteristics. They don't mention his name, they don't need to as both understand who is meant by "he". The likelihood of him cleaning the car twice in a week will thus help with the interpretation of the linguistic signal – the element of surprise in the voice of the speaker.

Finally, the conversation takes place within a particular cultural setting and the two speakers will also share cultural expectations about washing cars, doing the washing up, and the gardening. These cultural expectations will certainly be different in different societies and thus will not necessarily be shared by the second language learner participating in such an exchange. Thus cultural 'schema', knowledge of the social norms of the society, play a part in the interpretation of spoken messages and these schema are supplied from the LTM of the speakers.

The use of the wider context to interpret messages, and the use of schematic and episodic memory in particular is known as top-down processing. If we add these to our model, Figure 4.4 represents the fully functioning information processing system, showing the reverse information flow from the Long Term Memory as well as the incoming information from the senses.

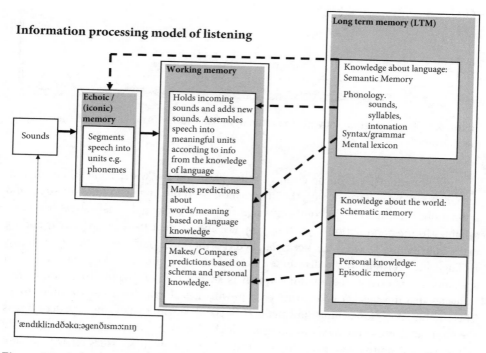

Figure 4.5. A diagram of the information processing involved in listening

It is clear from this analysis that a simple serial processing approach to the analysis of incoming sounds will not be sufficient. The process needs to be highly iterative, even within the limited domain of linguistic information. Information from the rules of phonotactics needs to be combined with syntactic, semantic and wider episodic/schematic information through parallel processing.

Areas such as semantics will be further explored when the structure of the lexicon is discussed in Chapter 5 and the role of schema in understanding messages is discussed in terms of reading strategies later in this chapter, but the most important aspect to note from this analysis is that the second language learner, in different degrees at different stages of the learning process will need to spend Working Memory processing capacity on linguistic parsing and analysis (see Workbook exercise 4.1 for an exploration of this aspect). This means having less capacity for

a.   holding longer stretches of language for integrating with incoming information and,
b.   thinking about the wider contextual environment with which to interpret the text.

These two factors lead to the complaints noted by second language teachers that:

1.   second language speakers face difficulties with longer spoken texts and,
2.   that learners try to interpret word by word and do not harness the wider context in interpreting the message.

The simple answer is that they do not have the processing capacity as it is utilized in 'lower' level processing tasks.

4.4   Top-down processing and reading comprehension

Since the mid-1970s there has been a great deal of interest in the use of context in reading comprehension. Frank Smith's seminal work emphasises the importance of context in comprehension, and many authors have emphasised the importance of what the reader brings to the text and the reading process as being an interactive process between the reader and the text (Smith, 1978). The recent applied linguistic interest in genre[1] has led again to an emphasis on top-down processes in reading comprehension. However, the use of such schema approaches to second language learners will have a definitive cost in terms of processing capacity. Does the second language learner have the capacity in WM to both analyse the incoming data and to relate this to larger schema? This is a major issue which will be examined in this chapter from the point of view of approaches to reading.

---

1.   Applied Linguistics and language teaching currently emphasise the importance of studying the macro-aspects of text organisation and the way that this organisation is different in different discourse situations, for example different academic genres, journalism, narratives etc.

Much of the work in psychology and in second language work in the area of textual comprehension has involved studies of memory. Typically, subjects are presented with some written language and then tested for what they can remember after differing amounts of time.

The importance of wider context in comprehension and recall can easily be demonstrated. Read through the following text quickly, shut the book and then write down what you can recall.

> If the balloons popped, the sound would not be able to carry since everything would be too far away from the correct floor. A closed window would also prevent the sound from carrying since most buildings tend to be well insulated. Since the whole operation depends on a steady flow of electricity, a break in the middle of the wire would also cause problems. Of course the fellow could shout, but the human voice is not loud enough to carry that far. An additional problem is that a string could break on the instrument. Then there could be no accompaniment to the message. It is clear that the best situation would involve less distance. Then there would be fewer potential problems. With face to face contact, the least number of things could go wrong.

Figure 4.6. From Bransford and Johnson, 1973

The text on the level of language (i.e. lexis and syntax) provides no problem at all. Yet on the level of coherence (making sense) it is highly incoherent. However, if the context is supplied, then the text becomes fully comprehensible (for the context, turn to Workbook 4.2). Bransford and Johnson (1973) presented texts such as this orally and then tested recall after some time. When subjects were exposed to such unusual passages without advanced knowledge of the context, memory, as measured by the number of details they were abler to recall, was severely impaired compared to situations in which they were provided with the context before they heard them. Provision of the context after exposure did not significantly increase the recall which suggests that the framework provided by the context plays an important role in constructing meaning and comprehension. Although the original Bransford and Johnson studies were carried out through listening rather than reading comprehension and with first language subjects rather than second language subjects, a large number of studies have indicated that background knowledge in terms of culture and topic are better predictors of comprehension than syntax or lexical knowledge (see Berhardt, 1991 for a discussion of these studies).

The above indicates the importance of full contextual understanding to comprehension. Other studies have shown the importance of meaning in remembering. One of the most consistent findings of this research is that L1 readers tend to remember the information content of messages rather than the actual form of sentences. In a typical experiment

Sachs (1967) presented subjects with a sentence in a text. After some time he presented subjects with a series of grammatically accurate but differently phrased sentences. He then asked which sentence they had seen. The responses demonstrated that as the time between the exposure to the sentence and the decision was increased, the subjects could not tell the difference between the words used in the sentence they had seen and the target sentences, but were quite clear when the meaning was changed (see Workbook activity 4.3). It would thus seem that although syntax must necessarily be involved in comprehension, it is the underlying meaning which is used to prompt recall rather than surface-level form. Other studies have shown that inference and what is considered to be important also play an important role in comprehension of text. For example Johnson et al (1973) found that subjects falsely thought they had heard the word "hammer" when presented with sentences such as;

> John was trying to fix the birdhouse. He was looking for a nail when his father came out to watch him and to help him do the work.
> (For another example of inference leading to false understanding see Workbook 4.4)

We noted in the above reading passage that the language of the text presented no difficulty to the first language listeners/readers; the difficulty lay in the lack of understanding of the context. A lack of correlation between syntactical complexity in the texts and comprehension in second language readers was also found by Bernhardt (1991), although her work demonstrated a strong effect of topic knowledge. Topic knowledge was found to be a strong determiner of accuracy of recall. However, as she points out, the syntactical complexity of the text does not necessarily tell us anything about the syntactic knowledge of the reader, which is the variable we are most interested in, and knowledge of syntax and topic may well be closely related, in that language form is often quite closely related to different topics.

When discussing the influence of context and prior knowledge on comprehension, we are, in fact, examining the way that information held in the LTM can be used to make sense of the text by setting up predictions about what is being expressed. This knowledge is the knowledge that the reader brings to the task of comprehension and is what has generally been characterised as top-down processing. It consists of at least two elements; the episodic memories of each individual (as we saw in our analysis of the conversation above) and the wider socio-cultural schema deriving from living within a particular society. These schema include the generally accepted ways that people act in specific societies, sometime separately classified as 'scripts'. If we examine the Bransford and Johnson text and the context on p 187 in the workbook, we can see that general cultural schema and scripts are involved. The idea of courtship and serenading is deeply embedded in European cultures, whereas it is absent in other cultures (such as Islamic cultures). In addition, these schema are used in widely known stories such as 'Romeo and Juliet' which again may not be available to the second language learner from a different cultural background. The lack of general schematic knowledge (courtship routines) and specific episodic memory (the story) will provide difficulties for the second language user.

One particular type of schema which has been investigated and which has specific language manifestations is that of story grammars. Again through investigation of recall, research has shown how the overall organisation of text can affect the retention of features within the story. Unfamiliar story schema have been used by Bartlett (1932) to investigate how people remember stories (see Workbook 4.5 for an example). Both the familiarity of story type (see activity 4.5a) and the different levels of detail within the story (see activity 4.5b) have been shown to effect memory for details. These findings mirror the interest in genre analysis in linguistic studies and the fact that different languages will have different overall text organisation structures. Thus, second language readers will need to be aware of these different genre conventions in order to be able to access texts in the second language. Some studies have shown that text structure is an important factor although the degree to which overall text structures differ from language to language is open to question (for a discussion see Bernhardt, 1991).

4.5   Bottom-up and top-down processes and the second language reader

As we have mentioned, for the last two decades, second language reading pedagogy has been driven largely by the importance that context plays in comprehension and consequently in training the second language learner in using the wider context to interpret texts. This is motivated by the research with first language readers which has emphasised the importance of what the reader brings to the text in terms of prior knowledge and by the observation of teachers and research findings which highlights the lack of such top-down processes in second language readers.

However, the fluent first language readers' use of top-down schema for interpreting texts rests on already well-established word recognition procedures. These procedures in fluent first language readers are highly automatic. Such procedures are not so highly proceduralised in the second language reader. Thus the bottom-up processing of text at a graphemic, morphological, phonological and syntactic level will occupy the reader's conscious attention and will take up precious processing capacity which as a result will not be available for analysing the text from the wider perspective. It is not solely the case that the reader is unaware of the processes of using top-down information in comprehension, but that such procedures may be impossible to implement due to the restricted capacity of WM and the tasks the second language learner has to perform. Indeed, if there is any transfer from first language reading to second language reading, then it is likely that such automatic, unconscious, top-down procedures are ones which will be transferred to the second language.

Whilst it is clear that fluent reading involves both top-down and bottom-up processes in an interactive manner, the extent of the reader's use of top-down approaches has been limited by the degree of that reader's language proficiency. Ridgway (1997) conducted a number of studies which showed that enhanced comprehension due to prior topic knowledge appeared to have a threshold level of language proficiency. Any improvements in comprehension due to prior knowledge were not detectable on ESL readers below this threshold level. This would support our conclusion that the reader with a lower level of language proficiency will need to devote more processing capacity to formal features of the text and will not have the processing capacity to pay attention to wider features of topic and context. The relationship between language level and the use of different LTM resources is represented diagrammatically in Figure 4.7.

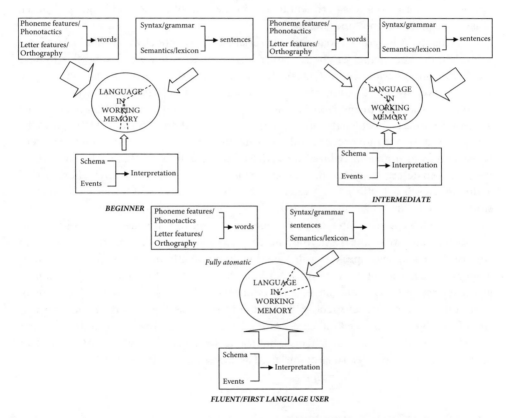

Figure 4.7. Diagrammatic representation of differing use of processing modules at different proficiency levels

The initial aim of the second language reader must be to develop automatic text and word recognition skills to the point at which they become sufficiently proceduralised to allow for efficient chunking of information. This will free up WM capacity for carrying out the integration of received information with incoming information and for matching and interpreting this information with information stored in the LTM.

4.5.1   Top-down and chunking the text

This chapter has examined the way that wider contextual features are believed to be utilized in the understanding of spoken and written language in WM. It has examined the processes which can be seen to operate on the oral comprehension of a dialogue and it has examined a number of studies with first language speakers on textual comprehension. It has demonstrated the importance of what are called 'top-down' processes in comprehension. Such 'top-down' processes are generally thought of as using the wider cultural and episodic memories, but it is pertinent to ask, in the light of the second language learner, what is meant by the 'bottom' and the 'top'.

In Chapter 2 we argued that a simple serial assembly model would not be sufficient to explain how phonemes can be recognised. Any model would need to be able to have feedback from the wider context, albeit the narrow linguistic context. In the same way in Chapter 3 we saw how the immediate context of letter features and letters would need to be taken into account in any model of decoding print. All of these models have described an iterative process in which the brain will need to feedback from further 'upstream' in the message and to take into account wider information at the feature, word, phrase or sentence level from stored procedures in the LTM. Feedback from the schematic level which we have been describing here is no different in kind, merely different in level. Thus learners at different levels will utilize to a greater or lesser extent the different forms of information stored in the LTM.

However, we have pointed out the problems that second language learners have with processing capacity in the WM. They need to consciously process at the level of form whereas first language speakers will have highly automatic processes for dealing with language form. The solution would seem to be for the second language learner to progressively process larger and larger chunks of text, either written or oral. The focus of attention, the top-down element, will increase in scope as the level of the learner and size of the chunks processed increases. At the advanced level, this will include active use of wider context and cultural schemas, but the less proficient learner top-down will be restricted to more complex rules of the language system (see Workbook 4.1).

4.6   Neuropsychological evidence

4.6.1   Different types of memory

From the point of view of explaining how languages are processed we have generally adopted a cognitive psychological viewpoint and considered the different memory stores as separate components of the information processing framework. As such they represent functions which the brain performs. They do not necessarily relate to any specific areas. The working memory, for example, does not necessarily reside in one particular place, although the areas associated with working memory are largely located in the temporal, parietal and frontal lobes (Aboitiz and Garcia, 1997, Smith et al, 1996). These different areas in the right and left frontal lobes have also shown to be coordinated by the prefrontal cortex (Goldman-Rakie, 1992). Thus it would seem to be better to conceive of the working memory as a complex interconnecting network of different areas coordinated by a controlling 'telephone exchange' of neurons directing and inhibiting different areas for different tasks. This system may well have evolved form a system for holding images and ideas temporarily while new ideas are added which then became adapted for use with language. For example, we would need such a structure for thinking about, planning and carrying out a series of instructions. Thus, it could be that language processing has taken advantage of a pre-existing structure. This is the argument put forward by Aboitiz and Garcia (1997), who argue that the language device is embedded within a wider neural network involving connections between the temporal, parietal and frontal cortices which comprise the Working Memory and is involved in immediate cognitive processing.

The idea of separate areas ('telephone exchanges') which coordinate the activation of other areas can also be used to explain other types of memory. It seems that medial temporal areas such as the hippocampus play an important role in the extraction of and the formation of the relatively more permanent neural connections that are necessary for forming longer term memories. For example research has shown that the hippocampus is sensitive to the degree of predictability of events. The hippocampus triggers an extensive network of areas when the person needs to search for events in order to make sense of visual messages. (Strange et al, 1999 and also see Byrnes, 2001: 69).

4.6.2   Limited capacity of the working memory

This chapter and previous chapters have suggested that one of the principle problems faced by second language learners is the increased cognitive load imposed on WM by the necessity to devote extra resources to language processing. The difficulties of restricted capacity and language processing are nowhere clearer than in reading. One of the central symptoms used to diagnose dyslexic children is that of restricted capacity in short term memory. The involvement of areas associated with working memory also show different activation patterns with dyslexics. Studies with dyslexic children, for example, indicate increased activation in Broca's area but lesser activation in other areas, Wernicke's area and the angular gyrus (Shaywitz et al, cited in Byrne, 2001). Similar results have also been obtained over a number of different languages (Karni et al, 2005 for Hebrew, Georgiewa et al, 2002 for German and Seki et al, 2001 for Japanese). Broca's area is located in the left frontal lobe, the area of the brain most associated with WM. This areas is also associated with task difficulty. For example, Burton et al (2005) in investigating the processing of auditory versus visual stimuli, found a similar increased activation in the frontal region for the processing of pseudowords relative to other types of stimulus. They also attribute this to task difficulty. Presumably both the dyslexics and the normal subjects needed to work much harder to process the incoming linguistic information and thus the increased activity in the WM.

4.7   Summary

This chapter has examined the way that information stored in Long Term Memory is used in the interpretation of language messages both oral and written. It has shown that native speakers of a language use stored schema from the LTM and events from their own episodic memories to interpret incoming information. There is considerable evidence that information is stored, manipulated and remembered as meaning rather than form and that the interpretation of language symbols relies heavily on schema drawn from the LTM. However, this top-down process of using information from the wider context to interpret the message in first language users rests on highly unconscious, automatic language recognition procedures. With second language users, these processes are not nearly so automatic, and valuable space will be taken up in the working memory for consciously processing the language code. Thus, second language users will have more problems using the context and schema to interpret messages. Contrary to many of the ideas contained in recent pedagogies which emphasise the use of top-down processes for interpreting messages, it would seem to be sensible to concentrate on the processes for increasing the processing of language itself by increasing the size of the language 'chunks' being held in the working memory and by helping the learner to comprehend larger chunks and transfer them into meaningful units (bottom-up processing). In the next chapter, we shall examine another crucial area concerning memory and language learning and that is the storage of vocabulary.

Suggested Further Reading

Elizabeth B. Bernhardt (1991). *Reading Development in a Second Language; Theoretical, Empirical & Classroom Perspectives.* Norwood NJ: Ablex.
An excellent review of research into second language reading connecting research with classroom practices.

Keiko Koda (2005). *Insights into Second Language reading: A Cross-Linguistic Account.* Cambridge: Cambridge University Press.
A very thorough discussion of the theoretical factors involved in reading which relates comprehension to differences between the first and second language. It covers a wide area of research into second language reading, examining both bottom-up and top-down processes.

Chapter 5

Making sense

The structure of semantic memory and the mental lexicon

So far we have examined the way that incoming stimuli are decoded via the extraction of features from the raw data (Chapters 2 & 3), and in the last chapter we discussed the part played by stored knowledge of the world in comprehending spoken and written texts. In this examination we discussed how individual units are then assembled into larger chunks (words, phrases and sentences/utterances) and meaning derived from these chunks. Of these larger units, words are arguably the most important. In the models of reading which we examined in Chapter 3, a crucial stage in the process was comparing the graphic images with the words stored in the lexicon. It is the content words which carry most significance for native speakers and the same goes for second language learners. The more words which are known, the better will be their language comprehension. Lexical items, their storage, retrieval and their associated structural relationships, will be the focus of this chapter.

The chapter will focus on the following questions:

1. What types of knowledge are involved in knowing a word?
2. What models have been proposed for the storage and retrieval of words with L1 users?

3. Do second language learners have a single integrated lexical store, or do they have separate stores for each language?

5.1   What does it mean to know a word? Types of word knowledge

The answer to this question may seem obvious, but there are a number of aspects to the answer. I might say I know a word if

1. I can pronounce it
2. I can use it in a sentence
3. I know how to add and subtract parts of it to make new words
4. And, most crucially, I know what it means.

These four simple answers give rise to the four different types of knowledge which are traditionally associated with knowing a word: phonological, syntactic, morphological and semantic.

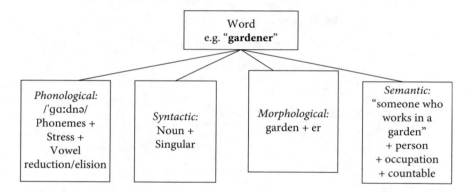

Figure 5.1. The types of knowledge involved in knowing a word

These areas of knowledge are similar to the language-specific modules which are hypothesised to be present in the long term memory. As we have suggested, they come from a symbolist view of language processing and are derived from linguistic descriptions of language.

Psychologists, by and large, have based their approach to lexical storage on investigating the psychological reality of these models. They have devised experiments based on these theories. Typical techniques involve reaction times to lexical decision tasks (e.g. deciding if a presented word or phrase is a word or is true/valid) and various memory retrieval tasks (for an example of a lexical decision task, see Workbook exercise 5.1). It is argued that such tasks can illuminate different storage patterns. For example, theoretical models which presuppose hierarchical semantic networks (see below, this chapter) can be tested against the time it takes subjects to make judgments on a statement such as "An ostrich is type of bird".

We shall use the types of knowledge derived from this symbolist tradition as a framework to examine what is known about the organization of the lexicon in native English speakers.

5.1.1 Phonological knowledge

The first of these, phonological knowledge is best illustrated by the 'Tip of the Tongue' (TOT) phenomenon, investigated by Brown and McNeil (1966). The TOT describes the thinking which we go through when trying to remember a word or name. In this situation, we remember fragments of words and are unable to access the full word or name. In their experiment Brown and McNeil induced TOT situations in their subjects and got them to report what features they knew about the word. They found that the subjects could report different parts of the words; the initial sounds, the final sounds, the number of syllables and the stress patterns, for example. They could also report similar-sounding words. Slips of the tongue are examples of speakers producing a similar-sounding word instead of the intended word and can also provide interesting speculation about how words are stored (see Aitchison, 1989).

The situation in which L1 speakers often confuse similar sounding words suggests that phonological features form a very significant part of the information stored about the word even though eventual access is not successful. If we examine the TOT phenomenon from a connectionist point of view such as the interactive activation model of McClelland and Rumelhart (1981) certain nodes are being activated at a phonological feature level, but fail to make sufficient connections at the lexical level to allow a particular word to be identified. Taking an example, the word "exacerbate", which I often have difficulty accessing (but is there "on the tip of my tongue"), the interaction between the various levels in my TOT state might look something like this:

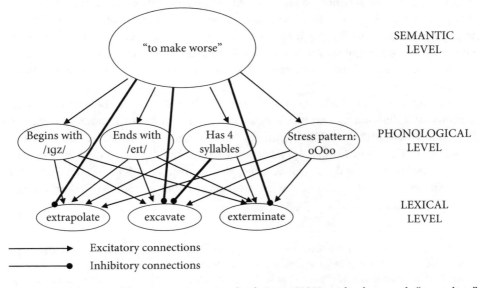

Figure includes labels:

SEMANTIC LEVEL — "to make worse"

PHONOLOGICAL LEVEL — Begins with /ɪgz/ · Ends with /eɪt/ · Has 4 syllables · Stress pattern: oOoo

LEXICAL LEVEL — extrapolate · excavate · exterminate

→ Excitatory connections
—● Inhibitory connections

Figure 5.2. The possible connections involved in a TOT with the word "exacerbate" (/ɪgzæzɛːbeɪt/)

The TOT study would imply that learning the phonological form of a word is crucial for lexical access. The L1 subjects used in the studies had acquired the language first of all orally, and thus the 'base form' of any lexical item for them is likely to be the phonological representation. As we have argued, this does not mean that L2 learners will necessarily use the same route. In the L1 users, the underlying meaning of the word will be closely associated with the spoken word in L1. In L2 learners, the underlying meaning may be associated with the spoken word in **their L1** (see the later discussion on separate versus unified lexicons), which will imply a very different access process. Therefore the pronunciation of words in the target language by the L2 learner may not be as central to storage and retrieval as they are in the L1.

5.1.2   Syntactic knowledge

Grammatical knowledge is closely associated with our knowledge of a word. At the crudest level, there is clearly a difference in the storage of grammatical/function words and that of open-class, content words. The existence of aphasic patients suffering from deep dyslexia (agrammaticism), where access to content words is unimpaired but access to all grammatical words is, in varying degrees, impaired, argues for, at the very least, different access pathways, if not actual storage systems, for the two types of word (see also Workbook exercise 3.2). However, we have seen in the fixation studies of reading in the last chapter that this separation between function and content words may not be so clear in L2 users.

In addition, there is also the knowledge of how to connect the content words together to make meaningful sentences. This will involve information about the role the word plays in the sentence; the part of speech. Is the word a noun, verb, adjective or adverb? All this information is either stored along with the words or has close connections to the words. This knowledge can be expressed symbolically, as a series of linguistic concepts (e.g. place in the sentence), or it can be related to wider conceptual/schematic knowledge (e.g. the concept of 'cleaning' involves objects (transitive verb) whereas the concept on 'leaning' doesn't (intransitive verb) – see discussion of understanding a sentence, Chapter 4, p 91).

For example, a word such as "water" will be stored along with the syntactical information that it does not take an indefinite article[1] or that, in most circumstances, it cannot be plural. Wisniewski et al (2003) point out this knowledge can either be viewed as a linguistic or a conceptual feature. Syntactic information could then be used by a sentence 'parser' (analyser) to build a sentence. Conceptual knowledge will involve retrieving general semantic information concerning the concepts or notions underlying countable objects

---

1.   "Water" is here used as the head noun of a noun phrase. It can be preceded by an indefinite article when it is used as part of a noun phrase e.g. "a water bucket" to pre-modify another, countable noun. In this situation the head noun "bucket" is countable and can take the indefinite article. Thus, "Bring me a water bucket" is acceptable, but *"Bring me a cold water" is not.

versus mass substances. This conceptual knowledge can then be converted into meaningful sentences through the use of syntactic rules which specify the language form, for example, concerning article use and verb agreement.

Word storage can also be understood as a series of interconnections between word nodes. These connections will be determined by the probability of a number of words occurring together as seen in the highly stable word collocations and colligations shown in large concordance studies. The syntactic knowledge stored with the word will be a series of connecting pathways to both associated function and content words. A connectionist account would argue that structural rules are built up implicitly by L1 speakers through repeated exposure to the language and the connections between the words. The mechanism by which they are consolidated is through repetition of different neural pathways which will establish connections between words. These connections will be based on frequency.

The three options concerning the storage of a word such as water can be represented as:

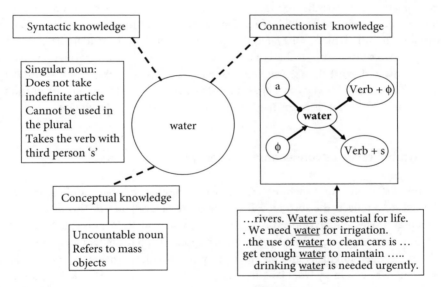

Figure 5.3. The different ways that the structural and semantic features of "water" can be represented

Increasingly, syntactic knowledge is also being seen as the way that one content word triggers a whole host of other connected words. At a basic level, words will activate prepositions and other grammatical features associated with them, to produce grammatically correct sentences as shown above. On a more refined level, words not only exist in correct grammatical sentences, they also have preferences for the type of grammatical environment. This type of grammatical knowledge about words is often based on the use of large-scale studies of corpora.

5.2   Use, usage and the natural use of language

Structural approaches to language processing emphasise the construction of utterances based on underlying syntactic rules. However, the language which we use depends on more than syntactic criteria. Language which is structurally correct but has no communicative purpose was famously characterised by Widdowson as 'usage', but when it is embedded in a communicative context, can be characterised as 'use' (Widdowson, 1978b). Learners need not only need to be accurate, they also need to use the language appropriately.

For example, Hoey (2003) gives the examples of the word *"convince"* and the phrase *"have enough information"* in a piece of writing by a second language learner. The way they were used by the SL learner was very awkward, yet not syntactically 'wrong'. The L2 writer used the phrase *"if the writer wants to convince the reader about something in the ad, it needs to have enough information"*. For the L1 speaker, *"convince"* will normally exist in the framework *"convince [someone] of [something]"* The framework *"convince [someone] about [something]"* is possible (syntactically correct), but much less common, yet the latter is the sentence produced by the learner. Similarly, *"have enough information"* is far more likely to occur with denial, *"don't have enough information"* yet the student used the phrase in the positive sense. Both of these native speaker 'feelings' for the correct environment for the words and word chunks were confirmed by a study of a 100-million-word corpus. *Convince [someone] of [something]* appeared 238 times as against 9 for *"about"* in and there were 11 out of 13 instances of the negative use of *"have enough information"*.

5.3   Symbolist versus connectionist memory models

The symbolist approach to memory storage would be that the shape and organization of the lexical store reflects the abstract way the languages are organized. This involves a belief that mental processes derive from rule-governed behaviour (Hulstijn, 2002, O'Halloran, 2003). Cognitive linguistics and the connectionist approach, on the other hand, emphasise the similarity between linguistic and other forms of information processing and sees knowledge of language emerging from language use (Croft and Cruse, 2004). Thus, "grammatical knowledge is the outcome of language use, not the other way round" (Foster 2001; 79). This approach to language comprehension on the lexical level emphasises the intricate connections between words within chunks.

However, as famously pointed out by Chomsky, language cannot be explained solely by 'blind' unmotivated connections between words. The problem with pure connectionist models is that they rely on associative learning and provide little room for creative learning based on rules. In order to make sense of novel utterances, we need to use a grammar to interpret what the language symbols mean. Thus, L1 speakers of English may use the concept of mass and count nouns to decide when to pluralise or to select the correct articles. From the symbolist, UG-influenced, point of view, such behaviour is generated by parameters (as we discussed earlier) in that article usage for count and mass nouns will be a parameter that is differentially "switched on" in different languages. The L2 learner will then have a different set of parameters switched on for the L1, and will need to reset these parameters in the L2 setting. The mechanism by which such parameter setting happens in the L1 is, as we have said, largely fueled by associative learning through extensive exposure. However, it is argued that such a mechanism will also need to be supplemented or controlled by some innate language parser; the essence of the modular approach to language learning. The question for the L2 learner must be whether such processes can work in the L2, or whether a more symbolic approach – the explicit use of syntactical information about the noun phrase in English – will be more successful. The different processes can be illustrated like this:

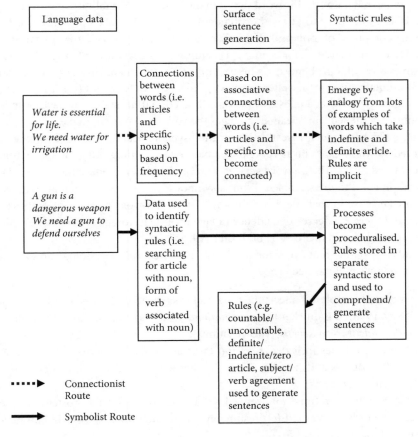

Figure 5.4. The way that syntactical information is used in symbolist versus connectionist approaches

The implications for word storage in the mental lexicon are clear in these two models. In the connectionist route, each word would be stored along with connections to a whole series of words which exist with it. In the symbolist route, words would be stored along with their grammatical characteristics and a separate syntactic module would be enacted to assemble the words into sentences. These two approaches will have important implications for the second language learner in the context of methodology and approaches to learning. This will be considered in the coming chapters. The different approaches are also important in the discussion of semantic networks, which will be considered later in this chapter, but before that we shall examine the issue of lexical storage and morphology, the third of the aspects of word knowledge.

5.3.1   Morphological knowledge

In addition to having a specific word stored in the lexicon, the symbolist approach suggests that it is also necessary to know the attendant parts which make up such a word. Many words are composed of roots and affixes. Each independent part is known as a morpheme. A word like "independent", for example, is composed of a root morpheme, "depend" plus two affixes (bound morphemes) – a prefix, "in" and a suffix, "ent". These affixes are known as 'derivational' affixes – they alter the class or meaning of the word (positive to negative, noun to verb etc.). Other affixes are known as 'inflectional' affixes – they have grammatical functions (e.g. the "ed" on "cleaned" changes the verb from present to past).

There has been much investigation in the psychological literature of whether words are stored as whole units or as roots plus affixes by examining different access times for different word forms. Thus, a word such as *decision* could be stored as the word *decide* plus the affix *–ion* and then assembled. From a symbolist point of view such an arrangement would make sense in that there is economy of storage involved in a root + affix storage system, and there is a degree of evidence in favour of such storage systems. The main proponents of such a system are Taft and Foster (1975).

A number of different experiments have shown effects of morphology on word recognition, production. It has been shown that

- derivational complexity affects the time subjects take to derive one word from another (McKay, 1978). It is quicker to derive *national* from *nation* (addition of one affix) than *interdependent* from *depend* (two additions);
- that response times in lexical decision tasks are longer for affixed than non-affixed words (Snodgrass and Jarvella, 1972). It takes longer to decide if *predetermined* is a word than *determined*;
- that lexical decision times for prefixed words such as *remind* are shorter than pseudo-prefixed words such as *relish* (presumably due to the time to affix strip and reject the latter) (Taft, 1981);
- and even that in such pseudoprefixed words such as *dissuade* and *persuade*, decision times are related to the frequency of the false root *suade* rather than the frequencies of the two words themselves (Taft, 1981).

However, although this decomposition route seems to work some of the time, at other times it seems that a holistic route is used for more frequent words (Rubin et al, 1979).

This does not necessarily mean that morphological decomposition is not used in lexical storage. The brain may not just use one route exclusively: it is quite possible that both routes can be operating in parallel and the one which comes up with the result in the quickest time in any particular circumstance will be the one used (Forster, 1979, provides a 'horse race' analogy, where the brain uses parallel competing strategies for each task). For example, economy of storage, the argument often used to support approaches from linguistics, is only one factor. It may well be a significant factor in a dictionary or computer, but not be pertinent to mental organisation. What is clear, however, is that morphological decomposition is a mechanism which is used, at least in part, by L1 users. For L2 users two issues arise.

First, their own language may use morphological decomposition in very different ways. English does not have an extended morphological derivation system compared to some other languages such as Arabic. Nagy and Anderson (1984) estimate the high school students' vocabulary store at about 45,000 word roots, in 88,533 word families. The figure of 45,000 is a huge number of root words when compared to Arabic, where the whole lexicon can be derived from a very small number of triliteral word roots by a highly regular and systematic series of derivational rules (around 5000, Dichy & Farghaly, 2003). Thus an L2 English Arabic speaker is likely to use morphological decomposition as a lexical access route quite differently from an L1 English user.[2]

Secondly, the L2 learner will need to be sensitive to the syllable structure of English; the way to divide up the word and the significance of the different parts of the word. This will involve both traditional syntactic knowledge (aspect, tense, agreement and plurality suffixes) and the role played by derivational affixes in altering the grammatical role of the word (e.g. the addition of *–ion* to a verb to make a noun).

5.3.2   Semantic knowledge

Many of the approaches to lexical storage and the structure of the lexicon have derived their models from the study of formal semantics. Generally, this area has been interested in attempting to explain the way that language relates to outside reality. There are three broad categories of models which we shall examine:

> Semantic networks – Hierarchical models and Prototypicality
> Categorisation and Conceptual Models.
> Spreading Activation Models

---

2.   Although note Abu-Rabia and Awwad (2004) did not find any evidence of a priming effect using similar word forms as primes in Arabic lexical decision/naming tasks. Also, in reading tasks, Koda (2005) reports no difference between Korean and Chinese first language ESL readers in morphological awareness to English words.

5.4   Hierarchical models

Semantic networks describe the organisation of the mental lexicon as a network of inter-connected elements. Words exist as nodes with connections between them. The connections represent the relationships between the words. In the classical networks, this relationship is between the word and its referent in the real world. The relationships involve the classical semantic distinctions of hyponymy, synonymy and antonymy. The most obvious example of such a model is the hierarchical network of Collins and Quillan (1969).

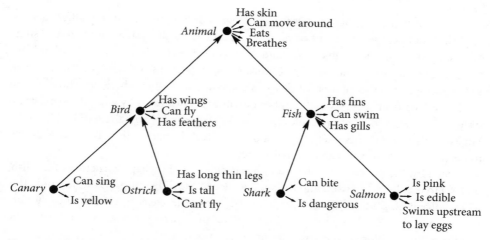

Figure 5.5. A hierarchical model of lexical storage from Collins and Quillan (1969: 241)

The existence of such a hierarchy was investigated by a series of semantic verification tasks where subjects were asked to decide as quickly as possible the truth of statements such as

| | a. | A sparrow is a bird |
| or | b. | A sparrow is an animal |

It was assumed that the speed of response to such statements would reflect the distance between the words or nodes in the hierarchy; the greater distance the longer the response. Sentence (a) should have a quicker response than sentence (b) as the second requires the connections to travel a greater distance across two levels in the hierarchy than the first (for an example of such statements, see Workbook 5.2). Whilst the predictions for the model were often born out, there were other times when the predictions were not. Sentences like

An ostrich is a bird
actually took a longer time to consider than
A robin is a bird
despite the similar positions within the hierarchy.

This led to the idea that there are differences in typicality between statements, and that certain features are prototypical of certain categories and that the degree of prototypicality of features (e.g. a bird has feathers, a bird can fly) will effect the way that such statements are processed. Prototypical relationships have been extensively investigated. In the seminal work in this area, Rosch and Mervis (1975) found family resemblances among a number of categories such as fruit, furniture and vehicles. The concept of protoypicality as concerns birds is illustrated in Figure 5.6.

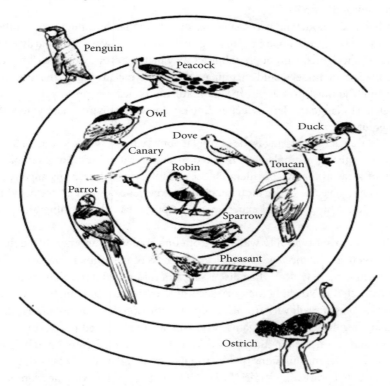

Figure 5.6. A diagrammatical representation of "birdiness" rankings as reported in Rosch and Mervis, 1975 (from Aitchison, 1989: 54)

The concept of prototypicality is not confined to lexical storage, but has also been developed to cover syntax as well (see O'Hallaran, 2003).

5.5   Categorisation and conceptual models

The approach to investigating lexical storage has generally involved asking subjects to place words in categories or to explore the characteristics of different categories. Rosenman and Sudweeks (1995) have suggested that categorisation can be seen in four different ways; as classical, probabilistic, exemplar and distributed.

Classical categorisation assumes that there are essential characteristics of any category and that all members need to possess these essential characteristics. This is the hierarchical model above and does not allow for members of classes which do not possess all the characteristics (e.g. birds which cannot fly). For second language learners this raises the question as to whether the characteristics of a particular item in one language are the same in another. For example, the categorisation of food terms, fruit, vegetables or verbs such as peel and skin will vary between languages. Languages may also employ different categories (see Workbook activity 5.4).

A probabilistic model, however, suggests that there may be a high probability of certain features in any member of a category but such features may not necessarily be present. In this model a weighted sum of probabilities may be the best way of describing category membership. Such a model would encompass the prototypicality effect (the most common features being the most prototypical). Again, for the L2 learner prototypicality will vary from language to language, largely depending on the wider environment where the L1 is used (different schema).

Another way of categorising is the exemplar approach (Mervis & Rosch, 1981). People often resort to giving examples when asked to define categories. For example, people will think of a car as a concept (hierarchical or prototypical) or an instance (e.g. Fred's car). This will involve use of the individual's own experience (Episodic Memory) in making the decision. Thus, personal experience is important in the learning and storage of vocabulary.

Finally, notions of typicality will vary from one context to another. If the discussion is of farms, then *cow* or *sheep* will be typical members of the animal category rather than *monkey*, which is more typical when discussing a rain forest context. Notions of typicality will be constructed in Working Memory according to the current situation. Thus, typical members of a category will vary from situation to situation. It is suggested that the lexical store in Long Term Memory is organised on a parallel distributed processing basis, with lexical items interconnected in different ways and then extracted as required by the Working Memory in different situations (the distributed model, Barsalou & Sewell, 1985).

The distributed processing models have a lot more in common with the frame semantics developed by Fillmore (1976). Within this approach to semantics, words are related, not by formal semantic relationships such as antinomy and hyponymy, but through experience. Thus, words such as WAITER, ORDER, MENU, BILL, STARTERS are connected through the concept of RESTAURANT; it is through experience that these words are primarily associated (for an example of this see Workbook exercise 5.3). Fillmore and others argue that a particular concept cannot be understood without an understanding of a wider concept with which it is intimately connected. Thus the word RADIUS cannot be comprehended without the base concept of CIRCLE. (for a discussion of Filmore's frame semantics see Petruck, 1996).

The importance of these categorisation models for the second language learner are twofold.

1.   Classical categorisation models are insufficiently flexible to adequately explain the way that speakers react to and associate words. Probabilistic models provide a better and more flexible explanation. However, are these semantic features universal or language-specific? If the latter is correct, the L1 speaker's knowledge schema derives from long experience with the language, yet L2 learners do not have this long experience.

2.   Equally, if we accept the view of the importance of semantic frames/domains as an organising factor in semantic processing and storage, then the question again arises as to whether such domains are language specific or are general to all cognitive processing.

5.5.1   Linguistic relativity and the Whorfian hypothesis

Although not traditionally associated with lexical access and retrieval, the above discussion raises a related issue which is the degree to which general concepts are linked to language. If the general cognitive conceptual view of language processing is accepted, then syntactic features will be determined by general cognitive concepts such as time, place, or, as above notions of countability and uncountability. These are 'notions' in notional/ functional grammars. The argument is that languages will have different ways of splitting up reality (e.g. Swahili does not have male and female pronouns, in French and German all nouns carry gender, languages differ in the number of colour terms, and many other examples). From the point of view of the learner, these notions or schematic frameworks for the second language will need to reset to the target language. However, an extension to this argument is that languages actually shape thought.

The ideas that languages may have a powerful influence on the way different groups view the world was first put forward by two American anthropologists and is known as the Whorfian or Sapir-Whorf hypothesis after the names of the two researchers who worked in this area. The original theory was developed from the study of indigenous American Indian languages such as Hopi. It was noticed, for example, that the Hopi language had very different ways of expressing time or of expressing physical properties such as rigidity (making a distinction between objects such as ropes and sticks based on their rigidity). Extensions of this work suggested that the Inuits, who spent much of their time in the arctic circle had a much larger vocabulary in their language for types of snow. It was hypothesised that these groups would comprehend the world differently from users of English or other languages. This theory was investigated in a number of different situations, most notably with colour terms. Languages vary in the number of colour terms they use and experiments have been carried out to find out if this effects the way that colours are perceived by different language users. For example, the Dani tribe of West Papua whose language contains a very restricted range of colour terms (3) was compared to L1 users of English (11 colour terms). Initial results from this comparison suggested that the ability to discriminate between different colours is affected by language, but the results of other studies have been less conclusive. Similarly, attempts on the syntactical level to link the ability to think hypothetically with the lack of a verb form which allows for this (e.g. Bloom, 1981 who looked at Chinese speakers in Hong Kong) have also been challenged (for discussion of evidence of lexical and grammatical issues see Carroll, 1999: 365–379). The lack of clear evidence for perceptual differences generally led to the abandonment of the strong version of the theory (i.e. that languages determine thought), but with the rise in interest in cognitive linguistics, increasing interest is being placed on the influences of language over thought (see Levinson, 2003).

It would thus seem that, if lexical knowledge is stored in hierarchical systems as suggested by linguistics, that the second language learner will need to re-organise underlying schema in order to be able to effectively store second language vocabulary, or to set up a separate storage system for the second language organised on different lines.

5.6   Spreading Activation Models

The model which attempts to bring together many of the observed phenomena of word associations is the spreading activation model, first proposed by Collins and Loftus (1975).

A possible semantic network for FIRE ENGINE is represented diagrammatically in Figure 5.7. This model has words represented as nodes as in the earlier network models and these nodes are connected to each other, but the connections are not necessarily hierarchical, they are determined by strength of associations. Similarly, categories are not determined by features, rather features appear as nodes within the network. Their relationship with any particular word and thus category membership and typicality are determined by the strength of association between the nodes and not the logical semantic relationships. The strength of the associations between the nodes is represented by the length of line connecting them. In the spreading activation model, any activation of one point in the network will lead to the increased activation of other nodes within the network. The nodes are similar to the logogens discussed earlier in the book; they can receive input from other nodes which will increase or decrease their level of activation. This raised level of activation will prepare the mind for the recognition of that particular word. The strength of association between words as represented by distance between the nodes in the model can provide an explanation for category effects (i.e. deciding if something is within a category), reverse category effects (deciding that it is not in a category) and typicality effects (deciding if it is typical) in categorisation and verification tasks. Similarly, such a network can explain semantic priming effects where, in a lexical decision task, preceding DOCTOR with NURSE will speed up recognition of the latter due to the fact that the node for DOCTOR will already have a level of activation due to the activation of NURSE. Evidence of stable language-specific connections such as this is provided by the strong stereotypical associations which have been found to the Kent-Rosanoff 100 word list (Palermo & Jenkins, 1964), which are different with second language speakers of English (Randall, 1980).

In an important extension of the spreading activation model, Bock and Levelt (1994) added a language level to what was essentially designed as a semantic network. This model

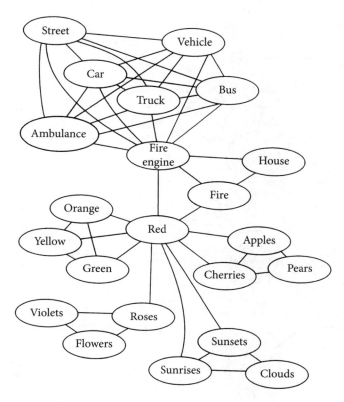

Figure 5.7. A Spreading Activation Model

operates at three levels: the conceptual level, the language (lexeme) level, and an intermediate level, the lemma level. Figure 5.8 represents part of the lexical network of the processes involved in either listening to or reading the words for SHEEP and GOAT in English and French.

The conceptual level operates as a semantic network, with concepts connected to each other in networks. The lexeme level contains nodes which contain all the features necessary to produce or recognise a word. In addition to the conceptual level and language levels, they added a 'hidden' abstract level of knowledge which they called the lemma level. Nodes at this level contain the syntactical information about a word, which act as an intermediate level between the concept and the actual word itself, the lexeme. The conceptual level operates in exactly the same way as the spreading activation model, but this semantic network is accessed from (or could provide access to) the 'lemma' level of abstract representation of the words. In the diagram, SHEEP and GOAT are both nouns in English and French and thus this syntactic category "Noun" is activated in both languages. However, in English there is no need for the activation of the gender node, whereas in French, MOUTON is masculine and CHÈVRE is feminine, so these nodes will be activated on the syntactic

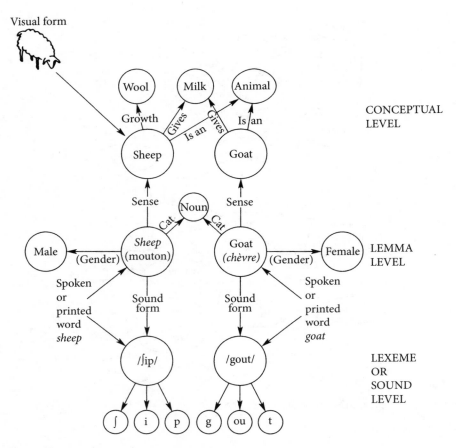

Figure 5.8. The Bock and Levelt network model

level in French. This lemma level will then activate specific word nodes at the lexeme level where phonological and/or graphical features are stored and the word can be produced. A reverse process would operate for the recognition of a word in writing or speech.

The Bock and Levelt model provides a very plausible explanation of the way that syntactic/structural information can become involved in lexical storage and recovery. As with all the network models, it places a great deal of emphasis on the strength of connections between words in the mental lexicon, but it attempts to integrate linguistic features as well. The semantic models describe the relations in terms of the semantics. The semantic systems operate independently of language, either the words used or the syntax involved. The Bock and Levelt model integrates all three processes.

The Bock and Levelt model combines aspects of symbolist and connectionist thinking. The mechanisms used to produce and understand language are those of activated nodes which is the same as connectionism. Features of the spoken or written word fire different lemma nodes, which, in turn activate lexemes. It is at the lemma level that more abstract, linguistic rules become involved, but again through a spreading of activation between actual word nodes and more general linguistic nodes such as gender, count and plurality. This 'hidden' lemma level involves symbolism through grammatical features. The task for the second language learner is to restructure the lemma level categories for the second language. An English native speaker learning French will need to both assign gender to nouns, but will also need to restructure the basic knowledge framework of nouns to allow for a new category which does not exist in English. This new category is an example of the language 'parameters' which according to UG proponents need to be reset for the new language.

The above model introduces the dimension of two languages, English and French rather than merely concentrating on the storage of one language. It suggests that both languages are stored in one place. However, there is also the possibility that two languages may not exist in one, but in separate stores, and this is the issue which will be examined next.

5.7   One store or two?

Much of the evidence we have drawn upon in our discussion of the semantic store and the mental lexicon has been derived from psychological studies carried out on English with English native speakers. However, the aim of this book is to discuss such evidence from the point of view of the second or foreign language learner. From the point of view of the second language learner the most important factor is that s/he has already acquired one language and we need to consider the effect that this will have on the learning of the second. In particular, we need to consider how knowledge of form from the existing language will effect the processing of the second. The learner will already have established and automated procedures deriving from the first language in LTM, and it is reasonable to assume that these are the routines which will automatically be called on to process the second language. This is nowhere more important than in the area of the mental lexicon.

There are two essential questions which we need to ask.

1. Do both languages share the same processes? i.e. Is the lexicon/are the lexicons accessed in the same manner?
2. Do both languages share the same structures? i.e. Do there exist separate stores for the L1 and L2?

In the Bock and Levelt model, both languages share the same conceptual store. It assumes that the concepts of sheep and goat and the associative network are common to both languages. It also seems to assume that the lemmas for the concepts [sheep] and [goat] contain both an English and French equivalent, i.e. both languages are represented in the same lemma. This model suggests that the lexicon of a bilingual stores the words in the two languages in the same lexicon. In such models it is often assumed that the two words are 'tagged' for language, one an English tag and the other French. However it is also possible to envisage a separate store for each language.

One of the early models to emerge was the dual-coding model (Paivio & Begg, 1981) which suggested that words are stored in two distinct ways: as a word (a 'logogen') or as an image (an 'imagen'). Linguistic information would be stored along with the word and non-linguistic information stored along with the image. The two systems would be separate, and one would call up a reference to another (i.e. the word GOAT would be linked to the image of goat and each would lead to the activation of the other). The bilingual would have two subsystems within the verbal store, one for each language and a node in the imagery system would activate words in both the subsystems. Such a model dealt well with a number of recall phenomena, particularly the speed of recall for simple repetition, synonym and word-image tasks (for a discussion see Hamer & Blanc, 2000: 185–186). However, the model only envisaged a common store for images, and dealt with more complex relationships via a series of associations between the words in the two language stores, associations which were determined by the way that the two languages were acquired.

The dual-coding model did not specifically deal with the issue of the relative 'strength' of the two languages. Asymmetrical storage models such as that proposed by Kroll and Stewart (1994) were developed from the dual-coding model, and take the differing degrees of fluency of the two languages into account. These models are hierarchical and propose a two-layer approach to thinking about words, with a separation between the form of the word and its concept. As with the dual-coding models, both the first and the second languages share a common conceptual store. L2 learners come to the task of learning second language vocabulary with an already well established bank of words from their first language, and an already established conceptual awareness of the world. Kroll and Stewart (1994) suggest there will be 2 components in the 'form' layer (one for each of the language) and these word forms will each have its own connection to the conceptual level (see Figure 5.9). The L1 learner has strong links between concepts and L1 lexical entries, and the linking of the L2 lexical item to its concept will, at the early stages of learning, be principally via the L1 lexicon. As learners become more proficient, stronger links will be formed between the L2 lexicon and the concepts.

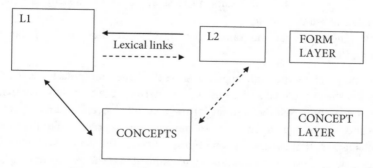

Figure 5.9. The assymetrical storage model. (Adapted from Kroll & Stewart, 1994. Solid arrows indicate strength of relationship and the size of boxes indicates relative size of lexicons)

This diagram shows the asymmetries which have been found to exist between tasks involving L1 and L2 processing. Translation is quicker from the L2 to the L1 than from the L1 to the L2. The structure also accounts for the fact that learning L2 words is easier when the two languages share concepts and more difficult when the languages do not share concepts as illustrated by Korean L1 learners and their problems with "take" and "put" (Ijaz, 1986). The above diagram suggests that access to the concepts of "take" and "put" will be principally mediated by the L1 lexicon in early bilinguals. If the L1 lexicon does not contain the lexical distinction, then access to the concepts will cause problems. The reliance on first language concepts was shown in another study with Korean students learning English (Jiang, 2004). Subjects were asked to decide in pairs of words were the same or different. If the word pairs in English shared the same Korean translation, the subjects reacted significantly faster than if they did not share the translation, suggesting that the subjects were using the semantic structures from the L1 to make the judgments. Similarly, the colour perception differences between the Dani tribe, who only have a two-colour system in their own language, and Americans, who have considerably more, may be more of a problem of translation rather than perception. The differences between the Dani and the Americans which is often taken to be evidence of the Whorfian Hypothesis that language affects thinking, becomes, not so much a problem of perception (as in the Whorfian hypothesis), but a problem of expressing themselves in languages which have a more complex colour system. It also allows for the links between the L2 lexicon and concepts to strengthen as the L2 learner becomes more proficient in the L2.[3]

Thus, in terms of memory usage and our understanding of how L2 users use and process language, it is quite clear from this discussion that in the early stages of language learning considerable processing capacity will be taken up with the 'translation' of lexical items in the L2 to access the concepts necessary for understanding the message.

5.7.1   Monitoring the process

There is another issue involved in the use of two languages which has received attention in the psychological literature and that is the decision as to which language to use; the issue of task direction. For example, should the output be in the first or second language?

---

3.   Although the above models were initially devised to account for order of acquisition (L1 and L2), not all results have shown an order of acquisition effect. Sometimes the L2 will become the dominant language. This led to a revision of this model where language dominance rather than order of acquisition is the controlling variable (Heredia, 1997). Hernandez (2002) found larger cross-linguistic lexical priming effects from the dominant language to the subordinate language than vice versa indicating that there was a stronger link between the concept and the L1 in the dominant language than between the concept and the L2 in the non-dominant language.

In terms of the mental process involved in bilingual tasks, Green proposes the following set of structures involved in such tasks:

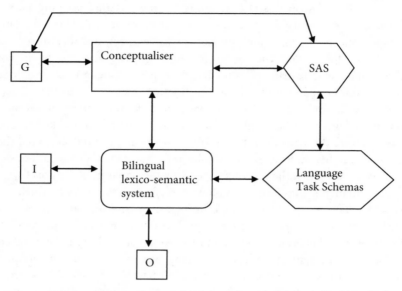

Figure 5.10. A diagram indicating the structures involved in controlling the bilingual lexico-semantic system (Green, 1998)

The mode envisages a bilingual lexical and semantic store which is acted upon by a number of other systems. One of these systems, the conceptualiser, decides on the general steps needed to perform a certain goal (G). This may be listening for information, preparing to speak, composing a letter or any other general task including translation. The language task schemas control both low-level schemas (e.g. the particular motor responses involved in producing a phoneme) through to higher-level schemes information (e.g. the appropriate register used to respond to the person speaking). These schemas and the control of the language to be used in the bilingual lexico-grammatical system are controlled by a supervisory attention system (SAS). The SAS plays a crucial role in directing the way that languages are used and as we have seen is an important element of the working memory.

Thus it would seem from the psychological literature that there is a good deal of evidence of a shared conceptual store and shared processes in both languages, but separate formal stores. These processes are overseen by the SAS.

5.8   Neuroscientific evidence

5.8.1   The structure of semantic stores

Examples of deep dyslexia in certain patients who are unable to access words which they clearly know provides evidence for a separate semantic store. Patients have been described who will respond FOREST when presented with the word TREE (A.W. Ellis, 1984) indicating the existence of neural networks of associated words such as the Spreading Activation Model proposed by Collins and Loftus (1975), but with the connections disrupted. Lesser and Milroy (1993) also report on patients who have lost the ability to produce a word but clearly have a lot of semantic knowledge about the word and will produce long circumlocutions in their attempt to cue the word and produce. As they point out, it is difficult to know whether this problem is due to the access to the semantic system, to the connection between the semantic store and the means of saying the word (the phonological output mechanism) or to a disruption of the phonological output system itself. However, it does indicate that there exists a semantic store and that it contains many of the organisational characteristics which we have discussed. One of the findings from studies of patients with deep dyslexia is that there can be selective impairment of different categories such as flowers, animals, household objects (Warrington and McCarthy, 1984), suggesting that these categories exist as organisational features in the semantic store.

In addition, brain imaging studies show that there is a degree of separation between the structures involved in phonological, morphological and semantic processing, although there is a large overlap. In terms of lexical processing, imaging studies suggest that words in the brain are connected in widely distributed networks (Pulvermüller, 1999) and that there is evidence that within these networks there are distinct category-related regions. Different areas concerned with body parts and numbers, animals and tools, a living/non-living distinction and colour terms as against action verbs, have been recorded (see Franceschini et al, 2003). These studies would seem to support the idea that words are stored in categories as suggested by the lexical storage models we have discussed.

5.8.2   Separate neural mechanisms for L1 and L2

The study of different types of aphasia following bilinguals who have experienced strokes is one way of trying to determine if languages use the same or different cerebral structures for the two languages. By studying the language loss following such a stroke (are both languages lost or only one?), and the recovery after such strokes (are both languages restored simultaneously or does one precede the other?), it is possible to speculate on the degree of overlap or otherwise between the areas involved in processing the two languages. On balance, the evidence would seem to suggest that there do not exist different areas for processing the two languages. In a review of a number of studies of polyglot aphasics 23% did show differential impairment and recovery (Whitaker, 1978), but in another review (Paradis, 1977) over half showed no difference; both languages were equally impaired or recovered at equal rates. This would argue for common processing mechanisms for both languages but does not, in itself, argue against there being separate lexical stores for the two languages. The factors involved in impairment, and, more importantly, recovery, are highly complex, but the fact that cases of selective impairment and recovery have been reported in the literature since as early as 1882 (Ribot, 1882), and the fact that 23% of cases did show some sort of differential aphasia, would suggest that certain aspects of the two languages, and vocabulary in particular, do have different stores, although processed by common language mechanisms (for a fuller debate of this issue, see Hamer & Blanc, 2000, Chapter 6).

Brain imaging studies are equally inconclusive on the issue of different lexical stores. Despite some early studies by Ojeman & Whitaker (1978) and Rapport et al (1983) which appeared to show that electrical simulation to different areas of the brain had differential inhibitory effects on the two languages spoken by the subjects, the evidence generally shows that the areas of the brain involved in the first and second languages are largely the same. We have already mentioned the Chee experiments with Chinese bilinguals which showed no substantial difference between bilingual English-Chinese subjects in terms of the areas used for the different language processing. Klein et al (1999) with Chinese-English subjects, Illes et al (1999) with English-Spanish bilinguals and Price et al (1999) with German-English bilinguals all failed to find evidence of separate cortical structures associated with the two languages (for discussion see Fabbro, 2001). These results have been replicated over a number of studies involving bilingual subjects with sentence comprehension, listening to stories and semantic judgment tasks (see Franceschini et al, 2003).

Investigations have paid particular attention to the level of bilingualism by comparing early and late bilinguals. One fact to emerge from studies of early and late bilinguals is that there is no solid evidence of differing use of the left and right brains in processing (laterality) as is suggested by Lenneberg's Critical Age Hypothesis (Hamer & Blanc, 2000). However, Fabbro (2001) suggests that there is evidence that while brain imaging indicated similar cerebral representations of lexicons in both early and late bilinguals, there would appear to be differences in the representations of these lexicons in declarative memory and there were differences in the languages acquired before and after the age of 7 in the areas concerned with grammatical aspects of the languages. This would suggest that adult second language learners use declarative memory (i.e. more explanatory processes) more than first language or early bilinguals (for a further discussion of declarative memory, see the next chapter and Anderson's ACT model of skill learning).

Although the areas activated are generally comparable, some studies have shown the activation of additional areas involved with late bilinguals (Chee, 1999a) in their less proficient language. Many of the studies also show increased activity of the common areas with late bilinguals, suggesting the extra processing costs arising from the more difficult task of second language manipulation. This would then suggest that second language learners need to employ extra resources to process language at an early stage, but that these resources are not used once greater fluency is attained. At this later stage of learning the second language learner uses the same resources as the first language speaker.

5.9   Summary

In this chapter we have reviewed different aspects of knowing a word and have seen that in many cases the categories of knowledge deriving from linguistic description have been shown to have psychological reality. However, we have also seen that ideas such as prototypicality and associative networks also provide powerful models for explaining the way that words are stored and retrieved, indicating the role played by frequency (through prototypicality) and connectivity (through associative networks) in the mental lexicon. The symbolist approach would indicate the importance of the use of higher-order, top-down linguistic schema in the use and understanding of words and would reinforce the importance to the second language learner of establishing such L2 categories in the LTM. The connectionist approach, on the other hand, would tend to emphasise the importance of the formation of strong inter-word connections and thus argue for a more bottom-up, associative learning approach to vocabulary. The degree to which the two approaches, the symbolist and the connectionist can be integrated into a single model is an interesting theoretical one (see Hulstijn, 2002), but it would seem from this discussion of lexical storage that both play a part in learning and teaching approaches will need to encourage both the establishment of connections between words and of the grouping of words on a more symbolic level. What remains to be decided is the methods by which such learning most effectively takes place and the memory implications involved. Is it best achieved through implicit or explicit learning?

The second issue which has emerged from our examination of the psychology of lexical storage is that in bilingual subjects, there is a lot of evidence for the use of separate lexical representations for the first and second languages, although brain imaging would suggest that these are not located separately in the brain. This raises the issue for the SL teacher of the role that translation and use of the first language in second language learning. This is an area which has received scant attention over the last fifty years of second language learning. Certainly, recent second language methodology has strongly frowned on any form of translation strategy, explicitly encouraging the sole use of the L2. From the stimulus-response procedures of the Audiolingualists to the meaning-based approaches of the mentalist and CLT approaches, the emphasis has been on almost exclusive use of the L2 with the implication that it is important to build up L2 specific connections rather than mediate the learning of the L2 through the L1. Yet such a situation does not seem to relate to the psychological evidence.

In terms of memory usage in the second language learner, what is important is that this interaction between the two languages is not without processing capacity costs. These costs are represented by the role played by the SAS in Green's model, and are again, going to compromise the amount of working memory available for such processes as storing chunks of text and using established schema from Long Term or Episodic Memory. Once again, the detailed discussion of the mechanisms by which second language speakers make sense of and use a second language, point to the difficulties they are likely to experience in trying to use higher order, top-down processes in language comprehension and production.

In the discussion so far, we have examined the processing costs involved in the WM in working in a second language. However, there is another crucial role that WM plays in learning a second language, the role of actually learning the language itself; of using experience to establish routines in LTM. It is this function of WM which will be examined in the next chapter.

Further Reading

Jean Aichison (1989). *Words in the Mind*. Oxford: Basill Blackwell.
An excellent and very readable account of different ways that words can be stored in the mental lexicon providing good accounts of the development of parallel distributed processing, spreading activation models in their different forms.

Josiane Hamer and Michel Blanc (2001). *Bilingualism and Bilinguality*. Cambridge: Cambridge University Press.
This is a very thorough examination of a wide range of issues concerning bilingualism, ranging from the socio-cultural through to the cognitive. In Chapters 6 and 7 they deal with the issues of neuropsychological evidence and information processing systems in bilinguals and review many studies in these areas.

Chapter 6

Making it stick
Learning theories applied to SL/FL learning

6.1 Working Memory: The main rehearsal space

6.2 Declarative and Procedural memory

6.3 Repetition and depth of processing

6.4 Repetition and attention: Implicit versus explicit learning

6.5 Gagné's hierarchy of learning

6.6 Neuroscientific evidence

6.7 Conclusion

So far in this book we have looked at the role that cognitive structures and memory play in language processing and comprehension. This is like describing a maze which sounds and symbols go through to be understood. However, memory has another crucial role in language learning; it is actively involved in learning the maze. Not only does it store information about the language used and use that information to make sense and communicate, but it also learns the maze, builds a framework in the brain. There are two, apparently opposing, learning processes which seem to be involved in such learning. One is the implicit, unconscious learning usually associated with the acquisition of the first language, and the other is a more explicit, conscious process involved when a second language learner studies a language, usually in a classroom. In this chapter we are going to turn our attention to the way memory is involved in learning, and, in particular, its role in the more conscious learning process associated with learning a second language in instructed second language learning (R. Ellis, 1990).

In this chapter we shall be seeking to answer the following questions:

- What role does WM play in learning language patterns?
- How do language patterns become automatic?
- What role does memory play in building up automatic procedures?
- What is the relationship between implicit and explicit knowledge of language?
- How can learning theories explain the different levels of language knowledge?

6.1   Working Memory: The main rehearsal space

6.1.1   Associative learning

In this book we have tried to examine the way that cognitive structures go about the process of language comprehension and learning. At every level, we have drawn attention to the importance of the Working Memory in the processes of comprehension and production, and the ramification that its limited capacity has for the second language learner. At all levels we have seen that a major part of efficient language processing is involved with the automatisation of procedures and in this chapter we wish to explore the methods by which automatisation may be achieved. On the simplest level, material to be learnt is repeated in Working Memory using the phonological loop. This is the main learning process involved in associative learning; the establishment of bonds between different items such as, on the simplest level, a picture and a word which represents it or a situation and an appropriate response. Such learning underlies the stimulus-response (S-R) of behaviourist psychology. The information processing framework, seen as an associative learning process looks like this:

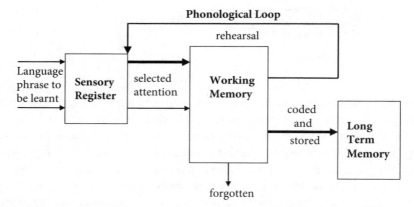

Figure 6.1. A model of how material can be learnt using the phonological loop in WM

As explained in Chapter 1, the phonological loop is a sub-system of Working Memory which allows verbal material to be repeated. Based on the way that we learn new material like telephone numbers by repetition, the phonological loop provides a verbal repetition process by which material in the Working Memory avoids decay. In terms of language comprehension, this will keep incoming material active whilst new material is integrated with it to form longer messages, but in terms of language **learning** this is the principle route by which new material is learnt. Material is learnt by repetition. In general, work on learning new material has shown that the greater the number of repetitions, the stronger the learning (the Power Law of Practice) and there has been considerable work done on associative learning and the effects of different patterns of repetition (spaced repetition in particular see Anderson, 1999). What emerges from these studies is the central role played by repetition in learning verbal material.

For the first language child learning a language, this repetition is provided by a huge amount of exposure to language input coupled with an almost unlimited amount of time within a five to six year period to practise the spoken output. Automatisation of language routines is implicit and unconscious and results from this long period of exposure to language input. The importance of the phonological loop in this learning process is shown, not only by the observations of children at play and their verbal repetitions, but also by a number of studies which show a correlation between the phonological working memory and either language success or failure in first language children (see Adams & Willis, 2001, for a review). This success is not solely at the phonological level, but also at the grammatical level.

With instructed second language learners, however, the situation is quite different. They do not have the huge amounts of exposure to the target language as first language speakers do. Neither do they have the huge amounts of time to dedicate to the process of repetition and practice. If, as N. Ellis suggests, the language acquisition process "favours a conclusion whereby the complexity of the final result stems from simple learning processes applied, over extended periods of practice in the learner's lifespan, to the rich and complex problem space of language evidence" (N.C. Ellis, 2001, p. 37), then the second language learner is at a severe disadvantage. Yet it is clear that second languages can be learnt and can be learnt in formal situations without the large amounts of naturalistic immersion in the second language which characterize the first language child's experience. What can replace the random and extensive unstructured experience of the first language child is a conscious, directed and targeted repetition of key language patterns. This repetition will take place in the Working Memory and will be consciously directed by some sort of attention mechanism.

An attention mechanism is also required by the first language learner if language is to be any more sophisticated than the simple 'parroting' of set phrases.

6.1.2   Devising and using rules: The LAD

The repetition of phrases and their allocation to Long Term Memory by a process of 'over-learning' is the basic building block of associative learning in behaviourist psychological approaches to learning. Yet this process, by itself, was found to be incapable of explaining the way that languages are learnt and used. Languages involve grammar and structure, not just a string of surface formats. The most famous attempt to provide an explanation for this phenomenon was the Language Acquisition Device (LAD) proposed by Chomsky (1959). He proposed, as we discussed in Chapter 1, that all human brains were predisposed to learn languages through a hard-wired device called the LAD.

The emergence of this concept was the result of a reaction within psychology to the refusal of behaviourist psychology to consider any contribution that cognition might play in the governing of human action. The mind was the famous 'black box' and only observable surface actions were considered to be valid evidence on which to build models of behaviour.

The LAD was a mental mechanism which worked on the surface data of experience in a suitable environment (Bruners' Language Acquisition Situation, LAS, Bruner, 1985) and provided the framework for learning and understanding languages. Attention switched to the discourse features of language acquisition; to inferring mental processes from analysis of the language produced. The micro-processes by which a language is 'acquired' were left rather vague. In many ways, from a cognitive point of view, the nativists, by ascribing language learning and acquisition to a hard-wired, innate system, turned their backs as effectively, as had the behaviourists before them, on the problem of how language is handled by the brain.

However, it is possible to argue that the monitoring system, the SAS, within the Working Memory is the mechanism by which abstract linguistic information can operate in language comprehension and learning. From an nativist viewpoint, this knowledge is innate. From a connectionist viewpoint, this knowledge is constructed from experience with the language and it is the way that such knowledge may operate in the Working Memory that we shall consider next.

6.1.3   Using and devising rules in Working Memory: The connectionist view

Connectionism, by arguing that complex structures can be derived from models derived from surface forms (for a review see Chater and Christiansen, 1999 & Ellis, N.C., 2001), offers both an explanation of how language structure can emerge from language use and also a mechanism by which these forms can be learnt. Ellis states that "the same systems which perceive language represent language" (N.C. Ellis, 2001, p. 42) and that WM is the key to understanding where and how this happens.

Ellis offers the following model to explain how working memory may act on language input and how learning/acquisition can take place (Figure 6.2).

This model shows how language and picture processing take place. Language input is first of all processed at a phoneme level and connections are formed between the nodes at this level and word nodes at the next level. These are again connected into established patterns at the phrase level. Through continuing exposure (in the case of the first language user), these neural pathways become more established. Language then becomes a network of interconnections between nodes at the different levels and the rules of the language are defined by these interconnections. Grammar, then emerges from the recurring chunks of language to which they are exposed ('emergent rules', Elman et al, 1996, MacWhinney, 1987). The whole process is governed by a monitoring SAS which directs attention within the Working Memory to the significant areas of input. This is where the rules of the language emerge.

With instructed second language learners the SAS also plays a part, not only in extracting the rules, but in directing the activity happening in the phonological loop. With structured input (from a teacher) and purposeful practice (through rehearsal), the SAS is able to establish language patterns through interconnections between the different levels of language.

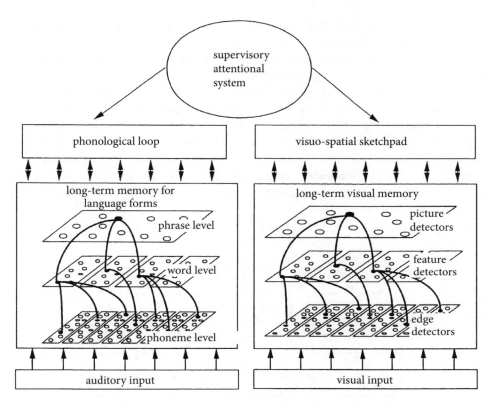

Figure 6.2. The model of working memory for language acquisition. From Ellis (2001), p. 36

6.1.4   Item-based versus rule-based memory

Throughout our discussion we have made the assumption that the LTM consists of modules (such as the phonological, semantic and syntactic) which store the 'rules' of the language and are used to interpret the incoming data according to these rules. However, there are other models of memory which have suggested that it is possible to explain language behaviour in terms of a large number of individual items (the item-based memory, Logan, 1988). Thus, the LTM acts rather like the Episodic Memory. Such an explanation would fit well with a prototypical approach to semantics (see Chapter 5) as applied to language. The language processing component of memory would consist of a series of frequent prototypical patterns, not a series of rules. Such an explanation would seem to deal well with highly frequent words and phrases (for a discussion see DeKeyser, 2001).

As with other aspects of the processing of language, it is not necessary to take a definite stand one way or the other about the organization of LTM. In some instances the item-based approach will yield the best explanation, in others a more modular approach will be more appropriate. Indeed as we have argued before, the brain systems are highly complex and so numerous are the neural resources available that one route may be acting in parallel with another in a 'horse race' situation, the winning strategy being chosen by the first to arrive at the answer. However, the processes we are describing for associative learning do favour, at least on the initial level, an item-based, episodic approach and it is necessary to re-examine the architecture of the WM in the light of such thinking.

The original model of working memory advanced by Baddeley and Hitch (1974) has not been without criticisms. In particular arguments have been put forward for a more integrated model of WM and LTM (for a critique of the WM, see Cowen, 1995 and Ward, 2001). The criticisms point out that some of the frequency and serial effects previously associated with WM alone can also be seen to operate in LTM under certain conditions. In response to these criticisms (in particular the necessity of integrating episodic and modular factors into his model of WM), Baddeley (2000) has produced the following adaptation of his original model.

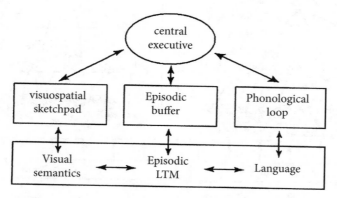

Figure 6.3. The multi-component model of working memory from Baddeley, 2000

This suggests that a section of the episodic LTM may also act as a temporary store for material expressed in a symbolic form (i.e. as language or visual semantics). Material from the WM is then passed on to this temporary episodic store in LTM via an Episodic Buffer. This temporary episodic memory then acts as an interface between the WM and the LTM. Stored information about language works on and receives information from the language module in the Episodic LTM (the item-based memory), which itself feeds to and has been fed from the Episodic Buffer in WM.

6.1.5   Connectionism and the second language learner

As regards the second language learner, there are two linked factors which we need to consider:

1. The second language learner has already learnt one language and this experience can be brought to bear on the task of learning the second language.
2. The second language learner is carrying out the learning process in a completely different environment.

Connectionists see language form as emerging from the surface structure of the input. Learners make sense of the language input and discover regularities in the input. In this sense the second language learner has a large advantage over the first language learner. Given the greater cognitive sophistication of the second language learner, and the experience of learning one language, it is likely that the learner will be able to examine the data in a more focused manner and thus recognise these recurring patterns at a much earlier stage than the naïve first language learner. Thus, the second language learner's SAS will already be trained to look out for significant chunks in the first language. Also, in the formal learning environment of the traditional language classroom, the second language learner will not be exposed to unstructured and random data; language lessons are highly structured events where the language data is laid out in a way to emphasise the significant chunks of which languages are built. Thus, the learners' exposure to the new language is highly mediated and in instructed second language settings, there will also be a teacher to direct the second language learner's attention to the salient features of the input.

It is also interesting to consider the role that repetition might play in learning rules. It is clear that in nearly all forms of second language learning, oral repetition forms a very significant element. If we accept the connectionist arguments that grammar and other schema emerge from surface form, this repetition may, by itself, allow the speaker to construct the formal schema (i.e. phonological and syntactical structures) which are necessary for comprehension. This argument can, for example, provide an explanation for the persistence of rote learning as a method employed in many cultures, in particular the Confucian methods which we shall explore further in Chapter 7. It should also be noted that connectionist explanations provide a theoretical basis from a learning perspective for the way that motor response pathways established for the production of sounds can also act as a means by which sounds are comprehended (see the Motor Theory of Speech Perception, Chapter 2).

Thus, connectionist explanations, with their emphasis on associative learning through repetition as the basic learning process and their arguments that rules emerge from such procedures provide an intuitively powerful framework for looking at learning a second language.

6.1.6 Chunking and repetition

Throughout our discussion of language comprehension we have referred to the importance of second language learners dealing with larger and larger chunks in order to maximize space in the WM for integration of new and received information; a comprehension perspective. However, we also need to consider the size of 'chunk' in terms of **learning**. What size of chunk should the learner be repeating?

At the beginner level, the learner will be concentrating on the establishment of low-level motor-neural pathways for the phonemes of the second language or the significant features of the writing systems (as exemplified by the lowest level of Figure 6.2; the phoneme and edge detectors). This will involve the repetition of words and short phrases which will be committed to memory in controlled contexts (e.g. as a response to a picture, to a spoken prompt, or a social situation). The process of repetition will simultaneously create links to the visual/social contexts in which the speech occurs. This allows for an appropriate response to be made in these situations. It also provides exposure to the phonological form, phonotactics and grammar of the second language. However, in addition to the amount of repetition, successful learning has also been shown to have strong links to attention. For effective learning to take place, the learner needs to pay attention to the salient features in the message (see 'noticing' Schmidt, 1990, and discussion in Chapter 7). Which features should be attended to will be under the control of the SAS, and this component of WM is highly important for the second language learner.

From the discussion so far we can draw some important conclusions about instructed second language.

1. The input to be memorized needs to be extensive if the learner is to have enough data to make connections between different patterns in the language;
2. This input should be meaningful to allow cross-modal connections to be made between the language form and meaning (connections between the language and social situations, for example);
3. The input should be selected to facilitate the noticing of the patterns;
4. The learner must be attending to the significant aspects of the input.

6.2   Declarative and Procedural memory

The discussion so far has concentrated on the role that WM plays in the learning of new material by repetition. It has suggested that the repetition of language in the WM either through exposure to large amounts of naturally occurring data as happens in language acquisition or to selected data in targeted language instruction, is one of the principal ways that material is passed to the LTM and stored. In each of the models discussed it is necessary to propose some sort of monitoring/analytical device for selecting significant information and directing the activity of the WM. In behaviourist associative learning, this mechanism would be concentrating on the surface form of the language and storing it as a series of individual examples without any analysis. This would suggest an item-based approach to memory, where individual instances are linked directly. From a nativist approach, the LAD would be using an innate language 'instinct' to process and analyse the language. This implies modular, symbolic structures in LTM. In connectionist thinking the SAS would be using the frequency distributions of the elements in the language to extract patterns and thus formulate an 'emergent grammar' of the language. Such approaches combine item-based and symbolic processes. In particular, connectionism can be seen to provide a mechanism by which language modules can be operationalised through connectionist networks.

However, underlying all three approaches (the behaviourist, nativist and connectionist) is the importance of maximizing the automatic nature of this process of linking concepts to language through the implementation of language patterns. We next examine a psychological model, drawn from the study of skill learning, which concentrates on this process of automatisation of skills. This model suggests there are two kinds of memory involved, the declarative and the procedural. This view of memory provides an important framework within which to conceptualise the way that languages, and especially second languages, are learnt.

6.2.1   Anderson's ACT model of skill learning

In the previous section we examined the way that the phonological loop and repetition of language chunks provided the central process for committing elements of language to memory. We also examined the way that formal, grammatical information about the language can emerge from the memorization of surface strings. This explanation, provides a useful core theory about language learning, and one which, by emphasizing the power of repetition in learning, is immediately appealing to the experience of second language learners. However, it is still unclear about the actual process by which the knowledge of form 'emerges' from the surface language. At best, the SAS, it can be argued, can be 'trained' in second language learners to attend to significant aspects of the language, but at its worst, as in first language acquisition studies, the way that the child constructs the grammar from the data is as vague as the nativist argument for the operation of the LAD. One view of memory which does try to provide an explanation for the way that immediate experience may be converted into automatic long-term memory routines (the underlying purpose of repetition in WM), is Anderson's ACT (Adaptive Control of Thought) model of skill learning (Anderson, 1983).

The model and its various modifications (see ACT-R Research Group, 2003) has been put forward as an explanation of the way that we learn routines of skilled behaviour

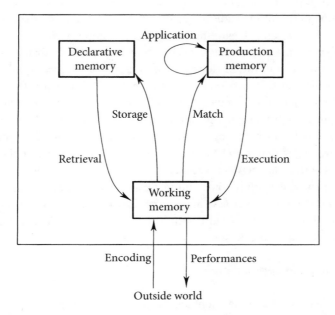

Figure 6.4. A schematic diagram of the major components and interlinking processes in Anderson's (1983, 1993) ACT models. From Eysenck & Keane, 1995, p. 386

and the way that these become automatic. It proposes two types of long term memory, the Declarative and the Production (also called "Procedural"), linked to an executor. Learning skilled behaviour gradually moves from conscious control, where verbally explicit sets of instructions need to be accessed from the Declarative Memory, to a situation where a stimulus from the environment directly accesses automatic procedures from the Production Memory. It provides an explanation for the common experience all of us have about learning skilled behaviours such as learning to drive a car. Initially, every action, such as changing gears, indicating when moving off, looking in the rear view mirror when pulling out, needs to be consciously thought about. Gradually these individual behaviours become chained into sequences of actions where the individual actions are automatically triggered by the previous action and ultimately the whole sequence is triggered by the desire to move off without any conscious thought being involved. In a final stage, added in Anderson's last model (Anderson et al, 1997), frequently encountered examples can be accessed directly from the declarative memory without the need to use procedural rules from the production memory. In this way the ACT model of skill automatisation converges to a degree with item-based approaches to memory as mentioned above.

Such an intuitively sound procedure for learning higher order skills such as driving also has clear relevance to language learning. It provides an explanation of learning in terms of 'higher order' analytical skills and to a degree 'lower order' motor-neural skills as well. The model also provides an explanation of the way that the SAS may operate, and a theoretical framework for the way that procedures for second language learning involve more than simple repetition; they involve the use of 'instructions' (formal language understanding), as part of the process of learning. It has generally been accepted that mere repetition is not sufficient (as audio-linguists found out) any more than simple immersion (as the CLT tradition is beginning to realize). Attention needs to be focused by the SAS, and Anderson's model provides a mechanism which could do that. At an initial stage of learning a new word in the L2, for example, 'peach', learners from different language backgrounds will need to pay conscious attention to the way that the sounds are pronounced. Arab learners, for example, may want to consciously 'devoice' the /b/ sound in their own language to produce the /p/ in English, or they might emphasize the aspiration of the /p/, as /pʰ/, both of which they may well have been directed to do through a language lesson. Initially, they will need to be conscious of this and may verbalise the task. Gradually, however, connections between various neurons in the sound production pathways (neuron-motor routines) will become automatic and will not need to be thought about. The sounds will be automatically assembled from the word 'lemma' (see Chapter 5) which will have connections to such procedures embedded in it. The lemma, then can be seen as the automatised entries in Anderson's Production Memory.

6.3 Repetition and depth of processing

Baddeley's model of WM and the phonological loop provide an explanation of how material can be transferred to LTM through a process of repetition and associative learning.

There is much evidence in the psychological literature of the power of frequency of repetition as an explanation of the strength of subsequent learning, but there is also another
area which can be shown to have an influence on the strength of learning, the depth of
processing involved. In a typical investigation of this, Eysenck and Eysenck (1980) demonstrated that recognition for words based on tasks which involved either semantic processing or involved distinctive features was better than recognition of words which had used
a shallow, non-distinctive, non-semantic process. Experiments such as these would seem
to suggest that the type of processing involved in the memory task will effect the efficiency
of the subsequent learning. However, the concept of depth of processing is one which
lacks clarity, and there are contradictory results provided in experiments which have tried
to demonstrate a facilitation of deeper processing. One study (Morris et al, 1977) found
no enhancement on tasks which involved apparently deeper processing, leading them to
suggest a transfer-appropriate learning theory. This suggests that enhancement will only
occur if the deeper processing is appropriate for the task in hand. This observation is a
key insight when we consider the appropriacy of rule-governed second language learning. It may well be that the added gains to learning expected from explicit rule instruction
(deeper processing) may not be realised due to the fact that the rules may not be appropriate for the task.

Linked to the concept of depth of processing, Ausubel developed a theory of cognition
which stipulates that there is a difference between pure rote learning and more cognitive
learning (Anderson & Ausubel, 1965, see discussion in Brown, 2000). He developed the
idea that material is better retained (and thus less easily forgotten) when it is both meaningful and cognitively related to previously learnt material.

If we accept that associative learning provides the basic process by which material
is learnt, the ACT model provides an explanation by which attention can be directed to
more than the surface features of the material to be learnt. It also provides a process by
which skills are automatised and provides a mechanism by which 'deeper' processing can
be seen to operate. In Baddeley's latest model of WM which includes an episodic buffer
and a section of the Episodic Memory LTM which can be devoted to short-term processing of language (see Figure 6.3 above), we have a mechanism which can explain both the
use of symbolic approaches and the depth of processing viewpoint. The transfer of language material from the phonological loop to this space in Episodic Memory will provide
deeper processing which is cognitively managed through symbolic representations. It also
provides a bridge to LTM, suggesting that material will first be learnt as a series of items or
exemplars and later form rules and be available to symbolic processing.

6.4   Repetition and attention: Implicit versus explicit learning

The models of WM which we have examined, and most of the theories derived from the
information processing framework involve the concepts of attending to and extracting
significant features of the language data. The architecture of the WM proposes a supervisory

system (the SAS) which can direct attention to different features. This SAS will need to be sensitive to the different features involved in the different languages being used. However, the question remains as to how this SAS may work. As we have shown nativists would argue that the SAS is hard-wired to notice certain features. In Chapter 2, we discussed evidence from studies of neonates which would suggest that children are born with an in-built mechanism for noticing phonetic features of languages. This innate mechanism, the LAD, it is argued, plays a powerful role in first language acquisition. Other powerful evidence for this method of understanding the emerging grammar of the first language has produced experiments such as the famous 'WUG' test (Berko, 1958). In this test young children were shown a picture of an unknown bird, a "Wug" (see Figure 6.5). They were told that it was a wug. They were then shown two similar birds and asked to orally complete a sentence such as "There are now two_____". Children were quite able to correctly produce the plural form, "wugs", showing that they could operate the addition of the plural morpheme in English without any formal understanding of grammar. This view of learning sees rule learning as implicit rather than explicit. However, although implicit, it still sees the process as rule governed.

Figure 6.5. Examples of the type of items used to test for knowledge of the plural morpheme. (Berko, 1958)

Arising from the approach which views language as rule-governed, the 'mentalist' approach emphasises the role that learning formal aspects of language play in learning a language. Mentalists argue that the attention mechanism can be trained to notice features by teaching the rules of the language, through understanding syntax, morphology and semantics.

Thus, the attention system can be under conscious control and use higher order processes to notice the significant features. In this approach, attention is controlled by explicit knowledge of the formal aspects of language. The explicit knowledge of form is one that has been close to many methods of formal second language instruction, which will be further explored in the next chapter.

Connectionists, on the other hand, would argue that the attention mechanism is trained to notice certain features from the structure of the data.

One of the most quoted pieces of evidence in favour of an innate language acquisition device is the way that English L1 children acquire the past tense of irregular verbs which we have already discussed in Chapter 1 (see Table 1, p. 9). As we discussed, in an early connectionist simulation Rumelhart and McClelland (1986) demonstrated the way that a connectionist approach could be used to model the normal past tense acquisition sequence of the L1 child. Thus, they were able to model a normal order of acquisition using a probabilistic model. However, although this demonstrates that a connectionist model can produce acquisition-like behaviour, it should be noted that it is modeling the implicit learning/acquisition of the L1 child, not the conscious learning of many L2 learners.

Thus we can see the following relationships between psychological approaches, learning processes and approaches to language form.

Psychological	Approaches	Learning processes	View of rules
Behaviourist		Associative links between stimulus and response.	IMPLICIT: rules learnt by analogy
Cognitive	nativist	Exposure to data in supportive environment.	IMPLICIT: rules fitted into innate framework
	mentalist	Exposure to data and rules	EXPLICIT: rules used to construct language
	connectionist	Exposure to data, associative connections between words in data	IMPLICIT: rules emerge from frequency of connections between words

Figure 6.6. Relationship between different approaches, learning processes and their implications for explicit or implicit knowledge of rules

Discussion of explicit versus implicit approaches to the learning of grammar in second language learning is a major issue in approaches to SL methodology. Similarly, the optimum methods for directing the attention of second language learners to important features of the language system through Focus on Form (noticing features in the language) or Focus on FormS (explicitly teaching grammar) has become one of the most important debates in recent SLA research (Doughty & Williams, 1998) and will be dealt with in the next chapter on recent methodological approaches to second language learning.

However, there is another way to view the cognitive processes involved in learning a language, and that is to consider different levels of learning and their relevance for different aspects of language knowledge/skills. Such an approach is that put forward by Gagné.

6.5   Gagné's hierarchy of learning

The connectionist framework provides an explanation of the way that meaning and conceptual understanding can be extracted from surface language features. The ACT model provides a general explanation of the way that language learning moves from conscious control to automatic production. The first rests on repetition and the second involves explicit use of rules. Teachers of second languages need to consider when it is appropriate to use repetition and when they should provide explanations. Throughout this discussion of language learning and teaching, a constant theme has been the different approaches to learning exemplified by the associative learning tradition (the straightforward association of one element with another) as against the symbolist, mentalist tradition (which provides explanations of the way languages work). Gagné's hierarchy of learning provides a useful model which can act as a framework for discussing this issue further (Gagné, 1985). Initially devised in 1965, this model stands at the interface between the earlier associative learning tradition of the first half of the last century and the later mentalist approaches. The model was also devised as a framework for curriculum development and, given this book's interest in learning second language in a formal classroom setting rather than acquiring a first or second language in a natural environment, it is thus particularly relevant.

Rather than conceptualizing learning as either associative or mentalist, Gagné outlines a hierarchy of learning types which build on each other. It is based on the premise that any intellectual skill can be broken down into simpler skills on which it rests. The ability to write a sentence, for example, rests on the ability to correctly form letters. In his model, each type of learning subsumes and requires prior learning in order to be successful. The learning types which he identifies (with possibly the exception of the most basic 'Classical Conditioning') all have relevance for language learning. A problem with this model is the implied strict hierarchical nature of the relationship between the levels. As we shall see both higher-order and lower-order learning types may be involved simultaneously, but the general concept of 'levels' of skill is a useful one. It is better to view his framework as a taxonomy of learning types many of which may operate simultaneously, but within a general hierarchical structure. However, all of the types have a clear relevance to language learning *per se* and, as a guide to the construction and understanding of classroom procedures used for second language instruction, they are a useful framework. The learning types involved in drilling a sentence pattern, for example, can be analysed in a quite different fashion from those involved in writing an essay or filling in a grammatical exercise (see Workbook exercise 6.1 and 6.2).

Gagné isolates 8 types of learning, divided into two levels, Intellectual Skills and Basic Forms of Learning.

Intellecual Skills	
TYPE 8 Higher Order Rules/ Problem solving require as prerequisites ↓	Problem solving is a kind of learning that requires internal thinking in which two or more rules are combined to produce a new capability that can be shown to depend on a new 'higher order' rule. These 'higher order' rules are procedures and one way for them to become more complex is for several simpler rules to be combined to make a *sequence of action steps*.
TYPE 7 Rules require as prerequisites ↓	The learner acquires a principle or rule which s/he may not be able to verbalise but which s/he is able to enact. For example, a learner becomes aware of the difference between the definite and indefinite article in English and has a general concept of definiteness versus indefiniteness. They then apply this concept to a written piece of discourse in which the first mention of a noun is indefinite and the later use is indefinite. The concept (Type 6) is then used to generate rules for use.
TYPE 6 Concepts require as prerequisites ↓	Concept learning involves becoming aware of a commonality between certain patterns and the concepts that bind them together. Thus, recognizing the common contexts in which a particular verb form is used in English, say the contexts in which the present continuous verb form is used to refer to future actions, will lead to a conscious or unconscious recognition of the concept involved when this verb form is used. Notice that, as with rule learning above, it is not necessary to be able to verbalise the concept to acquire the concept.
TYPE 5 Discriminations require as prerequisites ↓	This type of learning involves recognising that two classes of things are different. It is the basis of all the intellectual skill learning procedures. It is particularly relevant to learning coding and decoding skills by the second language learning. Each language will have its own features for distinguishing significant, meaningful distinctions between stimuli. This is particularly relevant to recognising the basic elements of the language code – the phonemes – but it is also relevant in terms of combinations of phonemes/graphemes in written and spoken language as well as significant grammatical and syntactical features. It is closely linked to 'noticing' language features.

⇓

Basic forms of learning Associations and chains	
TYPE 4 Verbal Associations require as prerequisites ↓	This is a special variety of chaining in which the responses are verbal. It is particularly important in human learning. The responses are happening within the brain and are thus covert. The simplest example of chaining is that of naming an object where the learner is involved in seeing a picture, accessing the concept, then the word for the picture, and then producing the word. Thus, the process of naming is not simply one of S-R, but is said to be mediated by another response. A good example of mediation would be the learning of a new vocabulary item by using its L1 equivalent as a mediated response which will then be retranslated into English.
TYPE 3 Chaining require as prerequisites ↓	This type of learning involves the addition of a number of individual learned responses to make a chain of actions. It is distinguished from verbal associations in that it does not lead to a verbal response, although the learning might be accompanied by internal or external verbalisation of the steps. A good example would be the learning of handwriting skills in an unfamiliar script.
TYPE 2 Instrumental (Operant) conditioning Associative Learning require as prerequisites ↓	This type of conditioning involves the reinforcement of a particular response to a stimulus by means of a reward in a S-R-R procedure. Thus, if a learner produces a correct response to a stimulus and is praised, this behaviour will be reinforced. Such procedures are the basis of language drills and are particularly important in the acquisition of automatic motor skills such as pronunciation.
TYPE 1 Classical Conditioning	This is the type of conditioning that is involved in the original Pavlovian experiments with dogs. An automatic response such as salivation at the sight of food can be conditioned to be made to another stimulus (e.g. a bell). It is really not that significant in language learning, although note that anxiety due to a negative response or failure may become a conditioned response to language lessons in general, or to some aspect of language learning such as comprehension, or speaking in the class.

Hierarchy of learning types and language learning adapted from Gagné (1985).

Taking this as a framework, we can then examine the memory implications for the learning types involved in his taxonomy.

Type 8 Problem solving	This is the type of learning which is most closely associated with Task based approaches. It is also the type of learning that Anderson used to develop his ACT model where experiments were done involving the learning of mathematical problems. In this type of learning the conscious mind is concerned with solving a problem and uses the WM to derive a solution, initially verbally, with explicit routines 'downloaded' from the Declarative Memory. In second language learning terms it is the type of learning which most clearly relies on prerequisites. Such problems are difficult to solve without a great number of automatised sub-routines such as word/sentence recognition and phonological decoding and encoding. To work on problem solving, the WM will be used to manipulate ideas and concepts with the language structure being supplied automatically from the Production Memory in LTM. If the learner does not have the necessary fluency in the language (lack of such automatic lower-order skills) the second language learner will probably use a translation strategy. S/he will use the automatic routines from the first language to provide the capacity within the WM to work on manipulating the ideas to solve the problem. It is likely that all but the most advanced second language users will heavily use the L1 for the 'thinking' part of problem solving, translating the output of the process into the L2. Whichever way the learner deals with the situation (either having to consciously work on the language input using 'lower' processing strategies (Types 6 and 7) or use translation (Type 4)), the capacity of the WM and the SAS will be taken up in these processes. The success of the problem solving will depend heavily on the 'code complexity' (Skehan, 1996a); with too high a code complexity, more resources will need to be devoted to decoding and encoding and thus fewer to the problem solving itself. The contribution of Type 8 skills to successful second language learning is likely to lie in the more efficient uses of Type 6 and 7 processes, but its success will rely to a great extent on automatised associations and chains.
Type 7 Rules	This type of learning most clearly underpins the post-Chomskian mentalist approaches to language learning and, to an extent, the traditional Grammar/Translation methods. It is still the foundation of much second language learning instruction in school settings. In a sense it can also be argued to be a possible component of the Declarative Memory stage of skill learning. Its implication for use of memory in L2 processing is that it is arguably highly 'memory-hungry' in both language comprehension and production. The conscious use of rules to decode and encode messages restricts the capacity of WM to store information and to integrate on-line information with that already received and to pay attention to the meaning content of messages. There is also an issue of the meta-language used in such procedures and the efficacy of grammatical terminology as a means of message comprehension and assembly.

The meta-language of grammatical description, itself, places a heavy memory burden on many learners; a burden which is not necessarily beneficial for rapid language processing. Here, the concept of emergent rules is an important one and one which may lessen the memory burden of rule use in the WM.

Type 6
Concepts

The role of schema has figured prominently in all the discussion of the LTM and the type of information which it contains. Schema range from cultural practices through to the way that languages conceive of the world (the linguistic relativity hypothesis). These schema, we have argued, need to be available to understand language input. On the language level, the types of meaning expressed by different structural patterns in each language will be different and these concepts need to be learnt. In instructed SLL, they can be learnt through the grouping of language patterns for the learner with their meaning either being explicitly named, or, more probably, by drawing attention to such features. Again, before they become automatic, they will occupy memory capacity in the WM.

Type 5
Discrimination

This type of learning has obvious relevance to the learning of phonology in a second language. It is also the type of learning which is most closely associated with the basic forms of learning. In learning to produce an unfamiliar sound through the establishment of motor-neural pathways which underlies Type 2 learning, it is also necessary to be able to discriminate between the sounds in one language and the other, or to notice the significant features of different phonemes in the SL. This type of discrimination is one which is well described by the ACT model, in the movement from a consciously-controlled declarative process on to an automatic production process. For successful learning, the learner will need to be made consciously aware of the significant differences between two sounds or two structural patterns alongside the actual practice of the forms (Type 2 learning). It is clear that discrimination does not necessarily follow from associative learning, but is more likely to proceed simultaneously with the basic forms of learning. This would suggest that although expressed as a hierarchy, the different levels of skills can be used simultaneously. Whilst relating closely to more basic learning processes, discrimination can be seen as a necessary pre-requisite for the higher learning processes as it is central to the decoding process. Learners who still need to work consciously on such discrimination will have severely restricted WM capacity for higher order processes.

Type 4
Verbal
Associations

The terminology for this type of learning and its Type 3 prerequisite reflect the attempt of behaviourists to encompass more complex behaviours from individual stimulus-response elements – the only basis for learning within their theory. However, this type of learning in its architecture, if not its detailed operation, reflects the importance of associative learning which underpins parallel distributed processing and general connectionist approaches to language learning. It perhaps occupies the interface between the connectionist and symbolist views of language, (Hulstijn, 2002). It stresses the importance of establishing strong associative ties between different words and networks of words through repeated exposure to such networks and through the use of the WM as mechanism for rehearsal. Thus, it is the phonological loop which is paramount in this type of learning rather than the SAS, which is more likely to be involved in the higher order learning processes. Verbal associations can also be used to explain the use of translation as a mediator for SL learning where the L2 word is linked to the L1 word and the concept.

Type 3 Chaining	This type of learning is distinguished from Type 4 in that there is no specific verbal output and is thus much less relevant to language learning *per se*. However, if by verbal we mean words which carry meaning, there are parts of language learning which involve specific motor-skill training (such as the production of sounds and their blending into words) which can arguably be seen as a chaining process. However, as with Type 4, the role of WM is more of a rehearsal space. The role of the SAS, then, is to direct the rehearsal rather than provide the more intellectual skills of comprehension/composition.
Type 2 Instrumental conditioning	This is the basic type of learning on which all behaviourist theory was built. The ultimate rejection of the theory as an all-embracing theory of language learning was arguably due to its over-emphasis on the S-R-R process as an explanation for all learning, and within that on the overemphasis on the role of reinforcement. However, the importance of stimulus and response as a basic mechanism for most language performance is attested to by the realisation of the importance of association and chunking in language production and comprehension. All explanations of language ability require highly automatic and unconscious responses to achieve fluency. Our issue here is not with the motivational factors involved in the reinforcement step (important as that is in language learning), but in the power of stimulus-response pairings as a way of learning a second language. The great advantage in the overlearning of such pairings is the emphasis it placed on automaticity, which, as we have argued, is an important element within all areas of language production and processing. By using large amounts of repetition of basic language forms produced as automatic responses to external stimuli the learner lays down a basis without which higher order skills are not able to operate. The use of the rehearsal space in the WM to provide new neural pathways to process the L2 at the decoding and encoding level must remain an essential prerequisite for all language learning.
Type 1 Classical conditioning	This type of learning really has no relevance to the subject of memory and language learning, although it may have some relevance to anxiety in language learning.

For a further examination of this hierarchy in terms of language learning see Workbook exercise 6.3.

6.6   Neuroscientific evidence

Neuropsychology and brain imaging can provide evidence of two of the important issues which have been central to the discussion in this chapter. The first concerns the evidence for some sort of executive control of attention and the second concerns the evidence for declarative memory.

6.6.1   Evidence for the SAS

The presence of an executive attention network is well documented. Studies have shown that an area known as the anterior cingulated gyrus (close to the motor area, at the base of the frontal lobes) is central to directing attention. Patients with damage to this find it difficult to initiate actions. Posner and Raichle (1994) report on a patient who was able to repeat an instruction after being given it (e.g. "I must press a key") but unable to carry it out, suggesting a lack of ability to send messages from the language area to the motor area to respond. PET scans of subjects performing the STROOP test show activation of the same area (Posner and Raichle, 1994). The STROOP test is one where colour words e.g. RED are presented in another colour (e.g. the word is written in blue) and the subjects are asked to read the word or say the colour. This tasks clearly leads to conflict between the different information being received by the brain and needs quite close control by the subject as to which information to attend to. Other neuroimaging studies have found that the majority of target detection tasks involve this area (Byrnes, 2001). Green (1998) also cites evidence from poorer performance of frontal lobe injured patients on STROOP tests (Perret, 1974) and sentence completion tasks (Burgess & Shallice, 1996) to show that frontal lobes play a part in unilingual language tasks, and suggests that such control is also used in bilingual speakers. Located as it is close to the back of the frontal lobe which is so important in WM tasks it seems that this area performs the functions of the SAS as has been described in the WM models.

6.6.2   Declarative and implicit memory

The second issue, that of declarative versus implicit memory, has also been partially borne out by neurological evidence. Based on evidence from patients with brain damage a number of areas in the medial temporal lobe and the thalamus have been found to be involved in declarative knowledge such as facts and events, whereas different areas are involved in the memory of sensory – motor skills, priming and reflex pathways (see Byrnes, 2001).

However, whilst indicating differences between declarative memory and more automatic, reflex areas, the definition of 'implicit' here is somewhat removed from the meaning as used in language studies, except perhaps for priming. Harley (2001) points out that there are two types of priming effect which can be shown to be operating in word recognition – one highly automatic and fast and the other requiring attention (attentional processing) which is much slower. The association of certain brain structures (the neocortex) with automatic priming in which implicit (highly automatised) knowledge is involved, would suggest that there does exist a separate area for this type of knowledge which is different from the declarative knowledge which would be involved in attentional priming.

6.7   Conclusion

This chapter has described the process by which basic learning of language takes place in Working Memory. It has been suggested that the phonological loop and repetition/rehearsal form a basic mechanism for transferring material into the LTM. For this to be successful, the material rehearsed must be selected and this selection will be made on the basis of significance to the language being studied. This selection would seem to be controlled by a monitor system, the SAS. The question then becomes of the source of information on which the SAS works. In nativist accounts of first language acquisition, the source of information would probably be supplied by a hard-wired innate language acquisition device. From a symbolist/mentalist point of view the source would be from language-specific modules in the LTM which contain the rules of the language. These rules can either be derived from the nature of the frequency information as suggested by the connectionists or specifically taught as grammar rules. We also explored a skill-learning model which suggests that skills move from conscious control to automatic procedures which would also suggest that some form of formal, declarative knowledge is a necessary stage in the automatisation of skills. Finally, we explored the suggestion that there might be different types of learning which are appropriate at different levels. What is clear from this discussion is the further cognitive load placed on the WM by its role, not only as the assembler and integrator of information but also in its learning role.

The task of the second language teacher is to enable the second language learner to make language processing in the second language automatic, in fact, to train the SAS. One of the major issues which has arisen is the exact nature of the knowledge used by the SAS in directing attention. To what extent is this knowledge explicit and to what extent is it implicit? The nature of the input provided by the teacher is crucial to the success or otherwise of the language learning process. The issue of explicit/implicit knowledge is one which has been central to much of the debate about second language teaching and learning in the last half century and it is to the subject of methodologies and their cognitive assumptions to which we turn in the next chapter.

Further Reading

H. Douglas Brown (2000). *Principles of Language Learning and Teaching (4th Edn)*. White Plaims NY: Longman Pearson.
This is a very accessible account of learning theories and their applicability to second language teaching. Chapter 4 gives a good overview of the development of psychological learning theories as applied to second language teaching.

Peter Robinson (ed.) (2001). *Cognition and Second Language Instruction*. Cambridge: Cambridge University Press.
This is an excellent collection of articles on many aspects of second language learning and, in particular, connectionist approaches.

Chapter 7

SL methodologies and cognitive processing

In the previous chapters we have examined the way that languages are processed by the brain, how these general cognitive structures may operate in second language speakers and finally how cognitive structures may participate in learning a second language. This chapter will examine the methodologies of second language teaching and the implications of such methodologies in terms of cognitive processing. It will answer the following questions:

1. What model of language processing is implied by the different methods and techniques used in second language teaching?
2. What models of learning underpin the different methods and techniques?
3. How do these relate to memory processes, in particular to the operation of WM?
4. All three of the above will be examined in the light of:
    a. Less traditional, well-resourced, small-group approaches to second language teaching
    b. more traditional techniques used in less well resourced language classrooms

7.1 Methods, approaches and underlying theories

Second language teaching and in particular, ELT, has undergone a number of radical changes over the last 150 years. We shall take as our general framework the distinction between methods and approaches as offered by Richards and Rogers (2001) where methods of teaching derive from theoretical models of language and learning. The first is the concern of linguistics and the second the concern of psychology. There has been much discussion throughout the book on the differences in models of language processing which derive from the different frameworks provided by linguistics (symbolist) as against psychology (neural networking and connectionism). We alluded early in the book to the profound shift in thinking between behaviourist psychology combined with structural linguistics to cognitive psychology combined with symbolist linguistics. These theories are reflected in learning processes; associative learning versus acquisition. These two interlocking sets of ideas from the two disciplines form the two major 'paradigms' which have dominated thinking about second language teaching for the last 50 years. However, they exist within emerging and changing thinking about second language teaching. The relationship between major methods, their characteristics and underlying theories of psychology and linguistics can be seen in the following table:

Methods/approaches	Characteristics	Linguistic Theories	Psychological Theories
Grammar-Translation	Written texts Formal study of language Translation L1/L2	Formal sentence grammar from study of different languages. Latin-based grammar	No explicit reference to learning or processing theory.
Reform movement/ Direct method	Spoken language Associations between elements in L2, not translation	Phonetic descriptions, structural linguistics	Behaviourist – associative learning
Audiolingualism	Spoken language – conversation Stimulus-response associations between phrases	Structural linguistics, phonetic descriptions. Error analysis Contrastive Analysis	Behaviourist – associative learning
Cognitive-code learning	Both oral and written Establishment of grammatical patterns leading to assembly of language	Symbolist Generative grammar, UG	Cognitive – Mentalist
Communicative Language Teaching (CLT)[1]	Emphasis on meaning, not form Functions of language, not grammar	Symbolist Socio-linguistic & Notional/functional descriptions	Cognitive – Nativist Acquisition via LAD
Interactionalist, Task-based Learning, Lexical syllabi, Focus on Form[2]	Oral and written. Tasks and negotiation of meaning. Establishing connections between 'chunks' of language	Corpus linguistics	Cognitive – Mentalist Connectionist

Figure 7.1. A table illustrating the development of and connections between some of the major methods and the underlying theories used in second language teaching over the last 150 years

1.   It is acknowledged that this term has both strong and weak versions. In the strong version, associated with immersion teaching, for example, learners were only exposed to naturally occurring texts and is most closely associated with acquisitional approaches. In the weak version (probably

Such a table only shows the major methodologies and there are, within these broad categories, a number of different approaches (for further discussion of methods in detail see Danesi, 2003, Nunan, 1991, Richards and Rogers, 2001). However, the point we wish to make is that there are clear connections between psychological and linguistic concepts and methods of teaching which together form interconnecting webs of thought.

This chapter will begin with an examination of small-group, often tertiary, approaches to second language teaching contained within the communicative language teaching (CLT) traditions. These approaches are characteristic of relatively well-resourced situations as compared to large class, often poorly resourced situations and have been adopted by teachers from certain cultural backgrounds, the BANA (British Australian and North American) cultures, (for a discussion of the socio-cultural background to such methods, see Holliday, 1994).[3] It is clear that the communicative movement, whilst being very influential in certain situations is far from dominant in many more traditional second language settings. Therefore, the chapter will also examine, in some detail, other more traditional techniques which exist in such settings. Such techniques are often ignored or openly criticised by the literature on second language learning, but they are worthy of examination, if only because they constitute a major proportion of the language teaching methods used in classroom language teaching throughout the world.

7.2 Communicative Language Learning and Teaching

In Chapter 1 we examined the development of psychological theories of language processing and particularly the shift from behaviourist explanations of how languages are processed and learnt to the more cognitive explanation of the mental processes involved. This revolution in thinking about cognition, the structure of the mind and language learning led to the formation of what may be characterised as the 'psycholinguistic' approach to understanding language. In this paradigm shift attention turned from micro-processes of learning to more meta-cognitive aspects and the concept of natural acquisition; hard-wired processes such as the Language Acquisition Device and modular explanations of language processing. This paradigm shift in psychology and linguistics provided a series

---

the most commonly adopted in classroom instruction, learners are exposed to more structured material in addition to naturally occurring texts (see Howatt, 1984 for an overview). However, throughout the ELT community, the CLT 'banner' is used to cover many approaches which involve any degree of exposure to communicative situations, and the LAD is often used to justify such approaches.

2. This category is used as a description of evolving mainstream ELT approaches. It is similar to the 'post-methods era' (Richards and Rogers, 2001).

3. The characterization of "BANA" approaches in the last 30 years as 'CLT' is clearly an oversimplification. It does not consider the cognitive code learning approaches, for example, as a separate movement, but in this discussion we shall consider these approaches as a transition between structuralist and communicative language teaching, partly because their impact on second language teaching (e.g. the use of transformational generative grammar and UG systems) had a minimal effect on the actual materials used to teach ESL.

of methods and approaches which can be generally labeled as Communicative Language Teaching (CLT) and in this section we shall examine the implications for memory and learning derived from some of these methodologies.

The broad spectrum of approaches which we shall characterise under the general umbrella of CLT emerged from the insights provided by psycholinguists about first language acquisition combined with an interest in the uses of language rather than its form as exemplified by sociolinguists such as Hymes (1964) and the Prague school of applied linguists. The principles of this movement can be seen in the work of Wilkins (1976), Brumfit & Johnson (1979), Brumfit (1984) and Widdowson (1978a). In this broad approach, the focus shifted from an emphasis on form to that of communication. Interest shifted from learning the system of language to the communicative processes involved. It was important to provide the context in which the learner needed to communicate and the language with which to communicate. In the strong version of CLT, meaning and use of language become more important than grammar. Through participation in this process, the language forms would be acquired by the learner, much as first languages are acquired. Methods became focused on providing the necessary task in the classroom to allow learners to communicate in the SL in order to achieve communicative goals. It is through successful communication that they would acquire the form of the language. The approaches to the learning of language form were thus implicit rather than explicit.

Therefore, the learner's attention was focused on communicative goals rather than learning the code. As part of this movement, a great deal of interest has been shown in the macro-processes and strategies used by learners. O'Malley and Chamot's (1990) analysis of the strategies used in communication and the language learning strategy research of Oxford (1990) both reflect the interest in the meta-cognitive aspects of language learning. Similarly, within SL reading methodologies, there can be seen a similar shift of attention from the bottom-up processes of decoding towards more top-down strategic approaches to text comprehension (see Chapter 4). Although strategies such as repetition and translation do appear within the taxonomies of strategies used by learners, the emphasis in the methodologies became that of strategy training, raising of the learner's awareness of different strategies; an emphasis on the higher-order learning types. In such approaches Declarative Memory is trained to provide wider strategic procedures such as, in reading, skimming, scanning and reading for gist. As we saw in the discussion of Gagné's hierarchy of learning types (Chapter 6), such skills need the automatisation of lower-order skills in order to be successful. Skimming and scanning rely on basic word recognition skills to be successful. By concentrating on the successful completion of meaningful tasks (i.e. the extraction of a specific piece of information) the communicative approach ignores the process by which the language code itself, the recognition of words, is learnt. The learning of the code was assumed to be through a process of acquisition and secondary to the task of communication.

This emphasis on communicative goals rather than language form places the motivation of the learner (either explicit or implicit) as the driving factor in language learning. The desire to communicate will drive the learner to use the language and to acquire the correct forms in order to communicate better. One of the most influential theories within the CLT/SLA tradition is that developed by Stephen Krashen and as such epitomises many aspects of the movement.

7.2.1   The input hypothesis

Stephen Krashen's work (1981, 1982, 1985) produced what was the first, and probably still the most complete, description of how second languages may be learnt, encapsulated in a series of five hypotheses. In the first of these hypotheses (the Acquisition-Learning Distinction) he makes a categorical distinction between conscious 'learning' and unconscious, innate 'acquisition', arguing that the latter is far more effective than the former. One pillar of his argument (the Natural Order Hypothesis) is based on evidence from first and second language studies of the order in which different structural patterns are acquired, pointing out that there are remarkably similar orders of acquisition across languages. Thus his work lies centrally within the psycholinguistic tradition of writers such as Slobin (1971) and owes much to Chomsky's concept of Universal Grammar (the tradition which is most persuasively expressed by Pinker, 1994).

Krashen's five hypotheses about second language acquisition	
1. The acquisition-learning Distinction	Adults have two distinct and independent ways of developing competence in a second language: an acquisition process similar to the way the first language was learnt in childhood and language learning through the conscious knowledge of a language. Acquisition is a powerful method by which adults can learn.
2. The Natural Order Hypothesis	The acquisition of grammatical structures follows a predictable order similar to that observed in children.
3. The Monitor Hypothesis	The two processes of learning and acquisition act differently. Acquisition allows the learner to "pick up" a language and is responsible for fluency, while learning acts as an 'editor' correcting and re-shaping the spontaneous response. This process is controlled by a monitor.
4. The Input Hypothesis	This states that comprehensible input is the only necessary condition for effective second language development. Input which is compressible allows for acquisition to take place.
5. The Affective Filter Hypothesis	This states that the acquisition process, to be successful should take place in a stress-free environment. It is suggested that many learners have an effective filter which militates against acquisition. One of the main causes of this filter derives from the over-monitoring of output which itself comes from learning language rules.

Figure 7.2. Krashen's five hypotheses (from Krashen, 1982)

Perhaps the most important of his hypotheses, and certainly the most controversial, is the comprehensible input hypothesis which states that comprehensible input is the principle and only necessary condition for successful acquisition. He argues that conscious learning will interfere with acquisition (the monitor hypothesis) and that the role of the classroom input is to reduce this interference, to produce a stress-free environment (the effective filter hypothesis) in order for the innate language learning mechanism to operate through exposure to comprehensible input. In addition, he states that any new material should be at a level just above that of the current level of the learner (his famous i + 1).

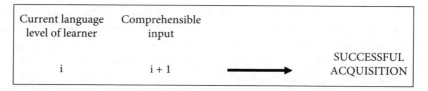

Figure 7.3. The process of acquisition according the Comprehensible Input Hypothesis

His arguments concerning comprehensible input have been much criticised in the language learning literature. One example is the impossibility of defining the 'i + 1' (McLaughlin, 1978 – for a discussion see Brown, 2000, Mitchell & Myles, 1998), and the lack of any attention to output is another (see Swain and Lapkin, 1995). However, the theory in its weak form has a clear appeal to language teaching practitioners and materials writers. This appeal is also explicable in terms of the operation of WM and other psychological processes which we have outlined in this book.

1.   **Cognitive load in WM.** We have argued that the restricted capacity of the WM places an added burden on second language learners who have to use the limited capacity to work on the decoding of language as well as manipulating the meaning and combining new input to that already received. For input which is too far above the learner's current level of language competence too much attention will need to be paid to the analysis and decoding of the input for effective comprehension to take place. By emphasising input close the leaner's level, more processing capacity will be available to the second language speaker for the processing of meaning and the integration of longer chunks of language.

2.   **Depth of processing.** Without meaningful comprehension, as argued by Ausubel (1965), retention and learning will be less effective. This hypothesis emphasises the importance of comprehension, thus increasing depth of processing.

3.   **Importance of input.** The emphasis on input (although not necessarily the complete exclusion of any production) echoes the constructionist argument that language understanding and grammar derive from language data not from the application of conscious rules.

Thus, aspects of Krashen's theory of second language acquisition are supported by models of language processing, particularly the restricted capacity of WM. However, the learning processes involved are underspecified. They rest entirely on an innate acquisition device which is argued to work in the same manner in the second as in the first language. There is no place for conscious learning within his theory of second language acquisition. Indeed, he argues that conscious learning as carried out in classrooms actually works in opposition to the process of acquisition, which he argues is the most effective means of becoming proficient in a second language.

It is interesting to speculate here about the combination of his *"i + 1"* model, the social constructivist idea of the Zone of Proximal Development (ZPD, Vygotsky, 1978) and the Declarative Memory concept from the ACT model of learning. The definition of the ZPD involves tasks which a learner can perform under guidance from another person such as a teacher (an 'expert'). Thus in social constructivism new learning is socially constructed through dialogue between the learner and an 'expert' where the latter is able to 'talk the learner through' tasks which the learner would be unable to perform without help (a process which has become known as 'scaffolding'). These instructions parallel the knowledge which is proposed to exist in the Declarative Memory in the ACT model of learning. Thus the *"1"* in *"i + 1"* is the learning zone on which the SAS, through classroom dialogue can construct learning, although the important difference in the Krashen model is that this learning does not have an explicit component as in the ACT and constructivist models.

Although defensible from within a cognitive information processing framework, it is interesting to note that Krashen does not use this framework to support his ideas. He relies on motivational arguments to support his hypotheses, which, as we have said earlier, is a feature of the CLT movement. He is also central to the CLT tradition in attributing language development to an unspecified, innate acquisition device which he sees as more powerful than conscious learning. However, developments within the CLT movement began to question the reliance on such a device to account for second language learning and have began to reassess the role that the understanding of form may play in developing second language competence.

7.2.2   Developing and re-structuring the learners knowledge

Although much criticised in the SLA literature, Krashen's controversial model has spawned a whole area of research into second language learning clustered around the investigation of how language input can be turned into language learning. Long (1985) and others began to question the idea that all input is equally significant in leading to learning and began to develop the notion of quality input, input that is particularly important in producing second language acquisition. This led to the question of what aspects of the input receive attention during processing and the difference between 'input' and 'uptake'. Van Patten (1996) suggests that the prime purpose for all SL learners is to process the input for meaning, attending to major content words such as nouns and verbs before attending to structural features. This comprehension-based process is different from process-based approaches where attention is given to the linguistic features of the text such as verb tenses.

Attention to form-meaning relationships will lead to a restructuring of the second language learner's hypotheses of the new language system and thus developing competence in the language.

Van Patten's model of the process involved in L2 acquisition involves three separate components; the intake, the uptake and the output mediated by a process of accommodation in which the learner's knowledge of the second language is re-structured based on information from the input.

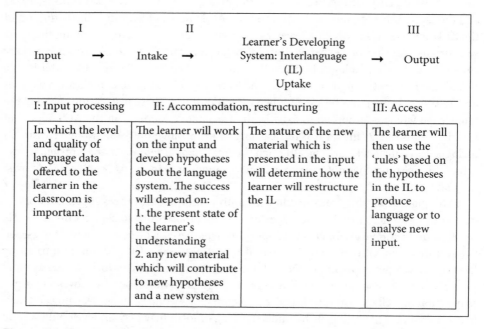

Figure 7.4. Processes involved in second language acquisition (adapted from Van Pattern, 1996: 164)

This model suggests that for successful learning to take place the input will need to be analysed in order to notice significant features which will then participate in re-structuring the understanding which the learner has of the rules of the second language, his/her interlanguage (IL). There are clear implications here of the need for input which is comprehensible and which has new features which will be attended to and used to re-formulate the learner's IL. In terms of the cognitive architecture involved, this process will take place in the WM. The WM will then be involved both in holding the incoming information for on-line processing and in extracting significant features for the re-training and development of the learner's IL. This new IL can then be used to structure output incorporating the new insights. This implies the operation of a supervisory attention mechanism, not just as a processing tool (i.e. understanding the incoming message), but also as a necessary component of the learning process (i.e. helping learners to learn the rules of the language).

Such a model is congruent with the depth of processing argument; the deeper the processing the more successful learning is likely to be. The more successful learner is thus one who not only processes language for comprehension, but one who is actively involved in noticing and analysing the input.

However, the processes by which this noticing take place are not specified. Is it a natural process built in to the SAS, or is it one that needs to be trained and taught to detect the significant features? To what extent are the new rules extracted implicit and to what extent are they available for inspection (i.e. part of the declarative knowledge of the learner)? How can learners be led to notice significant features or will exposure to the language be sufficient? These are some of the questions which have fuelled recent SLA research into the issues of Focus on Form or Focus on FormS. The former involves the direction of attention to language form in language data, whereas the latter refers to the more traditional methods of studying different language forms and providing examples of them in language texts (Long, 1996, and for a discussion, see Archard, 2004).

However, before looking at these issues, it is important to discuss another important hypothesis which underpins a lot of current less traditional language learning methods, the Interaction Hypothesis.

7.2.3   Learning through interaction

The strong version of CLT rested on the assumption that the best way to approach learning a second language was to provide the learners with large anounts of input and the opportunities to discuss and process the second language. The task-based learning approach of Prabhu (1987) and the earlier work of Breen (1984) and Candlin (1987) are good examples of this approach. Exposure to texts accompanied by discussion and group work has long formed the basis of language learning practices in the CLT classroom.

Thus, in the CLT tradition, interaction between students is considered to be the main mechanism by which languages are learnt. Whereas Krashen's Input Hypothesis agued that acquisition follows comprehensible input alone, others argued that output was also necessary for second language acquisition (Swain, 1985). The 'Interaction Hypothesis' argues that second languages will be acquired through communicative encounters and negotiation of meaning. Long (1983a, 1983b) proposed that learners will learn by adapting their speech to understand and will also learn from the adjustments made by other more competent speakers they are interacting with (interactional modifications in the negotiation for meaning). The argument is that the communicative pressure during these interactions will lead to the learners adjusting their language to overcome the problems of non-communication. In Long's (1996) revised version of the interaction hypothesis, greater emphasis is placed on the importance of feedback on form during interaction. Long incorporates Schmidt's concept of 'noticing' (Schmidt, 1990) and suggests that post-modified input (feedback that is a reformulation of the learner's preceeding incorrect utterance, i.e. a recast) is superior to pre-modified input (models of the correct forms provided to the learner). The benefit of post-modified input is that it allows learners to 'notice the gap'

(Schmidt & Frota, 1986, Swain, 1998) and the readjust then IL accordingly. Some concerns have been expressed about learners' ability to 'notice the gap' and some conditions may need to be fulfilled beforehand. For example, R. Ellis (1999) argues that learners must possess the necessary proficiency to process their reformulated utterance (i.e. recast) and the learner must be orientated to form rather than meaning. Loewen (2004) investigated uptake when the focus on form was incidental (i.e. lessons were primarily focused on the meaning, not the language) and found that there was a degree of uptake, but that it depended on a variety of factors such as complexity, timing and type of feedback.

As Doughty (2001) points out, this cognitive account of second language processing and learning places large cognitive demands on the learner, and, given the generally established limited capacity of the WM, questions must be asked as to the feasibility of such operations being implemented. To compare what they have said with what should have been said, learners would:

1.   need to be aware of the rules that they were using to make the utterance (have access to their own IL system)

2.   analyse the response which they received from their attempt to communicate (in itself not an easy task as the feedback may well not resemble in any way what was expected due to the miscommunication)

3.   then try to repair their utterance with reference to the Target Language (TL) rules (rather than using their own automatic IL rules)

4.   even if the last stage (access to the TL rules) was not necessary, if the response was a direct recast by a teacher or more fluent speaker, the cognitive demands on the WM for remembering what had been said, remembering the recast and making the comparison on-line is still extremely demanding.

The notion of cognitive demand has also been investigated within the task based language learning tradition. Skehan (1996a) and Robinson (2001a) examine the different issues of cognitive demand placed on the learner by the complexity of the task. This involves not only the linguistic difficulty of the text/task, but also the wider top-down problems involved with cultural schema and task familiarity. The familiarity or lack of it with such factors will place large cognitive demands on the second language learner which make it difficult for the learner to deploy cognitive resources to 'notice' the novel language features which are necessary for language development. Task-based learning is, as we suggested in the previous chapter, an example of Gagné's Type 8 higher order learning and rests, for it's success, on the automatisation of a whole raft of lower order skills.

In addition, the task based learning tradition has moved from an emphasis on negotiation of meaning to investigate a number of issues concerned with the timing and content of different phases of the pre-task, task, post-task framework (Willis, J., 1996, Bygate et al, 2001, and for a review, Skehan, 2003) and in this area mirrors the work which has been done within the Focus on Form area.

7.2.4   Focus on Form and Focus on FormS

The interest in interaction as the main site of language learning started from a descriptive base. The aim was to look at the interactions in the language classroom and describe what was happening. Language learning was assumed to be a natural acquisition process which emerged from the communicative event. However, as we described above, attention turned to the processes by which interaction could turn into learning, particularly in the instructed second language classroom. Within the notion of 'noticing' important aspects of the language, attention turned to the way that this noticing of form takes place in the learning process. According to Long (1991) there are three basic teaching options:

1.   Teaching can be based on meaning by providing a rich corpus of appropriate language material and the students acquire the language through using such material (Focus on Meaning);

2.   Teaching can be based on studying formal aspects of the language such as grammar in isolation (Focus on FormS);

3.   Teaching can be based on student output, using this output to provide examples of language form which will help students to communicate more effectively in the future, thus integrating meaning and form (Focus on Form).

Although useful categories it is clear that the actual classroom contains examples of more than one approach and some activities carried out in classrooms may not fit neatly into one or other of the categories. Thus R. Ellis (2001) suggests the term Form-focused Instruction (FFI) which encompasses a whole range of instructional types where instruction involves paying conscious attention to aspects of form in L2 learning.

What is important, though, is that there would appear to be a consensus on the need to raise awareness of language features for effective learning to take place. Focus on Form, however, can be manifested in a number of ways. It can range from awareness-raising exercises, recasts of different types, explicit correction with or without the explicit reference to grammatical rules. Others have investigated the role that pre-teaching of grammatical forms may have on intake (DeKeyser, 1998), and of prior practice on task performance. DeKeyser specifically links the success of the pre-teaching of form to the use of declarative memory in the ACT model of skill learning which we have discussed. It is a powerful argument for the success of explicit focus on form (see Norris and Ortega, 2000) and it is one we shall return to when discussing the persistence of traditional grammar teaching as an approach in many classroom situations throughout the world. A series of investigations into different aspects of focus on form, trying to ascertain which type might be more useful, are contained in Doughty and Williams (1998). Norris and Ortega (2000), in their meta-analysis of a large number L2 'type-of-instruction' research studies (i.e. studies which set out to see if a difference could be detected in the learning with different instruction types) found that there was clear evidence from all the studies examined of a sizeable

L2 instruction effect. In other words, from the 49 studies which they examined the students who underwent some sort of L2 instruction made more progress than students who did not have any instruction. On the issue of Focus on Form as against Focus on FormS both appeared to produce substantial gains compared to students who only concentrated on meaning but there was no clear difference between the two. However, there did appear to be an advantage in terms of learning for instruction which incorporated explicit rather than implicit learning, although it should be noted that, as indicated by Norris and Ortega, the majority of these numerical studies used tests which measured explicit knowledge of language rather than implicit knowledge. However, Ellis et al (2006) carried out a careful study which measured implicit and explicit knowledge following either implicit or explicit feedback. They found that both implicit and explicit knowledge benefited more from the use of explicit (use of metalinguistic explanation) rather than implicit feedback.

Focusing on form, noticing and restructuring of the IL can come from a variety of sources. In naturalistic settings it is driven by frequency and importance. It can also be directed by the learning situation. It can come though explicit rules (Ellis, 1994), through consciousness-raising activities leading to noticing (Adams, 2003) as well as communicative encounters and negotiation of meaning (Long, 1983b and Pica, 1994). Figure 7.5 represents some of the possible ways in which a learner might 'learn' the use of the present continuous used for future arrangements in either natural or instructional contexts.

Skehan (1998) has summed up these influences and the implications for WM and LTM and also adds the role of task demands and individual factors in the process (Figure 7.6).

The diagram shows how frequently encountered linguistic items are passed on to LTM. The frequency of an item is an important feature of the input. The more frequently a word or phrase is encountered, the more it is noticed and thus becomes an established part of the learner's lexical store. This, in turn, would get fed back to the noticing system/SAS as an individual difference (ID) in terms of what features to attend to in relation to the individual's language level (the more exposure the learner has had to features, the higher the level of language and the more features that particular individual will notice). The frequency of items in the input trains the mental lexicon or the grammatical module in LTM to notice these items. This results in an expanded lexicon or an expanded/re-structured language system. This expanded/developed IL produces a readiness in the learner to notice certain language features.

Whilst frequency and salience are important factors, especially in the acquisition of the first language, the model also indicates the importance of focused input such as instruction and tasks on the ability to notice language features. In the case of the second language learner, as we have discussed above, the noticing system will be heavily influenced by the structured nature of the classroom learning environment.

Despite the renewed interest in the learning of form, task-based approaches to language learning, growing out of communicative language learning, are central to most current BANA (British, Australian and North American) methodologies and are often seen as being at the 'cutting edge' of language learning approaches. These are exported, often inappropriately, to language teaching and learning situations for which they were not devised

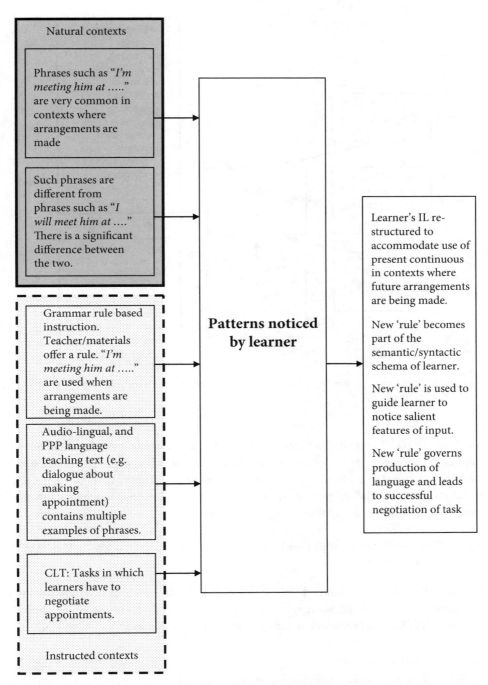

Figure 7.5. Different types of input and the learning of the present continuous as future

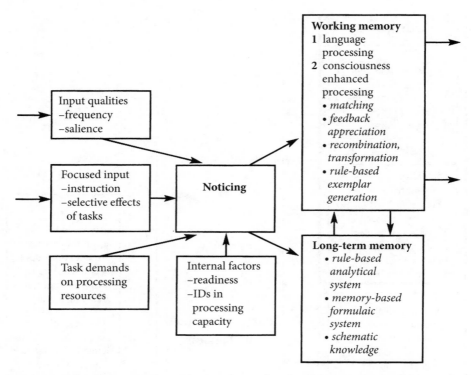

Figure 7.6. Influences on noticing and components of working memory and long-term memory. From Skehan, 1998: 57

(Holliday, 1994).[4] The centrality of the task and its role in learning means that more formal aspects of language learning which are undertaken in many language classrooms in the world are often not considered. Neither are alternative cultural approaches to learning. In the next section we shall assess more traditional methods of language learning in different learning cultures and the cognitive aspects involved.

7.2.5   The development of CLT and current approaches to learning in 'mainstream' ESL classrooms

In this section we have examined the current communicative view of language teaching and learning. In particular we noted the emphasis on meaning and communication as central factors involved in language learning. Present day CLT has moved from a primary

---

4.   It is important to note here that, as suggested earlier, these approaches are often used in tertiary or post-school private institutes and that the clientele for such institutions often come to the learning situation with an established grounding in formal grammar from their school study of the language.

concern with meaning to one that incorporates more attention to language form. This includes increased awareness of the importance of noticing as a criterion for devising tasks and learning procedures.

Nonetheless, these form-focused tasks and activities are provided within the context of communicative language activities. In the next section we wish to examine a range of different language teaching techniques which have been and are still used in more traditional second language teaching and learning situations and to evaluate then in the light of what we understand about the operation of the brain in language comprehension and learning.

As suggested earlier, whilst communicative and task-based approaches acknowledge the importance of attention fousing, they generally pay scant attention to the automation and proceduralisation of knowledge and skills (except see DeKeyser, 1998, 2001). Our examination of the processes involved in language comprehension and production have consistently emphasised the importance of the automatisation and proceduralisation of knowledge and skills in gaining effective language competence. The computational gains which can be made by a process of proceduralisation account, in a large degree, for the differences between the first and second language speakers. In Chapter 6 we found that proceduralisation of knowledge crucially involved rehearsal and repetition of material in the Working Memory. The connectionist argument is that such repetition is provided through exposure to the language, through the processes involved in comprehending and using the language. Thus, learning any particular feature is a function of its frequency of occurrence in the learning environment. In first language learning the sheer quantity of data produces the necessary frequency. In second language learning the frequency can be manipulated by focused instructional tasks, but the provision of sufficient repetition is another issue.

A model of learning which emphasises acquisition through exposure subsumes a great number of factors, some of which are clearly contextually and culturally bound. In order for the frequency effect to have an impact, learners need large amounts of contact with the language. In immersion or small-class private schools with access to high-tech resources, such contact is easier to arrange. In the standard low-resource school situation, contact with the language cannot be arranged in such 'naturalistic' settings. Contact with the language in many such learning situations is through conscious study rather than the more communication-driven, natural situations of small group learning.

7.3   More traditional views of learning and teaching

This discussion leads us to a highly important difference between traditional and more communicative methodologies. The assumed goal in the latter is that communication is the end-point of learning and that, by extension, communication should therefore be the ostensible goal of language exercises. Apart from the fact that most second language teaching takes place in formal school settings with often very different curriculum goals (c.f. the grammar-translation system in Japan), the 'exposure' approach disregards the role that conscious effort in general and repetition in particular can have on successful learning.

Many of the techniques which are used in traditional teaching methods do not appear in the communicative arsenal. Furthermore, despite the espoused communicative goals of task-based learning, many of the procedures actually used by students on more communicative programmes (such as simultaneous translation, silent repetition of words/phrases), are not seriously considered by teachers trained in the communicative tradition or by current research into second language learning. In the same way that cognitive theories of learning initially ignored the earlier behaviourist work on associative learning and conditioning, so too have the post-structuralist language methodologies ignored many of the techniques which were employed in more traditional methodologies and which are central to any learning of a new language.

In this section we shall examine a number of traditional techniques from the standpoint of the model of language processing and memory which we have been describing. In particular we shall examine four common procedures:

➢ Grammar study
➢ Translation
➢ Repetition, memorisation and 'rote learning'
➢ Reading aloud

To begin, we shall examine the approach of teaching grammar, so often given a high priority in traditional teaching situations.

7.4   Teaching grammar

As we have discussed, the CLT tradition emphasises the way that second languages are acquired and the mechanism suggested is one of 'noticing'. Students, as they carry out meaningful tasks, will become aware of their language deficits and alter their language accordingly. As we mentioned above, notions of unguided 'noticing' as a major mechanism for SL restructuring in naturalistic situations place large cognitive demands on WM, which is also trying to cope with problems of processing the input. In explicit grammar teaching such as used in the PPP (Presentation, Practice, Production) tradition, explanation/exposition of a grammar rule, is then followed by exemplar sentences to practice, and finally the application of the rule in a freer environment. Such a procedure is one which, as Skehan points out (Skehan, 1996b) is extremely persistent in very many language teaching contexts throughout the world. In such procedures, the cognitive load is much reduced.

a. The student's attention is drawn to important features of the language.
b. The declarative, or "learned" knowledge, is readily available for use following the demonstration or explanation of the rule.
c. The attention mechanism, the SAS, is thus "tuned" to notice the salient features of the structured TL input provided during the input and practice phases.

d. The SAS is trained to direct the production of SL output through the declarative rules contained in the presentation phase.

e. Through the practice, the learned or declarative knowledge can then become gradually more automatic and begin to be incorporated into the procedural, or "unconscious" knowledge.

As DeKeyser points out (DeKeyser, 1998), the terms implicit (unconscious) and explicit (conscious) are not necessarily distinct (or indeed, as Krashen (1985) suggested, in opposition). They are related. The process of automatisation in the ACT model provides an explanation of how implicit or apparently "acquired" knowledge is formed from explicit or conscious knowledge. As discussed above, N. Ellis (2005) argues from a cognitive and neurological viewpoint, that conscious processing acts as a necessary interface between input and the formation of implicit knowledge. Attention to grammatical form provides exactly that focus on form which can lead to successful implicit knowledge.

There is a lot of evidence to show that explicit teaching of grammar can be successful. As we have seen in the previous section, the Norris and Ortega meta-analysis of language instruction types and learning gains showed a general advantage for explicit as against implicit focus on form. N. Ellis (1993) demonstrated that the explicit teaching of grammar followed by systematic examples and practice was more effective than other forms of instruction for the learning of initial consonant changes in Welsh. Robinson (1996) showed that instructed ESL learners were more successful than others using different methods in learning certain simple grammar rules in English. These studies were carried out under highly manipulated experimental environments but in a longitudinal study of L2 German FL learners in an L1 university environment, Klapper and Rees (2003) found a substantial learning advantage for those learners who followed an explicit Focus on FormS approach over those who followed a more implicit, awareness-raising approach (Focus on Form). In a new book DeKeyser examines the effect of practice on language learning, indicating the growing interest in more traditional techniques (DeKeyser, 2007). In another study, Hu (2002) took students who had studied English in a highly metalinguistic fashion in China to see if the metalinguistic knowledge of the students was demonstrated in their production of English. China is one country in which systematic instruction in grammar is heavily utilised in the classroom. Hu found that explicit rule knowledge was demonstrated in free written output and that performance was enhanced following consciousness-raising tasks, suggesting again that attentional focus on rules transfers into improved IL performance.[5] The results, of course, as indicated earlier

---

[5]. He does, however, point out that his results may be influenced by cultural factors; that the learners in his study have received highly metalinguistic instruction and are from a culture of learning that stressed the importance of consciously applying knowledge (Cortazzi and Jin, 1996 and Wang, 2001).

about the Norton and Ortega meta-analysis (2000), may be due partly to the fact that explicit knowledge is often used in such studies to indicate language learning.

It would thus seem that, from a cognitive processing point of view, there are strong reasons for believing that the kind of pre-teaching of grammatical rules associated with traditional teaching methods can be effective in directing the attention of learners to salient factors in the input. It can also provide the declarative knowledge for early practice. However, one issue which needs to be considered is the nature and complexity of the features to be learnt. How useful are the grammar rules to the learner in terms of understanding or generating new utterances?

It would seem that rules work well for fairly simple structures and most of the studies have looked at the learning of simple morphosyntactic rules like past tenses, article usage or subject-verb agreement.[6] In these situations a simple rule can be expressed which allows correct utterances to be produced. For example, the use of the simple past tenses in a core, prototypical sentence such as *"He went out to the beach a great deal when we lived in France"* are fairly easy to explain. Where rules are more complex to formulate, such rule-governed behaviour may be less effective. For example, the use of the verb forms in more peripheral, less prototypical, sentences such as *"He would often walk on the beach in the evening when he lived in the bungalow"* is more difficult to explain. It may be the case that the latter sentences are best learnt as individual items rather than through rules. For example, both DeKeyser and Hu found a difference between judgments of their learners on prototypical as against peripheral sentence forms. It would appear that learning of rules did not help students to make decisions about less prototypical sentences.

Another issue which has traditionally been raised concerning the use of grammatical terminology is the additional cognitive load placed on the learner by the grammatical terminology itself. If the grammatical terminology is already familiar to the learner (through the study of grammar in the first language or from formal instruction in the second), then the use of grammatical terminology can be very effective. This is especially relevant when the second language is closely related to the first language as is the case of European languages. However, where the two languages differ radically in their structure (such as English and Arabic, English and Chinese etc.) not only is the grammatical terminology unfamiliar, but so are the basic grammatical concepts involved. The cognitive load involved in having to process both the language and the terminology will be much higher in the latter situation and thus formal grammar instruction will be less successful.

---

6. It should be acknowledged that the concept of a 'difficult' versus an 'easy' rule to learn is not an easy distinction to make with any real degree of delicacy. There are also issues concerning description (e.g. the third person 's' rule is easy to describe) versus acquisition (it is late to be acquired or learnt by many second language learners).

This would then suggest that

1. traditional grammar instruction works well on the use of prototypical language items (and may work best through their use as examples), and,
2. if the cognitive and memory load is increased by the learning of grammatical terminology with little concomitant payoff in terms of processing speed, then other forms of learning, (i.e. exemplars and simple surface analogy) may well be more profitable.

However, it would appear that there are good cognitive arguments for the teaching of grammar in order to train the learner's SAS to notice features in the SL. Grammar rules, understood in the widest sense as rules for understanding and producing a language, are the basis of Declarative Memory. They are useful provided the terminology used in the process does not, of itself, place too great a memory load on the learner. The rules also should be beneficial in language processing and production. The apparent failure of grammar teaching in SL classrooms may well be due to the inappropriate nature of the rules taught. Many of the grammar rules are descriptive rather than productive, deriving from early descriptive approaches to linguistics. They involve the analysis of languages and the naming of parts with little relationship to their use to generate language. Thus explicit grammar teaching in second language teaching suffers from placing an extra burden on WM in trying to analyse input and construct output using recipes which are not adequately designed for the task. Approaches to grammar which involve the noticing rather than the naming of patterns, are likely to be more successful.

7.5   Translation

Next, we would like to look briefly at the role that translation plays in second language teaching. Even more than the traditional study of grammar, translation (largely through its association with the Grammar Translation method), has generally been disregarded as a mainstream method for second language learning in less traditional settings.

Traditional word-for-word translation has rightly been criticised for its inefficiency as a method for text comprehension and language production. This is usually attributed to two main problems:

1. the difficulties involved in effective semantic mapping from the L1 and L2, and,
2. the extremely slow processing speeds that result from the use of the process of having to 'look up' the L2 word in the L1 and vice versa.

In terms of the information processing framework of language comprehension the costs involved in mentally having to "look up" each L2 word in an L1 lexicon and vice versa leave less capacity for integrating the new information with the old. The traditional word-for-word approach also diverts attention from trying to form an overall understanding of the text. However, the use of the L1 is clearly one of the central methods used by second language speakers in learning the SL and it must be considered seriously from the cognitive point of view.

A we discussed in Chapter 5, the issue of lexical storage and access via separate or integrated L1 and L2 lexicons has received a certain amount of attention. Although the situation is not black and white, there is clearly a lot of evidence that learners do use both languages for lexical access and storage. This, in itself, should make translation an important area to study, but here we wish to discuss the use of translation as a method of language processing and, in particular, its effect on processing costs in WM.

7.5.1 Translation and the reduction of processing costs

Although traditionally criticised for having high cognitive costs there is also a case for considering translation into L1 as being an efficient means of utilizing space within WM. In a study of SL learners of French in the US using think aloud protocols on a reading comprehension task, Kem (1994) found that

1. there was not a great deal of difference between more proficient and less proficient learners in the degree to which they used translation;

2. the difference between the two groups appeared to lie in the 'size' of the chunks they translated; less proficient readers translated word-for-word, but more proficient readers processed larger chunks of text and then translated them into English;

3. the students, especially the more proficient, reported that the reason for translation was to allow them 'space' to take in longer stretches of text.

The second language reader needs to take in information from the printed text. This involves decoding the symbols, assembling them into word units, assessing the meaning of these units and then integrating them into meaningful chunks. As the second language learner becomes more familiar with the second language, the degree of atomisation of these processes will increase, less attention will need to be paid to the decoding processes, and the less processing capacity will need to be devoted in WM to these processes. This will free up more space in WM for the storage and manipulation of incoming language and will allow for the incoming information to be handled in larger chunks. We have seen that evidence from native speaker studies suggests that language information is remembered for meaning, not form (Sachs, 1967), so these chunks will be units of meaning, not language. The meaning of these larger chunks can then be temporarily stored while the next language is input. Given the processing costs involved in using the L2, a much more efficient process would be for the second language learner to 'translate' the chunks into the L1 whilst taking in the new information from the text. In this way, the use of the L1 to store meaning is a much more efficient mechanism in terms of using the capacity of WM in reading than is exclusive use of the L2.

This can be represented like this:

| Sentence Input | *The previous week's information was still waiting to be processed when the new data was received by the system.* |

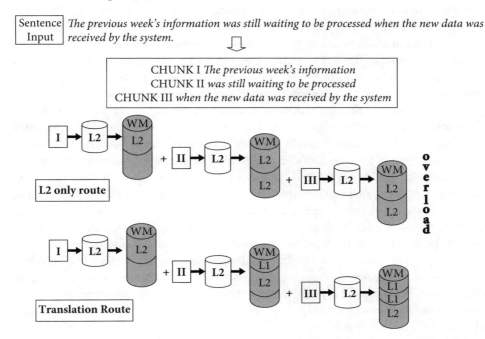

Figure 7.7. Diagrammatic portrayal of taking in the 3 chunks of the sentence and processing implications for translation

Studies such as Kern (1994) suggest that the role of translation as a second language technique need to be reconsidered. Serious consideration of and research into the use of translation as a method of L2 learning and teaching has been largely ignored by mainstream SLA research, yet such studies show that not only do all learners, both good and bad, use the strategy equally, but that there are good reasons from a cognitive point of view to consider translation into L1 as a beneficial strategy. Psychological studies also indicate that the L1 lexicon acts as a mediator between the L2 lexicon and the semantic store. That translation persists in all language classes, albeit in some in a clandestine fashion, attests to its perceived power from the point of view of the learner. For these reasons, it needs to be reintegrated into mainstream SL methodologies and the cognitive implications need to be examined more closely.

7.6   Repetition, memorisation and 'rote learning'

If there is one area that characterises the gulf between the communicative methodologies and their more traditional counterparts and between the learning approaches used in 'Western' and 'Eastern' classrooms, it is the use of and belief in repetition as a means of learning.

At the lowest level of language processing there can be no argument about the need to use repetition in one guise or another to produce fully automated responses. We noted in Chapter 2 that there is some evidence that recognition of phonemes may involve the passive activation of motor speech programmes, so the ability to rapidly associate a motor response to a stimulus through repetition may well be a vital foundation skill in language perception as well as production. To do this in a second language which is being learnt in an instructed language classroom rather than acquired in a naturalistic setting involves providing a targeted rehearsal task in which enough repetition can be undertaken to automatise the response. Studies of associative learning indicate that the speed of response is a function of the amount of repetition. The ACT model further suggests that the process of proceduralisation involves breaking the learnt routine into smaller units. The process of S-R language drilling of individual language items and chaining these into larger units was the core of the audio lingual method. It is still the core of many traditional classrooms, and fits the sorts of successful learning patterns derived from associative learning theory. Similarly, the private, silent, inner rehearsal which characterizes rote learning approaches, also functions to provide the repetition needed for proceduralisation to take place.

Perhaps such observations are almost unnecessary. They are obvious to all involved in language teaching. Yet the communicative task-based approaches do not include such procedures. Their attention is firmly fixed on the task and assume that the automatisation and proceduralisation of knowledge and skills will necessarily flow from the drive to complete the task. In this case, learning will be implicit rather than explicit. Learning clearly does take place in such conditions, but the question must be the amount of repetition and practice that can be provided by task-based approaches against the relative ease by which a great deal of rehearsal can be generated by drill and silent rehearsal associated with formal study procedures. Gatbonton and Segalowitz (2005) identify the rhetoric/reality gap between the espoused use of CLT methods around the world and the actual activities in the classroom, which are far from those which would normally be classed as communicative. Even in the communicative classroom, the successful student is the one who uses a whole range of learning strategies (Abraham and Vann, 1987, Oxford, 1990, 1996). Common to all these strategy inventories are such 'basic' strategies as word and sentence repetition.

7.6.1   Confucian concepts of learning

If the preceding discussion of the importance of repetition/rote learning is relatively uncontroversial in terms of the acquisition of 'base skills' such as the ability to correctly articulate certain sounds, the use of such techniques for more advanced learning is much more controversial. A number of observers have dubbed repetition and rote learning as useful for learning 'surface skills' or that the rote learning/repetition leads to 'superficial' learning, rather than 'deep' learning (see discussion in Watkins, 1996). Brown exemplifies the attitude of CLT towards rote learning and memorisation:

> "In a meaningful process like second language acquisition, mindless repetition and other rote practices in the language classroom have no place" (Brown, 2000: 125)

We have seen in Chapter 6 that sensory information which is more shallowly processed is more easily forgotten. In Western eyes, rote memorisation is associated with such processing systems. In our model of the working memory, this involves merely the activation of the phonological loop. As such, repetition is likely to be a highly inefficient means of learning. If rote learning is, in fact, only superficial learning, then it may indeed be one which is dysfunctional for successful language learning.

If we examine the concept of memorisation as it appears in Confucian thought, it is seen as an important pre-requisite for successful learning. Memorisation precedes understanding which itself precedes reflecting and questioning (Lee, 1996). This connection between memorisation and understanding was further explored by Marton et al (1996) through a series of interviews with teacher educators from China where they were probed about what constituted successful learning and how they went about it. Although there was a range of beliefs about the topic (we must be careful not to fall into the trap of building a stereotype which covers all learners from 'Confucian cultures' (Ho, 1986)), the views expressed on memorisation as a stepping stone to learning indicate that the process of rote memorisation involves more than the activation of the phonological loop as suggested by the term 'rote learning'. The teacher educators emphasised the importance of understanding as an essential element of what they meant by memorisation. They either expressed the view that understanding would follow from sufficient memorisation or that understanding and memorisation tend to be synchronous. The belief is summed up by Chu (1990)

> Learning is reciting. If we recite it then we think it over, think it over then recite it, naturally it'll become meaningful to us. If we recite but don't think it over, we still won't appreciate its meaning. If we think it over but don't recite it, even though we might understand it, our understanding will be precarious (Chu, 1990: 38)

This quotation, although related to concept development rather than language learning *per se*, incorporates two important cognitive principles which we have identified with regard to learning and language learning in particular.

1.   **Depth of processing**. Reciting the message involves more than mere operation of the mechanics of sound production, it involves 'thinking it over'. This is not 'mindless repetition' but involves the processes of thinking and association which are associated with deeper processing.

2.   **Sufficient practice.** 'Thinking it over' (the sort of activity which would be associated with a mentalist/analytical approach to language learning) and 'understanding' (the principle activity involved in Input-driven approaches) are, in themselves, insufficient. Without repetition, understanding is 'precarious'. Without sufficient practice the material will be only temporarily stored. Repetition is the principle route to storage in the LTM.

In a study of the vocabulary learning strategies of two highly successful Chinese learners of English from Beijing, Gu (2003) points to the high degree of intentional learning undertaken by both learners and the extensive use of memorisation strategies such as list learning undertaken by both subjects. These two successful learners utilised a number of different 'elaboration' strategies as part of their memorisation/study process. For example, as part of the memorisation process for words, one of the subjects annotated cards with the word on one side and then other 'facts' about the word on the other such as sample sentences in which the word could occur. The other candidate would read through word lists, making up sentences for words commonly used. Thus, for both subjects, the study and memorisation process involved much more than superficial rote learning and involved a great deal of elaboration.

As an interesting comparison between cultures of learning, in the Oxford learning strategy research mentioned above, one of the strategies which characterises the more successful learner is the willingness to seek out contact with the language. A successful learner is one who has a lot of exposure to the language, or, to rephrase the trait from a different cultural paradigm, one who invests a great deal of time on learning. Thus, perhaps, the question is ultimately one of motivation. The task-based CLT methods would argue, drawing on first language acquisition studies, that the drive to successfully communicate is central to learning a language. However, within many other cultures, for example Confucian cultures, much greater emphasis is placed on the amount of effort put in by the individual (Lee, 1996).

Thus, hard work and repetition of material can prove as effective as desire to communicate and extensive exposure.

7.6.2   Learning language chunks in the school classroom

Further evidence of the efficacy of memorisation of prefabricated chunks comes from Mitchell and Martin (1997) who followed a number of classes of children learning French in secondary schools in the UK. Whilst this study is set in a Western cultural environment, it is within the setting of general second language learning in schools where there is little access to the target language outside the classroom. They noted that early learning of the second language was almost entirely devoted to the rote memorisation of unanalysed chunks of language and that children "who did not internalize and retain a corpus of phrases of this kind, at this early stage, were highly unlikely to make any real progress subsequently, and in particular were never seen to move on from pragmatic communication strategies to grammatical control" (Mitchell and Martin, 1997: 23, emphasis in the original). They also noted that, amongst the children they observed over a long period of study, the better pupils began to notice and explore various aspects of the grammar of the chunks. The learning of chunks by heart without any specific focus on form was producing, of its own, an understanding/awareness of the different language elements involved in the chunks.

Although taking place over a different time-scale and without the extra dimension of the self-determination and effort exemplified by the Chinese examples (the main rationale provided by the teachers for learning of prefabricated chunks in the UK study was to make learning 'fun' and less challenging for the learners) the learning processes in both studies call on similar cognitive processes. They rely on the establishment of automatic response patterns to linguistic stimuli through repetition and practice. They rely for their success on deeper processing rather than just the exercising of acoustic and articulatory processes (in the Chinese study by extensive elaboration and the UK study by the attachment to the social and pragmatic meaning of the chunks). As this process of repetition takes place, not only do neural pathways become more established through use, but as the words (in the Chinese study) and the chunks (in the UK study) become recombined in different configurations, a neural network of interconnections begins to emerge as is described earlier in the spreading activation models. Part of this spreading activation will also involve syntactic as well as lexical knowledge. For example, the article system in English is extremely difficult for the Chinese speaker to grasp and the rules difficult to explain. Through the memorisation of pre-fabricated correct chunks of language, the learner will build up a corpus of language data which can be used then to 'set' their language parameter to the English article usage. Similarly children in the school will have a corpus of data on which to begin to explore the gender aspect of the French article system (an equally difficult problem for English learners of French).

The difference between effective and less effective use of repetition would appear to lie in the depth of processing and the type of cognitive processes employed and not in the technique itself. The differences between the two are illustrated in Figure 7.8.

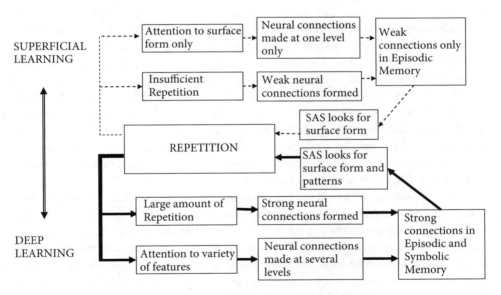

Figure 7.8. Cognitive processes involved in superficial and deep learning

In this section we have looked at the role that memorisation plays in second language learning in low-intensity, low-exposure situations. We examined the belief in memorisation exemplified by attitudes and practices in Confucian societies. Some of the specific study habits utilized in these societies will be heavily shaped by cultural attitudes to learning and their effect on individual motivation, and are not the central concern of this book, despite being very important. However, we explored the importance of memorisation in second language teaching in these societies and found the process to be important. This process has good justification from the model of language learning which we have outlined in this book, and would suggest that language learning methodologies would do well to pay more attention to the process of memorisation rather than ignoring it. It is clear from our discussion that not all memorisation is effective, as it is clear from psychological studies that not all repetition will automatically produce effective learning. Second language methodologies need to pay attention to how memorisation is approached and what needs to be memorised.

Finally, we shall examine the use of reading aloud through a cognitive/memory framework.

7.7   Reading aloud

Nearly all mainstream SL methodologies since the 1950s have been highly critical of reading aloud as a technique for learning the language. All mainstream methodologies from audio lingualism though to CLT have rested on the either implicit or explicit assumption that languages are first of all learnt in an oral/aural mode and that reading and writing are a later addition once some level of oral mastery has been achieved. Reading aloud has been criticised in that it supposedly ignores meaning as part of the decoding process; that the reader is often primarily processing words through a simple grapheme to phoneme decoding process (the non-lexical route, Coltheart et al, 2001). Skills approaches highlight the lack of reading speed implied by reading aloud: skilled L1 readers achieve reading speeds roughly double that of reading aloud and do not, generally subvocalise when reading quickly. CLT theorists also point to the low communicative value of reading aloud; it is not a common method of communication in most natural language situations, except for certain professions such as teaching and news reading.

Yet reading aloud of text in the classroom and private reading aloud of text by individual learners remains a highly popular method of second language teaching in many traditional contexts and in the individual strategies of learners as attested by its appearance on lists of learning strategies. One of the reasons for its popularity and persistence may well be cultural; its familiarity as a technique in early literacy in L1. However, in view of its frequency and persistence as a learning strategy, it is important to examine the memory implications of its use in second language teaching.

In Chapter 3 we discussed the issue of lexical access routes in SL learners and the possibility that different scriptal systems might have on lexical access. It was suggested that readers of logographic scripts might place less reliance on phonological access routes than readers of alphabetic scripts and that L2 readers are different from L1 readers in that they do not have an established and highly developed oral knowledge of the language on which to base the visual word recognition procedure. Both factors would suggest that the matching of phonological shape to orthographical features would be less useful than it is in L1 reading development. However, the power and persistence of reading aloud as a learning technique in the second language teaching may be related, not to the development of word recognition and reading skills as in the L1 learner, but may be more related to factors of learning the SL system itself.

The first benefit of reading aloud is that of rehearsal of the language and the activation of the phonological loop, which, as we have discussed, is a prime mechanism for the automatisation of language skills. By reading the SL material, either out loud or subvocally, the learner is activating the phonological loop and thus rehearsing the language and helping to move the material into LTM. The absolute prohibition with classical audiolingualism of any mediation by print during the initial rehearsal stage (no material could be read before it had been thoroughly drilled orally) rested on the belief that each outside stimulus needed to be connected to a unique oral response. This is the one-step item-based memory process of Logan (Logan, 1988). However, as we have discussed, there is a lot of evidence that such a simple process is not the sole process for providing automatisation and that reading aloud, rehearsal mediated by print decoding, is probably a powerful technique in providing the opportunity for such rehearsal. Evidence from L1 reading development shows that reading aloud is an essential stage in the learning to read process, and that, with greater practice, procedures such as phonological encoding, reduce in importance. With increasing routinisation and practice, the necessity for vocalisation becomes reduced. The same could be argued for SL learners using print as a rehearsal mechanism for oral language production. Initially spoken language will rely heavily on the visual prompt, but with increasing practice, chunks will be internalized and the learner will be able to dispense with the prompting from print input. This is particularly true in instructed second language teaching in traditional low resourced contexts where access to oral models for learning are highly restricted or almost non-existent. Print may be the principal access that the SL learner has to the language in large classes, and probably the only real access outside the classroom. Thus its use through reading aloud to provide the stimulus for rehearsal via the phonological loop is important.

The cognitive processes involved in the use of the phonological loop in reading aloud are also quite complex. In terms of the depth of processing argument, the process involves a number of different language mechanisms see Figure 7.9.

Reading aloud, then, can be used as a mediator for oral production when little opportunity exists for other methods of oral production. Another benefit of print as a mediator of SL oral production is that it can overcome the problems in language processing of having to store information in WM while taking in new information. As discussed in Chapter 2, this is particularly critical in listening and speaking. If the extra demands of planning and assembly are added to this, the ability to produce and rehearse substantial chunks of the SL will become severely restricted. The fact that printed text is permanent means that the temporary storage function of the WM can be replaced by the written word, allowing longer stretches of language to be rehearsed. The written word acts as a temporary store in place of WM. Thus, the reading aloud of dialogue and other material in classes persists in

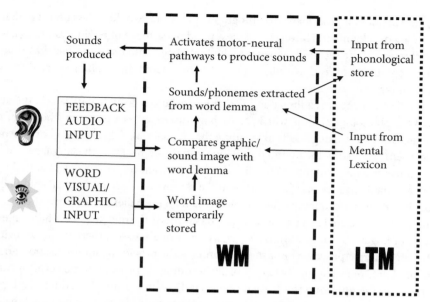

Figure 7.9. The cognitive processes involved in reading aloud

language classes, despite the theoretical problems often expressed about reading aloud as a language learning technique which lacks communicative purpose.

7.8 Conclusion

In this chapter we have examined the cognitive processing implications involved in current mainstream communicative approaches to second language learning. We have seen how the communicative movement has evolved from the ideas of the psycholinguists of the 60s and 70s, emphasising acquisition as the process of gaining competence in a second language. We have noted that the interests of this movement were not on the cognitive structures involved or, in any detail, on the processes involved in learning rules. Communication of meaning became the goal and this goal, for second as well as first language learners, was sufficient to lead to acquisition. We noted that the ideas contained in second language acquisition approaches, particularly the concept of comprehensible input, were highly congruent with the information processing framework for language, although such explanations were not offered by CLT theorists at the time. Motivational factors deriving from the successful achievement of communicational goals are more important within these approaches.

We also suggested that the acquisition of language needs to be guided by some sort of attention mechanism, the SAS, and we examined the way that such a mechanism might operate. Within the SLA tradition, this might be characterised as the LAD, with the principles driven by built-in, innate guidelines. However, we also examined the way that evolving mainstream ELT theory is beginning to focus on this area and the role that explicit teaching of language form can play in second language learning as against acquisition. It was noted that the cultural contexts in which CLT operated favoured a more inductive, if not implicit, approach to language form than the often more explicit approaches and traditional methods employed in other contexts.

We then examined four learning techniques which are employed in more traditional classroom settings; rote learning, reading aloud, teaching grammar and translation. We examined each from a cognitive point of view and found that each had considerable merits as an approach to second language teaching. The fact that they have not found favour within the recent mainstream approaches does not mean that they should not be considered seriously. Their merits rest on learning and study rather than acquisition and exposure and as such have a lot to offer to the second language teacher in many contexts.

Further Reading

Patsy Lightbown and Nina Spada (2006). *How Languages are Learned.* Oxford: Oxford University Press. A thoroughly approachable overview of the way that languages are learned and the way that different methodologies reflect such theories.

Rosalind Mitchell and Florence Myles (2004). *Second Language Learning (2nd Edn).* Oxford: Oxford University Press.
This provides a sound discussion of different approaches to theories second language learning.

Peter Skehan (1998). *A Cognitive Approach to Language Learning.* Oxford: Oxford University Press.
This provides a comprehensive framework of issues involved with the cognitive processes involved in both language comprehension and production.

Catherine Doughty and Jessica Williams (eds) (1998). *Focus on Form in Classroom SLA.* Cambridge: Cambridge University Press.
This provides an interesting set of papers on the issue of Focus on Form. The introduction lays out the ground of this growing area of study and a number of papers report on research into the effectiveness of different ways of focusing on form.

Rod Ellis (1997). *SLA Research and Language Teaching.* Oxford: Oxford University Press.
This provides a thorough overview of SLA research with lots of evidence from data collected in the classroom. It exemplifies the methods used in SLA and the evidence on which interactionalist thinking is based.

Stephen Pinker (1994). *The Language Instinct: How the Mind Creates Language.* New York NY: William Morrow.
Although not about second language *per se* this is an extremely articulate and persuasive exposition of the nativist argument. It summarises all of the evidence of the three decades following on from Chomsky's first ideas about the innateness of language and makes a compelling argument for an innate language device.

Endnote

Modular and non-modular approaches

Acquisition versus learning

Implicit and explicit learning

Automaticity

Symbolic versus connectionist views of language

The changing paradigms in psychology, linguistics and SLL methodologies have formed a backdrop to the discussion of the role of memory in language learning in this book. The initial concepts of behaviourism, structural linguistics and audiolingualism formed an interlocking network of ideas which concentrated on surface features; in learning theories the emphasis was on associative learning and in language description on surface structures. This paradigm was replaced by cognitivist views of psychology, by symbolicist approaches in linguistics and by mentalist and communicative approaches to language learning. This second paradigm concentrated attention on innate processes involved in language learning and in language description on the role that generative grammars and, in particular, universal grammars played in the comprehension and production of languages. The view of language learning taken by this approach was that exposure to language would, of itself, cause learning to take place using innate brain mechanisms.

We are now standing at the beginning of a new paradigm in which connectionist concepts from psychology combined with studies of corpora in linguistics are producing a model of language processing and description which is based, not on abstract rules but on the probability that certain surface features co-occur. The connectionist models rest on the view of the brain as interconnecting neural networks which cooperate in solving tasks, a view which is broadly supported by neuropsychology and brain imaging studies. The implications for learning theory from the connectionist ideas are a renewed interest in the training of neural networks and associative learning. The methodological implications of this new paradigm for second language learning are still to be seen, but the different views of language learning and memory processes we have addressed in this book have raised a number of issues which we need to consider. We shall consider them from the point of view of the WM model and suggest how consideration of this model may provide a resolution to some of the issues. The issues concern:

- modular versus non-modular approaches to language,
- the acquisition/learning dichotomy,
- implicit and explicit learning,
- automaticty,
- symbolic versus connectionist views of language.

Modular and non-modular approaches

The approach taken in this book is that language processing and learning can be explained through the use of an information processing framework i.e. a common cognitive process for all types of information. Within this framework attention has been directed to the role of the WM in language comprehension and learning. We have found that current views of the structure and operation of WM provide a useful model for explaining the way that languages are perceived (through the extraction of significant features from data) and learnt (through the use of repetition). These findings have largely been supported by anatomical, neuropsychological and brain imaging research. The existence of a specific language-processing module separate from general cognitive structures for processing information is not necessarily ruled out by the information processing framework. The WM functions of the brain are located in the front parietal lobes, but consist of a number of different brain areas which are activated differently and cooperate in different ways on different tasks. Within the left frontal region there are areas which are specifically and universally involved in all language tasks, the prime example being Broca's area. Brain imaging does not as yet provide sufficient detail to allow any detailed examination of what is actually happening within such areas: it can only indicate the areas which are principally involved in such tasks. However, it is possible to argue that such language specific areas and their combinations in processing language do provide something of a language-specific module. The fact that brain imaging studies show different combinations of areas on language-related tasks such as phonological, morphological and semantic processing is further evidence of language-specific processing structures. However, the important issue for second language learning is the operation of these areas and in particular, the degree to which language learning is innate or learnt.

Acquisition versus learning

As we have discussed, this issue has dominated second language learning thinking for the last 30 years. There does seem to be a strong case for believing that first languages are acquired rather than learnt. However, due to the plasticity of the developing brain this facility may not be so easily available to adult second language learners. Again, it is possible to explain acquisition and learning through the model of WM which we have developed. The model suggests a three part structure, a phonological short term store, a visual short term store and a supervisory system which directs attention. It is this system (the SAS) which directs attention to salient features of incoming information. There is considerable evidence that this SAS in early childhood is tuned to notice the types of features involved in language processing, but that after a while this SAS becomes tuned in to the features of a specific language (the first language) and is not so sensitive to features in other languages. Connectionist views of language suggest that the SAS is trained by the input. It learns to respond to different language features based on the frequency of such features in the data from the language experienced. In this way, connectionist approaches offer a mechanism by which acquisition takes place and a location of the place where it takes place: the SAS. However, the connectionist learning processes need a large amount of data to work on which is provided by the naturalistic environment of first language acquisition. What is less clear is the way that the SAS can be trained in second language learning where much less data is available to train the system.

Implicit and explicit learning

If the SAS is trained to notice significant features as described above, the SAS in second language learners will be tuned to notice features in the first not the second language. The degree to which 'noticing' can best be achieved is one that is the centre of much SLA research at the moment. The emphasis within CLT has been the concentration of extracting meaning from text. The effect of this meaning-focused attention on the uptake of grammatical form focus of attention is not clear from SLA research studies. It relies on the assumption that the SAS is tuned to universal properties of language, or is tuned to frequency effects as suggested by connectionists. These frequency effects can be enhanced in second language learning by the selection of specific instances (prototypical patterns) which exemplify certain language features such as grammatical patterns. The alternative argument would be that the use of instruction in language forms provides declarative knowledge which can be used in a two-stage memorisation process as put forward in the ACT model of skill learning. This model works with general motor and other intellectual skills, but is perhaps more questionable with language skills, particularly automatic feature detection skills as used in the SAS. However, the addition of an Episodic buffer with access to a temporary part of the Episodic memory would provide an opportunity for more declarative type knowledge to be involved in processing and production.

Automaticity

Perhaps the greatest challenge faced by SL learners is that of achieving anything like the levels of automaticity that first language users achieve. Our analysis of the workings of memory on language has highlighted the complexities involved in all levels of processing from raw feature detection through to semantic and syntactic processing. Effective processing involves the recall of permanent memory files into the WM for processing. Thus, the establishment of neural connections between the WM and appropriate nodes in LTM are crucial. The more automatic such links are, the less capacity will be taken up in the WM and the more the SAS will be able to concentrate on directing integration of different sources of information for the comprehension of messages or on higher order cognition. The behaviourist and audiolingual approach to the problem was the establishment of links between a stimulus and the response by substantial repetition and practice, a one-step memory process. Later models such as the ACT suggest that skill acquisition involves intermediate steps involving conscious control followed by proceduralisation. Again, the model of the WM with the SAS providing some direction to the work carried out by the phonological loop provides a mechanism for skill practice to take place. It is clear that both memory systems (the one-step and the two-step) are used by SL learners and are perhaps differentially applied to different types of sentence. What is unquestionable, however, is the importance of automaticity and the role that rehearsal and practice play in this process. This rehearsal can only take place in the WM and thus its role in learning through repetition is unchallenged.

Symbolic versus connectionist views of language

The neural networking model of brain operation is now generally accepted. It fits with neuropsychological studies and is strongly supported by brain imaging. Together with parallel processing and spreading activation models it would appear to provide explanations for both feature detection at the lowest level and semantic processing at the highest level. The question remains, however, of the way that information is stored within the nodes of the various models. Connectionists argue that information is stored in non-symbolic form as a series of probabilities. However, much of the discussion of more complex networking models characterises the information stored as symbolic. From the point of view of the second language learner or teacher, it is important to know if symbolic representation (such as teaching grammar or concepts) does facilitate understanding. Do symbolic representations have a psychological reality, and if so, what representations are pertinent? The possibility of 'emergent' grammar constructed by the learner from selected language input is an important idea, and is one way to approach the problem without the learner needing to use the highly abstract metalanguage of grammars. There is perhaps a need, as Hulstijn (2002) points out, to unify the two approaches. However, it is also possible to suggest that symbolic and non-symbolic representations can be used at different levels. The labeling of nodes as 'words', for example, is probably useful when discussing the storage of lexical information, even if these 'words', themselves are actually interconnecting features of individual nodes. The argument which we have made is that for successful second language use, larger prefabricated chunks need to be used by the learner, and the automatic access to larger symbolic units is part of that process.

Finally, we have traced the journey of psychologists and linguists from external factors into the internal workings of the mind and identified the crucial role played by the concept of memory and WM in particular. Perhaps the most important restraint on effective second language processing we have uncovered is the limited capacity of the WM. This limited capacity makes it difficult for the SLL to pay attention to top-down factors as well as bottom-up factors involved in decoding and encoding. Yet recent approaches to second language learning, especially EFL/ESL have urged learners to make a greater use of top-down factors from an early stage. Whilst accepting the importance of such factors in comprehension, this enquiry suggests that the architecture of memory makes this very difficult, if not impossible.

Future directions in language teaching methodologies need to take this into account to a greater degree than they do at the moment. Methodologies also need to pay greater attention to the basic learning mechanisms and the workings of memory than they do at the moment. Emphasis on such factors is still present in much of the low-resourced large class language teaching which takes place in the world and of the strategies used by individual learners. The challenge now is to re-integrate such well tried and sound factors into second language learning methodologies whilst still retaining the importance of meaning in language communication which was supplied from the communicative language learning tradition.

Workbook

Activities

2.1 Visual Perception. WYSIWYG or is it?

2.1.1 Look at the following illusions. What do you see? What factors change your view from one perception to another? How easily can you 'switch'? Consider cultural factors which might be involved.

Figure 1

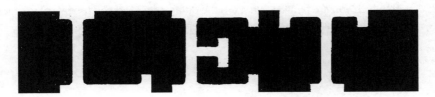

Figure 2

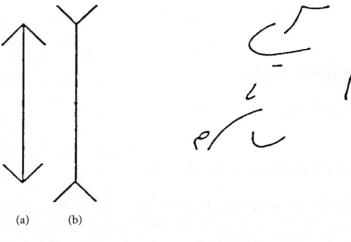

(a)   (b)

Figure 3   Figure 4

2.2 Short Term Memory; Digit span

2.2.1 EITHER read out the following lists of numbers to a partner one by one and ask them to repeat the numbers to you immediately without rehearsal. Note when they make a mistake. Now get your partner to do the same to you. OR
Read the numbers silently to yourself once, cover up the list and try to repeat the number. Note when you hesitate/make a mistake. How many could you repeat?

3 8 7 4
5 1 3 4 9
6 2 8 7 4 1
9 5 0 2 1 3 6
2 9 4 0 1 7 5 8
3 0 1 4 9 6 8 2 5
1 4 8 2 5 3 1 7 8 4

2.2.2 If English is not your first language, do the exercise again, using your first language, or, if English is your first language, try to repeat the exercise in a second language with which you are familiar. What are the differences? Did you repeat more or less? Discuss the possible reasons for any differences you encountered.

4 9 5 3
7 5 2 4 9
1 8 2 6 4 7
9 5 2 3 5 7 4
2 1 0 9 4 6 7 3
8 6 4 1 9 5 4 3 0
5 0 3 7 8 1 2 6 4 1

2.2.3   Tell your partner your telephone number or say your telephone number out loud to yourself. How did you do it?
The following are telephone numbers. Try to remember them. How did you go about it?

0 6 7 3 6 4 2 9 9
6 5 9 3 8 9 9 6 6 4
0 0 4 4 7 7 5 9 9 7 6 6
0 0 6 3 9 8 5 0 1 3 0 3 1

3.1   Contextual effects on letter recognition

3.1.1   Note the way that the central image changes from that of a letter to a number depending on the environment (horizontal or vertical)

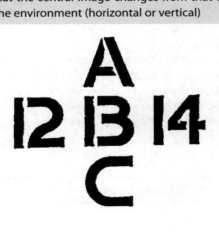

3.2   Holistic or analytic?

3.2.1   Read the following sentence and count the number of letter "f"s it contains.

FINISHED FILES ARE THE
RESULT OF YEARS OF SCIENTIFIC
STUDY COMBINED WITH THE
EXPERIENCE OF MANY YEARS

3.3   Context and words

3.3.1   Look very quickly at the following. Do you notice anything strange?

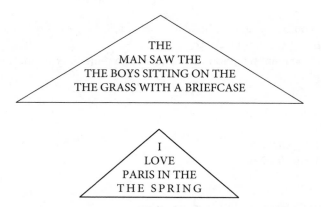

4.1   Automatic Language processing

4.1.1   Think about the utterance "And he cleaned the car again this morning", 'ændɪkliːndðəkɑːəgenðɪsmɔːnɪŋ.
With regard to a particular first language group/speaker decide
1.   Which features of the message would cause comprehension problems for learners at different levels of competence?
2.   What features would be automatically processed?
3.   Which features would the learners need to think about in order to understand the message?

	AUTOMATIC	NEED TO BE THOUGHT ABOUT
Beginner ESL learner		
Intermediate ESL learner		
Fluent Bilingual		

4.2   The context for the balloon text (Chapter 4, p @@)

Bransford et al., 1973

4.3 Memory for surface structure versus meaning

Johannes Kepler was debating with a number of influential scientists in Austria about the motion of the inner planets. He was particularly interested in the movement of Mars, which was clearly visible with the naked eye. However, he could not measure the movement as accurately as he would like. He wanted to verify that the orbit was not a circle but an ellipsis. He sent a letter about it to Galileo, the great Italian scientist. Gallileo was known to have developed a telescope which was capable of making much more accurate observations than could be made with the naked eye or any of the instruments available to Kepler.

1. He sent Galileo, the great Italian scientist, a letter about it.
2. A letter about it was sent to Galileo, the great Italian scientist.
3. He sent a letter about it to Galileo, the great Italian scientist.
4. Galileo, the great Italian scientist, sent him a letter about it.

4.4 Inferencing and shallow processing

There was a tourist flight on its way from Vienna to Barcelona. On the last leg of the journey, the plane developed severe engine trouble over the Pyrenees. The pilot lost control, and it crashed, right on the border. Wreckage was equally strewn in France and Spain, and one question facing the authorities was where the survivors should be buried. What was the solution?

Barton & Sanford (1993)

4.4 Story grammars and text structure

☐ One night two young men ☐ from Egulac ☐ went down to the river ☐ to hunt seals and ☐ while they were there it became foggy and calm. ☐ Then they heard war-cries, and ☐ they thought, "Maybe this is a war party." ☐ They escaped to the shore, and ☐ hid behind a log. ☐ Now canoes came up, and they heard the noise of paddles, and ☐ saw one canoe coming up to them. ☐ There were five men in the canoe, and they said,

☐ "What do you think? We wish to take you along. ☐ We are going up the river to make war on people."

☐ One of the young men said, "I have no arrows."

☐ "Arrows are in the canoe," they said.

☐ "I will not go along. I might be killed. ☐ My relatives do not know where I have gone. ☐ But you," he said, turning to the other, "may go with them."

☐ So one of the young men went, but ☐ the other returned home.

And ☐ the warriors went on up the river ☐ to a town on the other side of Kalama. ☐ The people came down to the water, and they began to fight, and ☐ many were killed. But presently ☐ the young man heard one of the warriors say, "☐ Quick, let us go home, that Indian has been hit." ☐ Now he thought, " Oh, they are ghosts." ☐ He did not feel sick, but ☐ they said he had been shot.

So ☐ the canoes went back to Egulac, and ☐ the young man went ashore to his house and made a fire. And ☐ he told everybody and said, "☐ Behold I accompanied the ghosts, and ☐ we went to fight. ☐ Many of our fellows were killed, and ☐ many of those who attacked us were killed. ☐ I was hit, and I did not feel sick."

☐ He told it all, and ☐ then he became quiet. ☐ When the sun rose he fell down. ☐Something black came out of his mouth. ☐ His face became contorted. ☐ The people jumped up and cried.

☐ He was dead.

4.4b   Read the following passage and then turn the paper over and tell the story to the next person in your team. They should then tell the story to the next person in the team and so on. When the last person tells the story, tick off the ideas which they have got correct. OR
Read the story, go away and do something else, and then come back and jot down all you can remember about it. Tick off the ideas you remember.

☐ Circle island is located in the middle of the Atlantic Ocean, ☐ north of Ronald Island. ☐ The main occupations on the island are farming and ranching. ☐ Circle Island has good soil, ☐ but few rivers and ☐ hence a shortage of water. ☐ The island is run democratically. ☐ All issues are decided by a majority vote of the islanders.☐ The governing body is a senate, ☐ whose job is to carry out the will of the majority. ☐ Recently, an island scientist discovered a cheap method of ☐ converting salt water into fresh water. ☐ As a result, the island farmers wanted ☐ to build a canal across the island, ☐ so that they could use water from the canal. ☐ to cultivate the island's central region. ☐ Therefore, the farmers formed a pro-canal association ☐ and persuaded a few senators ☐ to join. ☐ The pro-canal association brought the construction idea to a vote. ☐ All the islanders voted. ☐ The majority voted in favour of construction. ☐ The senate, however, decided that ☐ the farmers' proposal was ecologically unsound. ☐ The senators agreed ☐ to build a smaller canal ☐ that was two feet wide and one foot deep. ☐ After starting construction on the smaller canal, ☐ the islanders discovered that ☐ no water would flow into it. ☐ Thus, the project was abandoned. ☐ The farmers were angry ☐ because of the failure of the canal project. ☐ Civil war seemed inevitable.

adapted from Bartlett, 1932

5.1   Lexical decision task

> **5.1.1**   Read each of the words silently on the following lists one by one and say immediately "yes" if it is a word and "no" if it isn't. Time yourself or your partner for the whole list. Discuss the results

List 1

gambastya, revery, voitle, chard, wefe, cratify, decoy, puldow, raflot, oriole, voluble, bovle, chalt, awry, signet, trave, crock, cryptic, ewe, himpola

List 2

mulvow, governor, bless, tuglety, gate, relief, ruftily, history, pindle, develop, garlot, norve, busy, effort, garvola, match, sard, pleasant, coin, maisle

From Carroll (1999), p. 120

5.2   Semantic verification task

> **5.2.1**   Say the following to a partner. Ask them to say yes or no. See how quickly they respond. Discuss what happened and why

A robin is a bird
A butterfly is a bird
A robin can fly
A goose is a computer
A horse is a mammal
A tomatoe is a vegetable
A muse has teeth
A monkey can read
A pickle has fingernails

Thomas Edison invented the telescope
An octopus runs on batteries
Abraham Lincoln had a beard.

From Carroll (1999), p. 115

5.3   Frame semantics

5.3.1   1.   Write down one word which you associate with each the 6 words in the box.
2.   Compare your associations with others if possible.
3.   Place each of the words in the box into the semantic fields in the table.
4.   What aspects of the meanings of the words are NOT captured by this analysis?

man, boy, woman, girl, spinster bachelor.

Semantic fields:

[MALE]	[FEMALE]	
		[ADULT]
		[YOUNG]
		[UNMARRIED]

From Croft & Cruse (2004) p. 8

5.4   Collocation/Concept

5.4.1   Decide which verbs go with which foods in English.
How does this compare with any other language you know?

Which words go with which foods?

	shell	peel	skin
potatoes			
oranges			
eggs			
shrimps			
nuts			
tomatoes			
grapes			
fish			

From Hubbard et al (1983) p. 52

6.1 Processes used in learning a language

> 6.1.1 Think of a language which you have learnt or interview someone who has learnt another language. Try to think of the mental processes and procedures which you went through as a beginner in the language (or ask your informant).

What things did you have to think about as a beginner?

What things did you need to pay attention to when you were an intermediate user? Are they different now?

Can you identify areas which have become automatic now which you had to think about when you were at an earlier stage of language development?

6.2 Use of memorization in language learning

> 6.2.1 Either get a class of learners to reflect on the following
> Or reflect on your own experience of learning a second language

1. Make a list of the different ways in which you approached learning different aspects of a second language. Particularly concentrate on the early stages of learning.

2. Using this list:

   - How many steps involved using memorization in some form or another?
   - How important were simple procedures of memorisation?
   - How successful were they?
   - Can you identify any instances where memorisation leads to understanding?

6.3 Hierarchy of skills in language learning

> 6.3.1 Relate the following language learning activities to Gagne's hierarchy of learning types, giving your reasons for your choice.

Activity	Learning type
1. A Japanese student trying to produce the sounds /l/ and /r/	

2. Students practising the intonation and stress patterns in: *Hello, how are you?* *Fine, thanks. How are you?*	
3. A blank-filling grammar exercise which involves the difference between the present perfect and the simple past.	
4. A drill involving the teacher in holding up two pictures and asking the students to produce sentences like: *I like potatoes but I don't like meat.*	
5. A parallel writing exercise in which the student has to write about her/his own town based on a paragraph about a town in Britain.	
6. A minimal pair phonological exercise.	
7. Pre-questions on a reading passage which direct the student's attention to the most important points in the passage.	
8. An exercise asking students to divide adjectives into two groups; those which refer to women and those which refer to men.	
9. An exercise in which students are given a lot of advertisements and are asked to find which job is suitable for a given person.	

Notes on activities

Notes on activity 2.1

Figure 1   This is the famous illusion, thought to derive from a German postcard in 1888, in which the brain alternates between seeing a young woman looking away from the picture to an old woman looking to the left of the picture. The switching depends, among other things, on us seeing the lines in the middle as the jaw line of the young woman, or the bottom of the nose of the old woman. Note the importance of cultural images in the dress of the young woman (the feathered cap, the necklace) and the scarf and fur coat of the old woman. This illusion may not be so successful in other than European cultures.

Figure 2   As with the illusion in Chapter 2, p 32, this illusion depends on the 'normal' interpretation of the black areas as the foreground and the white as the background. It may take quite a while to 'see' the word, but once it is seen, it is then often difficult to see the original shapes. You need to consciously 'shift' from one to the other.

Figure 3   The famous Müller-Lyer illusion is said to be due to our experience of the world which teaches us that objects further from us are smaller, thus the line which appears to be the 'far' corner of the room (the line on the right) must be longer than the line which appears as the 'near' corner of the room (the line on the left), even though both are exactly the same length. It is almost impossible for us to override this impression.

Figure 4   This is an example of the Gestalt psychological principle of 'closure'. The mind interprets the lines as a face with a hat and a pipe, closing the gaps in the drawing. Notice, again, the culturally-bound images of the pipe and hat which may not be available to all cultures.

Notes on Activity 2.2

2.2.1   For most people the number of items which can be held and repeated like this varies between 5 and 9. It is the famous Miller constant of 7 ± 2 as the capacity for short term memory. It appears that all humans have a limited STM capacity of this number of units of information, although it appears to be related to the number of syllables (see 1.4.2 and the phonological loop, Chapter 1). One of the central symptoms for diagnosing dyslexic children is a restricted digit span (see Chapter 1).

2.2.2   This is an interesting exercise to discuss, and the results may well vary considerably from individual to individual. Many balanced bilinguals report that despite their proficiency in English, they still prefer to carry out 'mathematical' manipulations such as this in their first language. If this is the case, then translation processes when the exercise is carried out in English may well effect the storage capacity of STM and thus limit the number of items which can be stored in the second language. There is also evidence that different language speakers may have different digit spans. The mean for Chinese is 9.9, for English, 6.6 and for Welsh 5.8 (Hoosain & Salili, 1988, Ellis & Hennelly, 1980). This has been argued to be related to the different articulation rates between the three languages: Chinese is 265 msec/digit, English is 321 msec/digit, and Welsh 385. This is further evidence of the phonological loop model of Working Memory (see Chapter 1)

2.2.3   Telephone numbers are 'chunked' into groups of two, three or four digits and these chunks are remembered. Chunking considerably increases the capacity of STM.

Notes on activity 3.1

This illustrates the way that the immediate context effects the way that our brain interprets the central letter. It also illustrates the Gestalt 'closure' principle discussed with the visual illusions.

Notes on activity 3.2

Most fluent readers of this text can only see 3 "f"s. In fact there are 6. A number of explanations can be given for this.

1.   the failure to see the "f"s in the 3 instances of "of" could be a confusion between the phonological and graphical representations of "f". Although written with an "f" the sound in the weak form is, in fact, /v/.
2.   we tend to read a text for meaning and thus concentrate on the content words, not the function words (see Chapter 5).
3.   function words are stored differently from content words. They are read "holistically" and are thus not available for internal inspection as separate letters sounds. Content words, on the other hand, are available for inspection.

Notes on activity 3.3

It is quite common for readers not to notice the repeated words when reading quickly. The reader tends to take in the whole sentence by looking at the content words and not look at the function words.

Notes on activity 4.1

These are possible areas where learners may experience problems and have to use up Working Memory capacity to comprehend the message. Note that a full understanding of the message, with the integration of past memories is arguably only possible with more advanced learners; at earlier stages Working Memory will be taken up with trying to "decode" the message form.

	AUTOMATIC	NEED TO BE THOUGHT ABOUT
Beginner ESL learner	Phonemes which do not differ markedly from learner's first language. Many of the individual consonants in this are common to many languages and are relatively "unmarked" – c.f. /n/, /m/, /k/, /d/, /g/. However, clusters are not universal to many languages (/kl/, /nd/) and may cause processing problems. (e.g. for Malays, Chinese)	The differentiation of phonemes; length (/ɑː/, /ɪ/, /iː/) quality (/e/, / æ/) The assignment of sounds to words (e.g. "and" or "end"). The segmentation of the sounds into syllables/words "an di" or "andi" or "and (h)e" The identification of the major content words and the grammar function words. The identification of the grammatical structure SVO + adv phrase
Intermediate ESL learner	The identification of the significant sounds, their assembly into words, and the general syntactic structure of the utterance.	Verb and tense forms and deletion of sounds (e.g. he → /ɪ/, cleaned → clean). The intonation pattern of the sentence and the implication of the tonic stress on "And". The ambiguity of "Andy" versus "And he"; reference to preceding context.
Fluent Bilingual	All of the above language features would be automatically processed, including the contrastive/marked tonic stress on "And"	The ambiguity between the interpretations "And he …" or "Andy…" would be checked against the immediate discourse context. Knowledge of the person under discussion derived from personal episodic memory can be used to realize the implication of the statement.

Notes on activity 4.2

See discussion in Chapter 4, p. 10

Notes on activity 4.3

It should be clear that sentence 4 is not one that you read/heard, however, it is probably unlikely that you could be certain about whether you had read/heard 1, 2 or 3. The longer between the reading/hearing and the sentences, the less certain you could be.

(Sachs, 1967.) tested memory for actual sentence immediately on reading, and after 25 or 50 sec delays. People rapidly forget the surface structure, but can tell the different semantic content (i.e. knew when meaning had been changed as in #4).

Notes on Activity 4.4

Many readers do not process the details of the passage and the individual words. Thus, they do not notice the anomaly of burying "survivors". Thus, the text was processed by assigning the meaning of the text as quickly as possible to background knowledge and using this to interpret what is being said. Only 33% were able to detect the anomaly in Barton & Salford's experiment, yet when the context was changed to riding a bicycle, the detection rate increased to 80%.

Notes on activity 4.4a

This is a highly unfamiliar story structure. Most western readers will have few cultural schema to fit the story into. It is thus likely that many of the details will not get transferred/be remembered.

Notes on activity 4.4b

To a western reader this has a much more familiar structure. It is a typical semi-academic text that might be found in many textbooks in schools/universities. It has a clear hierarchical, structure which is illustrated in 4.4c. It was found that facts at the higher levels of the story structure were better recalled than those at the bottom as the higher level facts played a more important part in the general meaning of the passage.

4.4c

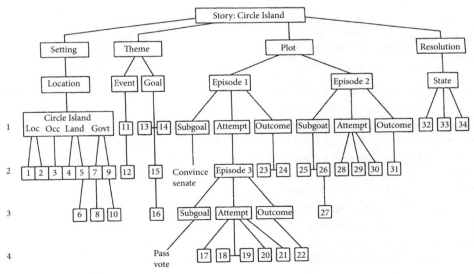

Plot structure for the Circle Island story

Notes on activity 5.1

List 1 probably took longer to complete than List 2. The words in List 1 are of a much lower frequency than in List 2 and thus take longer to access and decide if they are a real word or not. This would indicate that word frequency is a factor in lexical access. Another factor which you may have felt was important was the degree of 'legality' of the pseudo-words. For example, "bovle" is further from a word in English than "sard" and might be quicker to reject.

Notes on activity 5.2

Times taken to decide on the truth do vary. "A robin is a bird" is very quick – a bird is within the same category as bird and only one level down, therefore the search 'distance' is short and decision time will be quick. Similarly "A robin can fly" will be fast – flying will be associated closely with bird. Sentences like "A goose is a computer" take a long time to refute because the mind needs to travel between hierarchies – up to bird, then animal, across to machines and down to computer. However, there are problems if only distance in hierarchies are considered as the only principle. There is also the issue of 'typicality'. A sentence like "A tomatoe is a vegetable" often takes longer to decide upon as a tomatoe is not the most typical vegetable. In fact, it is somewhere between a fruit and a vegetable. Thus, despite being only one level below vegetable in a semantic hierarchy, it takes longer to make a decision.

Notes on activity 5.3

The words fit into the semantic grid in the following way:

[MALE]	[FEMALE]	
man	woman	[ADULT]
boy	girl	[YOUNG]
bachelor	spinster	[UNMARRIED]

You will find that there are many ideas which you have associated with each of the words which do not fit into the grid.
For example, associations for the word "man" might include, in addition to those in the grid: strong, work, trousers, beard, old, husband, father, dominant, sex, drive.
It is likely that you will have a great deal in common with others in your associations to this word.
Spinster (a much less common word) might generate:
old, haggard, Dickens, Victorian, wedding cake, veil, sad.
These associations will belong to different semantic "frames" and will depend, to some extent, on each individual's experience and viewpoint.
You may find that there will be a greater variation in the associations to this word.

Notes on activity 5.4

	shell	peel	skin
potatoes		✓	
oranges		✓	
eggs	✓		
shrimps		✓	
nuts	✓		
tomatoes		✓	
grapes		✓	
fish			✓

This exercise illustrates the particular collocations between nouns and verbs within the simple semantic domain of food and food preparation. Notice that the verbs and the nouns for the surfaces of foods do not necessarily go together. Thus we peel potatoes, but potatoes have skins. These collocations are a good example of neural networks which exist in one language but are quite different in other languages. It is useful to speculate how such networks might be set up for a second language speaker who has different collocation networks. Are the collocations connected to the way that the surface of foods are viewed in English as against other languages or are they simply superficial word associations?

Notes on activity 6.1

This activity concentrates on the way the more advanced learners are able to call on earlier leant routines as automatic 'packages' without having to be consciously think about them. The examples will usually come from phonology (the thinking about how to produce a sound, place the tongue in the mouth etc.) and grammar, structure (thinking of the correct endings for verbs, putting verbs into the correct tense, having to think of correct prepositions etc.). The discussion will probably illustrate the phenomenon of 'chunking' smaller units into larger units.

Notes on activity 6.2

This is an awareness-raising exercise to elicit the 'inner voice' of the learner, to reflect on the silent processes which learners use when participating in a language activity. The activity as suggested by the course book or the teacher's plan may, for example, be reading or listening comprehension, for example, yet the learner may well notice certain chunks in the text which s/he repeats and tries to remember. This can be easily demonstrated by asking students what they have learnt at the end of a lesson which might, for example, have as its aim to listen or read for gist (a metacognitive skill). Invariably, students will report the content of the text (e.g. 'spiders') rather than the skill aim. Learning strategy taxonomies (e.g. Oxford, 1990) have memorisation as one of the strategies, yet these taxonomies often do not reflect the degree to which such strategies are employed.

Notes on activity 6.3

There are a number of possible suggestions as to the types of learning involved in these exercises. One of the differences is between the function – is the activity designed for learning in the sense of understanding a concept or rule, or is it for reinforcement, the memorisation/practice of a rule. It is also important to note the learning types are not necessarily strictly hierarchical; in most activities basic and intellectual skills are involved at the same time. However, it is important to note that the activities involving intellectual skills are not possible without the automatisation of the skills at the lower levels.

Activity	Learning type
1. A Japanese student trying to produce the sounds /l/ and /r/	In its base form, the learning of how to **produce** the sounds this is Type 2, basic associative learning. It involves the establishment of motor neural pathways to make the muscles in the mouth place the tongue etc. in the correct places. However, as approached in the classroom, it may also be linked to Type 5, discriminatory learning (learning to hear the difference between the sounds). This illustrates the fact that the types are not necessarily strictly hierarchical in nature, but they interact with each other.
2. Students practising the intonation and stress patterns in: Hello, how are you? Fine, thanks. How are you?	Again, on one level this can be seen as either a Type 2, associative, or a Type 4, verbal, learning type. However, it can also involve Type 6,concept and Type 7, rule, learning involving concepts of 'given' and 'new' in information processing and contrastive stress patterns in discourse intonation.
3. A blank-filling grammar exercise which involves the difference between the present perfect and the simple past	Type 7, rule learning and Type 6, concepts (the notion of time in the English tense system). It also involves Type 5, discrimination between the forms. It is often used, however, in language teaching as reinforcement of learning (Type 2).
4. A drill involving the teacher in holding up two pictures and asking the students to produce sentences like: I like potatoes but I don't like meat.	Type 4, verbal associations.

5. A parallel writing exercise in which the student has to write about her/his own town based on a paragraph about a town in Britain.

Type 6, concepts, or Type 7, rules. It involves the understanding of cultural schema, of lexis and semantics and the structural rules involved in constructing a descriptive passage.

6. A minimal pair phonological exercise.

Type 5, discrimination.

7. Pre-questions on a reading passage which direct the student's attention to the most important points in the passage.

Type 5, concepts. As an exercise in metacognition it is directing the reading strategies for a reader to help them develop reading skills.

8. An exercise asking students to divide adjectives into two groups; those which refer to women and those which refer to men.

This is mainly Type 4, verbal associations (linking words together), but it may also involve Type 6, concept development.

9. An exercise in which students are given a lot of advertisements and are asked to find which job is suitable for a given person.

This is a Type 8 exercise, typical of task based learning approaches. This rests for its success on the acquisition of skills from most of the 'lower' types of learning.

Bibliography

ACT-R Research Group. 2003. *Models*. Department of Psychology, Carnegie Mellon University. http://act-r.psy.cmu.edu/models/

Aboitiz, F. & García, R.V. 1997. The evolutionary origin of the language areas in the human brain. A neuroanatomical perspective. *Brain Research Reviews* 25(3): 381–396.

Abraham, R.G. & Vann, R.J. 1987. Strategies of two language students: A case study. In *Learner Strategies in Language Learning*, A. Wenden & R. Rubens (eds), Englewood Cliffs NJ: Prentice-Hall.

Abramson, A.S. & Lisker, L. 1970. Discriminability along the voicing continuum: Cross-language tests. In *Proceedings of the 6th International Congress of Phonetic Sciences, September, Prague 1967*, B. Hàla, M. Romportl & P. Jonata, 569–573. Prague: Academia.

Abu-Rabia, S. & Awwad, J.S. 2004. Morphological structures in visual word recognition: The case of Arabic. *Journal of Research in Reading* 27(3): 321–336.

Achard, M. 2004. Grammatical instruction in the natural approach: A cognitive grammar view. In *Cognitive Linguistics, Second Language Acquisition, and Foreign Language Teaching* [Studies on Language Acquisition 18], M. Achard & S. Niemeier (eds). Berlin: Mouton de Gruyter.

Adams, M. 1990. *Beginning to Read: Thinking and learning about print*. Cambridge MA: The MIT Press.

Adams, A.-M. & Willis, C. 2001. Language processing and working memory: A developmental perspective. In *Working Memory in Perspective*, J. Andrade (ed.), 79–100. Hove: Psychology Press.

Adams, R. 2003. L2 output, reformulation and noticing: Implications for IL development. *Language Teaching Research* 7(3): 347–376.

Aitchison, J. 1989. *Words in the Mind*. Oxford: Basil Blackwell.

Aitchison, J. 1998. *The Articulate Mammal. An introduction to psycholinguistics*. 4th edn. London: Routledge.

Al-Hamouri, F., Maestu, F., Rio, D. del, Fernandez, S., Campo, P., Capilla, A., Garcia, E., Gonzalez-Marques, J. & Ortiz, T. 2005. Brain dynamics of Arabic reading: A magnetoencephalographic study. *Neuroreport* 16(16): 1861–1864.

Anderson, J.R. 1983. *The Architecture of Cognition*. Harvard MA: Harvard University Press.

Anderson, J.R. 1993. *Rules of the Mind*. Hillsdale NJ: Lawrence Erlbaum.

Anderson, J.R. 1999. *Learning and Memory: An integrated approach*. 2nd edn. New York NY: John Wiley.

Anderson, J.R. 2000. *Cognitive Psychology and its Implications (5th Edition)*. St Martin Press.

Anderson, J.R, Fincham, J.M. & Douglas, S. 1997. The role of examples and rules in the development of a cognitive skill. *Journal of Experimental Psychology: Learning, Memory and Cognition* 23: 932–945.

Anderson, R.C. & Ausubel, D.A. (eds). 1965. *Readings in the Psychology of Cognition*. New York NY: Holt, Rinehart & Winston.

Andrade, J. (ed.). 2001. *Working Memory in Perspective*. Hove: Psychology Press.

Arab-Moghaddam, N. & Sénéchal, M. 2001. Orthographic and phonological processing skills in reading and spelling in Persian/English bilinguals. *Journal of Behavioral Development* 25(2): 140–147.

Aslin, R.N., Pisoni, D.B., Henessey, B.L. & Perey, A.J. 1981. Discrimination of voice onset time in human infants: New findings and implications for the effects of early experience. *Child Development* 52: 1135–1145.

Atkinson, R.C. & Shiffrin, R.M. 1968. Human memory: A proposed system and its control processes. In *The Psychology of Learning and Motivation*, Vol. 2, K.W. Spence & J.T. Spence (eds). London: Academic Press.

Ausubel, D.A. 1965. Introduction to part one. In *Readings in the Psychology of Cognition*, R.C. Anderson & D.P. Ansubel (eds). New York NY: Holt, Rinehart & Winston.

Baddeley, A.D. 1986. *Working Memory*. Oxford: OUP.

Baddeley, A.D. 2000. The episodic buffer: A new concept of working memory? *Trends in Cognitive Sciences* 4(11): 417–423.

Baddeley, A.D. & Hitch, G.J. 1974. Working Memory. In *The Psychology of Learning and Motivation*, Vol. 8, G.H. Bower (ed.). London: Academic Press.

Baddeley, A.D. & Warrington, E.K. 1970. Amnesia and the distinction between long- and short-term memory. *Journal of Verbal Learning and Verbal Behavior* 9: 176–189.

Barsalou, L.W. & Sewell, D.R. 1985. Contrasting the representation of scripts and categories. *Journal of Memory and Language* 24(6): 646–665.

Bartlett, F.C. 1932. *Remembering: A study in experimental and social psychology*. Cambridge: CUP.

Barton, S.B. & Sanford, A.J. 1993. A case study of pragmatic anomaly detection: Relevance-driven cohesion patterns. *Memory and Cognition* 21: 477–487.

Berko, J. 1958. The child's learning of English morphology. *Word* 14: 150–177.

Bernhardt, E.B. 1991. *Reading Development in a Second Language: Theoretical, empirical & classroom perspectives*. Norwood NJ: Ablex.

Best, C.T., McRoberts, G.W. & Sithole, N.M. 1988. Examination of perceptual reorganization for nonnative speech contrasts: Zulu click discrimination by English-speaking adults and infants. *J. Exp. Psychol. Hum. Percept. Perform.* 14(3): 345–360.

Bialystock, E., Majumder, S. & Martin, M. 2003. Developing phonological awareness: Is there a bilingual advantage? *Applied Psycholinguistics* 24: 27–44.

Binder, J.R., Medler, D.A., Desai, R., Conant, L.L. & Liebenthal, E. 2005. Some neuropsychological constraints on models of word naming. *Neuroimage* 27: 677–693.

Birch, B.M. 2002. *English L2 Reading: Getting to the bottom*. Mahwah NJ: Lawrence Erlbaum.

Bleuler, M. & Bleuler, R. 1935. Rorschach ink-blot tests and social psychology. *Character and Personality* 4: 99–114.

Bloom, A.H. 1981. *The Linguistic Shaping of Thought: A study in the impact of language on thinking in China and the West*. Hillsdale NJ: Lawrence Erlbaum.

Bock, K. & Levelt, W. 1994. Language production, grammatical encoding. In *Handbook of Psycholinguistics*, M.A. Gernsbacher (ed.). San Diego CA: Academic Press.

Bransford, J. & Johnson, M. 1973. Consideration of some problems of comprehension. In *Visual Information Processing*, W. Chase (ed.), 383–438. New York NY: Academic Press.

Bransford, J.D., Stein, B.D. & Shelton, T. 1984. Learning from the perspective of the comprehender. In *Reading in a Foreign Language*, J.C. Alderson & A.H. Urguhart (eds). London: Longman.

Brazil, D. 1997. *The Communicative Value of Intonation*. Cambridge: CUP.

Breen, M.P. 1984. Process syllabuses for the language classroom. In *General English Syllabus Design*, C.J. Brumfit (ed.). New York NY: Pergamon Press.

Brown, H.D. 2000. *Principles of Language Learning and Teaching*. 4th edn. White Plains NY: Pearson.

Brown, G., Malkjær & Williams, J. (eds). 1996. *Performance and Competence in Second Language Acquisition*. Cambridge: CUP.

Brown, R. & MacNeil, D. 1966. The 'tip of the tongue' phenomenon. *Journal of Verbal Learning and Behavior* 5: 325–327.

Brumfit, C.J. 1984. *Communicative Methodology in Language Teaching: The roles of fluency and accuracy.* Cambridge: CUP.

Brumfit, C.J. & Johnson, K. (eds). 1979. *The Communicative Approach to Language Teaching.* Oxford: OUP.

Bruner, J.S. 1985. *Child's Talk: Learning to use language.* New York NY: Norton.

Burgess, P.W. & Shallice, T. 1996. Response suppression, initiation and strategy use following frontal lobe lesions. *Neuropsychologia* 34: 263–273.

Burton, M.W., LoCasto, P.C., Krebs-Noble, D. & Gullapalli, R.P. 2005. A systematic investigation of the functional neuroanatomy of auditory and visual phonological processing. *NeuroImage* 26(3): 647–661.

Byagate, M., Skehan, P. & Swain, M. (eds). 2001. *Researching Pedagogic Tasks: Second language learning, teaching and testing.* London: Longman.

Byrnes, J.P. 2001. *Minds, Brains and Learning.* New York NY: The Guilford Press.

Candlin, C. 1987. *Language Learning Tasks.* Englewood Cliffs NJ: Prentice-Hall.

Carroll, D.W. 1999. *Psychology of Language.* 3rd edn. Pacific Grove CA: Brooks/Cole Publishing.

Chater, N. & Christiansen, M.H. 1999. Connectionism and natural language processing. In *Language Processing*, S. Garrod & M. Pickery (eds), 233–279. Hove: Psychology Press.

Chee, M.W.L., Caplan, D., Soon, C.S., Sriram, N., Tan, E.W.L., Thiel, T. & Weekesk, B. 1999a. Processing of visually presented sentences in Mandarin and English studied with fMRI. *Neuron* 23(1): 127–137.

Chee, M.W.L., Tan, E.W. & Thiel, T. 1999b. Mandarin and English single word processing studied with functional magnetic resonance imaging. *The Journal of Neuroscience* 19(8): 3050–3056.

Chomsky, N. 1959. Review of *Verbal Behaviour*. *Language* 35(1): 26–58.

Chomsky, N. 1964. *Current Issues in Linguistic Theory.* The Hague: Mouton.

Chomsky, N. 1972. *Language and Mind.* New York NY: Harcourt Brace, Jovanovitch.

Chomsky, N. & Halle, M. 1968. *The Sound Pattern of English.* New York NY: Harper & Row.

Chu, H. 1990. *Learning to be a Sage: Selections from the conversations of Master Chu, arranged topically,* transl. by D.K. Gardner. Berkeley CA: University of California Press.

Clark, H.H. & Clark, E.V. 1977. *Psychology and Language: An introduction to psycholinguistics.* New York NY: Harcourt Brace Jovanovich.

Collins, A.M. & Loftus, E.F. 1975. A spreading activation of semantic processing. *Psychological Review* 82: 407–428.

Collins, A.M. & Quillan, M.R. 1969. Retrieval time from semantic memory. *Journal of Verbal Learning and Verbal Behavior* 8: 240–247.

Coltheart, M., Rastle, K., Perry, C., Langdon, R. & Ziegler, J. 2001. DRC. A computational model of visual word recognition and reading aloud. *Psychological Review* 108(1): 204–256.

Condon, W.S. & Sadler, L.W. 1974. Synchrony demonstrated between the movements of the neonate and adult speech. *Child Development* 45: 456–462.

Cook, V. 1993. *Linguistics and Second Language Acquisition.* London: Macmillan.

Cook, V. & Bassetti, B. (eds). 2005. *Second Language Writing Systems.* Clevedon: Multilingual Matters.

Cortazzi, M. & Jin, L.X. 1996. English teaching and learning in China. *Language Learning* 2: 61–80.

Cowen, N. 1995. *Attention and Memory: An integrated framework.* Oxford: OUP.

Croft, W. & Cruse, D.A. 2004. *Cognitive Linguistics.* Cambridge: CUP.

Danesi, M. 2003. *Second Language Teaching: A view from the right side of the brain.* Dordrecht: Kluwer.

Darwin, C.J., Turvey, M.T. & Crowder, R.G. 1972. An auditory analogue of the Sperling partial report procedure: Evidence for brief auditory storage. *Cognitive Psychology* 3: 255–267.

DeKeyser, R.M. 1998. Beyond focus on form. In *Focus of Form in Second Classroom Language Acquisition*, C. Doughty & J. Williams (eds), 42–63. Cambridge: CUP.

DeKeyser, R.M. 2001. Automaticity and automatization. In *Cognition and Second Language Instruction*, P. Robinson (ed.), 125–151. Cambridge: CUP.

DeKeyser, R.M. 2007. *Practice in a Second Language: Perspectives from applied linguistics and cognitive psychology*. New York NY: CUP.

Dichy, J. & Farghaly, A. 2003. Roots & patterns vs. stems plus grammar-lexis specifications: On what basis should a multilingual lexical database centred on Arabic be built? MT Summit IX, New Orleans, USA, 23–27. September 2003. http://www.amtaweb.org/summit/WS2/Dichy+Farghaly_paper.pdf

Doughty, C. 2001. Cognitive underpinnings of focus on form. In *Cognition and Second Language Instruction,* P. Robinson (ed.), 207–257. Cambridge: CUP.

Doughty, C. & Williams, J. (eds). 1998. *Focus on Form in Classroom SLA*. Cambridge: CUP.

Eimas, P.D., Siqueland, E.R., Juscyk, P. & Vogorito, J. 1971. Speech perception in infants. *Science* 171: 303–306.

Ellis, A. & Young, A.W. 1995. *Human Cognitive Neuropsychology: A textbook with readings*. Hove: Psychology Press.

Ellis, A.W. 1984. *Reading, Writing and Dyslexia: A cognitive analysis*. Hillsdale NJ: Lawrence Erlbaum.

Ellis, N.C. 1993. Rules and instances in foreign language learning: Interaction of implicit and explicit knowledge. *European Journal of Cognitive Psychology* 5: 289–319.

Ellis, N.C. 2001. Memory for language. In *Cognition and Second Language Instruction*, P. Robinson, 33–68. Cambridge: CUP.

Ellis, N.C. 2005. At the interface: Dynamic interpretations of explicit and implicit language knowledge. *Studies in Second Language Acquisition* 27: 305–362.

Ellis, N.C. & Hennelly, R.A. 1980. A bilingual word-length effect: Implications for intelligence testing and the relative ease of mental education in Welsh and English. *British Journal of Psychology* 71: 43–52.

Ellis, R. 1990. *Instructed Second Language Acquisition: Learning in the classroom*. Oxford: Basil Blackwell.

Ellis, R. 1994. *The Study of Second Language Acquisition*. Oxford: OUP.

Ellis, R. 1997. *SLA Research and Language Teaching*. Oxford: OUP.

Ellis, R. 1999. *Learning a Second Language through Interaction*. Amsterdam: John Benjamins.

Ellis, R.S. 2001. Investigating form-focused instruction. *Language Learning* 51(Supplement 1): 1–46.

Ellis, R.S., Loewen, S. & Erlam, R. 2006. Implicit and explicit corrective feedback and the acquisition of L2 grammar. *Studies in Second Language Acquisition* 28: 339–368.

Elman, J.L., Bates, E.A., Johnson, M.H., Kamiloff-Smith, A., Parisi, D. & Plunkett, K. 1996. *Rethinking Innateness: A connectionist perspective on development*. Cambridge MA: The MIT Press.

Eviatar, Z. & Ibrahim, R. 2004. Morphological and orthographic effects on hemispheric processing of nonwords: A cross-linguistic study. *Reading and Writing* 17(7–8): 691–705.

Eviatar, Z., Ibrahim, R. & Ganayim, D. 2004. Orthography and the hemispheres: Visual and linguistic aspects of letter processing. *Neuropsychology* 18(1): 174–184.

Eysenck, M.W. & Eysenck, M.C. 1980. Effects of processing depth, distinctiveness, and word frequency on retention. *British Journal of Psychology* 71: 263–274.

Eysenck, M.W. & Keane, M.T. 1995. *Cognitive Psychology*. Hove: Taylor & Francis.

Fabbro, F. 2001. The bilingual brain: Cerebral representation of languages. *Brain and Language* 79(2): 211–222.

Fadiga, L. & Craighero, L. 2003. New insights on sensorimotor integration: From hand action to speech perception. *Brain and Cognition* 53(3): 514–524.

Fantz, R.L. 1963. Pattern vision in newborn infants. *Science* 140: 296–297.

Farrag, A.F., Khedr, E.M. & Abel-Naser, W. 2002. Impaired parvocellular pathway in dyslexic children. *European Journal of Neurology* 9(4): 359–363.

Fender, M. 2003. English word recognition and word integration skills of native Arabic- and Japanese-speaking learners of English as a second language. *Applied Psycholinguistics* 24: 289–315.

Felser, C., Roberts, L., Martins, T. & Gross, R. 2003. The processing of ambiguous sentences by first and second language learners of English. *Applied Psycholinguistics* 24: 453–489.

Filmore, C.J. 1976. Frame semantics and the nature of language. In *Origins and Evolution of Language and Speech*, S.R. Harnad, H.D. Steklis & J. Lancaster (eds). *Annals of the NY Academy of Sciences* 280: 20–32.

Fitch, W.T, Hauser, M.D & Chomsky, N. 2005. The evolution of the language faculty: Clarifications and implications. *Cognition* 97: 179–210.

Forster, K.I. 1976. Accessing the mental lexicon. In *New Approaches to Language Mechanisms*, R.J. Wales & E.C.T. Walker (eds), 257–287. Amsterdam: North Holland.

Forster, K.I. 1979. Levels of processing and the structure of the language processor. In *Psycholinguistic Studies Presented to Merrill Garrett*, W.E. Cooper & E.C.T. Walker (eds), 27–85. Hillsdale NJ: Lawrence Erlbaum.

Forster, K.I. 1994. Computational modeling and elementary process analysis in visual word recognition. *Journal of Experimental Psychology: Human Perception and Performance* 20: 1292–1310.

Foster, P. 2001. Rules and routines: A consideration of their role in the task-based language production of native and non-native speakers. In *Researching Pedagogic Tasks: Second language learning, teaching and testing*, M. Bygate, P. Skehan & M. Swain (eds). Harlow: Pearson.

Franceschini, R., Zappatore, D. & Nitsch, Z. 2003. Lexicon in the brain: What neurobiology has to say about languages. In *The Multilingual Lexicon*, J. Cenoz, U. Jessner & B. Hufeisen (eds). Dordrecht: Kluwer.

Frost, R. 1998. Toward a strong phonological theory of visual word recognition: True issues and false trails. *Psychological Bulletin* 123: 71–99.

Gagné, R.M. 1985. *The Conditions of Learning and Theory of Instruction*. 4th edn. New York NY: Holt, Rinehart and Winston.

Gaillard, R., Naccache, L., Pinel, P., Clémenceau, S., Volle, E., Hasboun, D., Dupont, S., Baulac, M., Dehaene, S., Adam, C. & Cohen, L. 2006. Direct intracranial, fMRI, and lesion evidence for the causal role of left inferotemporal cortex in reading. *Neuron* 50(2): 191–204.

Gatbonton, E. & Segalowitz, N. 2005. Rethinking communicative language teaching: A focus on access to fluency. *The Canadian Modern Language Review* 61: 325–353.

Georgiewa, P., Rzanny, R., Gaser, C., Gerhard, U.-J., Vieweg, U., Freesmeyer, D., Mentzel, H.-J., Kaiser, W.A. & Blanz, B. 2002. Phonological processing in dyslexic children: A study combining functional imaging and event related potentials. *Neuroscience Letters* 318(1): 5–8.

Goldman-Rakie, P.S. 1992. Working memory and the mind. *Scientific American* 90: 111–117.

Goodman, K.S. 1967. Reading: A psycholinguistic guessing game. *Journal of the Reading Specialist* 6(1): 126–135.

Goswani, U., Gombert, J.E. & de Barrera, L.F. 1998. Children's orthographic representations and linguistic transparency. Nonsense word reading in English, French and Spanish. *Applied Psycholinguistics* 19(1): 19–52.

Goswani, U., Porpodas, C. & Wheelwright, S. 1997. Children's orthographic representations in English and Greek. *European Journal of Psychology of Education* 12(3): 273–292.

Goswami, U., Ziegler, J.C., Dalton, L. & Schneider, W. 2001. Pseudohomophone effects and phonological recoding procedures in reading development in English and German. *Journal of Memory and Language* 45(4): 648–664.

Goswani, U., Ziegler, J.C., Dalton, L. & Schneider, W. 2003. Nonword reading across orthographies: How flexible is the choice of reading units? *Applied Psycholinguistics* 24(2): 235–247.

Green, D. (1998). Mental control of the bilingual lexico-grammatical system. *Bilingualism: Language and Cognition* 1: 67–81.

Green, D.W., Hammond, E.J. & Supramanian, S. 1983. Letters and shapes: Developmental changes in search strategies. *British Journal of Psychology* 3(2): 101–117.

Green, D.W. & Meara, P. 1987. The effects of script on visual search. *Second Language Research* 3(2): 101–117.

Greenfield, S. 1997. *The Human Brain: A guided tour*. London: Weidenfeld & Nicolson.

Gu, P.Y. 2003. Fine brush and freehand: The vocabulary learning art of two successful Chinese EFL students. *TESOL Quarterly* 37(1): 73–104.

Halle, M. 2002. *From Memory to Speech and Back: Papers on phonetics and phonology 1954–2002*. New York NY: Mouton de Gruyter.

Hamer, J.F. & Blanc, M.H.A. 2000. *Bilinguality and Bilingualism*. 2nd edn. Cambridge: CUP.

Harley, T.A. 2001. *The Psychology of Language: From data to theory*. 2nd edn. Hove: Psychology Press.

Hauser, M.D., Chomsky, N. & Fitch, W.T. 2002. The faculty of language: What is it, who has it, and how did it evolve? *Science* 298: 1569–1579.

Hayward, K. 2000. *Experimental Phonetics*. Harlow: Pearson.

Heath, R.L., Mahmasanni, O., Rouhana, A. & Nassif, N. (2005). Comparison of aesthetic preferences among Roman and Arabic script readers Laterality: Asymmetries of body. *Brain and Cognition* 10(5): 399–411.

Henson, R. 2001. Neural working memory. In *Working Memory in Perspective*, J. Andrade (ed.). Hove: Psychology Press.

Heredia, R. 1997. Bilingual memory and hierarchical models: A case for language dominance. *Current Directions in Psychological Science* 6(2): 34–39.

Hernández, A.E. 2002. Exploring language asymmetries in early Spanish-English bilinguals: The role of lexical and sentential context effects. In *Bilingual Sentence Processing*, R.R. Heredia & J. Altarriba (eds). Amsterdam: Elsevier.

Ho, D.Y.F. 1986. Chinese patterns of socialization: A critical review. In *The Psychology of the Chinese People*, M.H. Bond (ed.), 1–37. Hong Kong: OUP.

Hoey, M. 2001. *Textual Interaction*. London: Routledge.

Hoey, M. 2003. What has research got to offer ELT (and what has ELT got to offer research)? Proceedings of ELT Confernce, School of Liberal Arts, King Mongkut's University of Technology Thonburi, Bangkok, Thailand.

Holliday, A. 1994. *Appropriate Methodology and Social Context*. Cambridge: CUP.

Hoosain, R. & Salili, F. 1988. Language differences, working memory and mathematical ability. In *Practical Aspects of Memory: Current research and issues*. Vol. 2: *Clinical and educational implications*, M.M. Gruneberg, P.E. Morris & R.N. Sykes (eds), 512–517. Chichester: Wiley.

Howatt, A. 1984. *A History of English Language Teaching*. Oxford: OUP.

Hu, G. 2002. Metalinguistic knowledge at work: The case of written production by Chinese Learners of English. *Asian Journal of English Language Teaching* 12: 6–44.

Hubbard, P., Jones, H., Thornton, B., & Wheeler, R. 1983. *A Training Course for TEFL*. Oxford: OUP.

Hulstijn, J. 2002. Towards a unified account of the representation, processing and acquisition of second language knowledge. *Second Language Research* 18(3): 193–223.

Hymes, D.H. 1964. *Language in Culture and Society: A reader in linguistics and anthropology*. New York NY: Harper & Row.

Ibrahim, R., Eviatar, Z. & Aharon-Peretz, J. 2002. The characteristics of Arabic orthography slow its processing. *Neuropsychology* 16: 322–326.

Ijaz, I.H. 1986. Linguistic and cognitive determinants of lexical acquisition in a second language. *Language Learning* 36(4): 401–451.

Illes, J., Francis, W.S., Desmond, J.E., Gabrieli, J.D.E., Glover, G.H., Poldrack, R. & Lee, C.J. 1999. Convergent cortical representation of semantic processing in bilinguals. *Brain and Language* 70: 347–363.

Jackendoff, R. & Pinker, S. 2005. The nature of the language faculty and its implications for the evolution of language. (Reply to Fitch, Hauser, and Chomsky). *Cognition* 97: 211–225.

James, W. 1890. *Principles of Psychology*. New York NY: Holt.

Jiang, N. 2004. Semantic transfer and its implications for vocabulary teaching in a second language. *Modern Language Journal* 88(3): 416–432.

Jobard, G., Crivello, F. & Tzourio-Mazoyer, N. 2003. Evaluation of the dual route theory of reading: A metanalysis of 35 neuroimaging studies. *Neuroimage* 20(2): 693–712.

Joubert, S., Beauregard, M., Walter, N., Bourgouin, P., Beaudoin, G., Leroux, J.-M., Karama, S. & Lecours, A.R. 2004. Neural correlates of sublexical processes in reading. *Brain and Language* 89(1): 9–20.

Johnson, M.K., Bransford, J.D. & Solomon, S.K. 1973. Memory for tacit implications of sentences. *Journal of Experimental Psychology* 98: 203–205.

Karni, A., Morocz, I.A., Bitan, T., Shaul, S., Kushnir, T. & Breznitz, Z. 2005. An fMRI study of the differential effects of word presentation rates (reading acceleration) on dyslexic readers' brain activity patterns. *Journal of Neurolinguistics* 18(2): 197–219.

Kem, R.G. 1994. The role of mental translation in second language reading. *Studies in Second Language Acquisition* 16: 441–461.

Klapper, J. & Rees, J. 2003. Reviewing the case for explicit grammar instruction in the university foreign language learning context. *Language Teaching Research* 7(3): 285–314.

Klein, D., Milner, B., Zatorre, R.J., Zhao, V. & Nikelski, J. 1999. Cerebral organization in bilinguals: A PET study of Chinese–English verb generation. *NeuroReport* 10: 2841–2846.

Klein, D., Milner, B., Zatorre, R.J., Meyer, E. & Evans, A.C. 1995. The neural substrates underlying word generation: A bilingual functional-imaging study. *Proceedings of the National Academy of Sciences* 92: 2899–2903.

Koda, K. 1989. Effects of L1 orthographic representation on L2 phonological coding strategies. *Journal of Psychological Research* 18: 201–222.

Koda, K. 2005. *Insights into Second Language reading: A cross-linguistic account*. Cambridge: CUP.

Krashen, S. 1981. *Second Language Acquisition and Second Language Learning*. Oxford: Pergamon Press.

Krashen, S. 1982. *Principles and Practice in Second Language Acquisition*. Oxford: Pergamon Press.

Krashen, S. 1985. *The Input Hypothesis*. London: Longman.

Kroll, J.F. & Stewart, E. 1994. Category influence in translation and picture naming: Evidence for asymmetric connections between bilingual memory representations. *Journal of Memory and Language* 33: 149–174.

Kuhl, P.K. & Miller, J.D. 1978. Speech perception in the chinchilla: Identifying functions for synthetic VOT stimuli. *Journal of the Acoustical Society of America* 63: 905–917.

Larsen-Freeman, D. 2000. *Techniques and Principles in Language Teaching*. 2nd edn. Oxford: OUP.

Lasky, R.E., Syrdal-Lasky, A. & Klein, R.E. 1975. VOT discriminations by four to six and a half month old infants from Spanish environments. *Journal of Experimental Child Psychology* 20: 215–225.

Lee Wing On. 1996. The cultural context for Chinese learners: Conceptions of learning in the Confucian tradition. In *The Chinese Learner: Cultural, psychological and contextual influences*, D.A. Watkins & J.B. Biggs (eds). Hong Kong: CERC & ACER.

Leker, R.R. & Biran, I. 1999. Unidirectional dyslexia in a polyglot. *Journal of Neurology, Neurosurgery and Psychiatry* 66: 517–519.

Lenneberg, E.H. 1967. *The Biological Foundations of Language*. New York NY: John Wiley.

Lesser, R. & Milroy, L. 1993. *Linguistics and Aphasia: Psycholinguistics and pragmatic aspects of intervention*. London: Longman.

Levinson, S.C. 2003. Language and mind: Let's get the issues straight. In *Language in Mind*, D. Gentner & S. Goldwin-Meadow (eds). Cambridge MA: The MIT Press.

Liberman, A.M., Cooper, F.S., Shankweiler, D.P. & Studdert-Kennedy, M. 1967. Perception of speech code. *Psychological Review* 74: 431–461.

Lightbown, P.M. & Spada, N. 2006. *How Languages are Learned*. Oxford: OUP.

Loewen, S. 2004. Uptake in incidental focus on form in meaning-focused ESL lessons. *Language Learning* 54(1): 153–188.

Logan, G.D. 1988. Towards an instance theory of automatisation. *Psychological Review* 95: 492–527.

Long, M.H. 1983a. Native speaker/non-native speaker conversation and the negotiation of comprehensible input. *Applied Linguistics* 4(2): 126–141.

Long, M.H. 1983b. Linguistic and conversational adjustments to non-native speakers. *Studies in Second Language Acquisition* 5(2): 177–193.

Long, M.H. 1985. A role for instruction in second language acquisition. In *Modelling and Assessing Second Language Acquisition*, K. Hyltenstam & M. Pienemann (eds), 115–141. Clevedon: Multingual Matters.

Long, M.H. 1991. Focus on form: A design feature in language teaching methodology. In *Foreign Language Research in Crosscultural Perspective*, K. de Bot, R. Ginsberg & C. Kramsch (eds), pp. 39–52. Amsterdam: John Benjamins.

Long, M.H. 1996. The role of the linguistic environment in second language acquisition. In *Handbook of Second Language Acquisition*, W. Ritchie & T.K. Bhatia (eds). San Diego CA: Academic Press.

Lyons, J. 1996. On competence and performance and related notions. In *Performance and Competence in Second Language Acquisition*, G. Brown, K. Malkj'ær & J. Williams (eds). Cambridge: CUP.

McCandliss, B.D., Cohen, L. & Dehaene, S. 2003. The visual word form area: Expertise for reading in the fusiform gyrus. *Trends in Cognitive Sciences* 7(7): 293–299.

McLaughlin, B. 1978. The monitor model: Some methodological considerations. *Language Learning* 28: 309–332.

McClelland, J.L. & Rumelhart, D.E. 1981. An interactive activation model of context effects in letter perception. Part 1. An account of the basic findings. *Psychological Review* 88: 375–407.

MacDonald, J. & McGurk, H. 1978. Visual influences on speech perception processes. *Perception & Psychophysics* 24: 253–257.

MacKay, D.G. 1978. Derivational rules and the internal lexicon. *Journal of Verbal Learning and Verbal Behaviour* 17: 61–71.

MacWhinney, B. 1987. The competition model. In *Mechanisms of Language Acquisition*, B. MacWhinney (ed.), 249–308. Hillsdale NJ: Lawrence Erlbaum.

MacWhinney, B. 2001. The competition model: The input, the context and the brain. In *Cognition and Second Language Instruction*, P. Robinson (ed.). Cambridge: CUP.

MacWhinney, B. 2002. Expanding the competition model. In *Bilingual Sentence Processing*, R.R. Heredia & J. Altarriba (eds). Amsterdam: Elsevier.

Martin, A. 2006. Shades of Déjerine – Forging a causal link between the visual word form area and reading. *Neuron* 50(2): 173–175.

Marton, F., Dall'Alba, G. & Tse, L.K. 1996. Memorizing and understanding: The keys to the paradox? In *The Chinese Learner: Cultural, psychological and contextual Influences*, D.A. Watkins & J.B. Biggs (eds). Hong Kong: CERC & ACER.

Meara, P. 1984. Word recognition in foreign languages. In *Reading for Professional Purposes: Studies and practices in native and foreign languages*, A.K. Pugh & J.M. Ulijn (eds), 97–105. London: Heineman Educational Books.

Meara, P. 1985. Hidden reading problems in ESL learners. *TESL Canada Journal* 3(1): 29–36.

Mervis, C. & Rosch, E. 1981. Categorization of natural objects. *Annual Review of Psychology* 32: 89–115.

Miller, G.A. 1956. The magical number seven plus or minus two: Some limits on our capacity for processing information. *Psychological Review* 63: 81–87.

Mitchell, R. & Martin, C. 1997. Rote learning, creativity and 'understanding' in classroom foreign language teaching. *Language Teaching Research* 1(1): 1–27.

Mitchell, R. & Myles, F. 1998. *Second Language Learning Theories*. Oxford: OUP.

Miyake, A. & Shah, P. (eds). 1999. *Models of Working Memory: Mechanisms of active maintenance and executive control*. New York NY: CUP.

Morris, C.D., Bransford, J.D. & Franks, J.J. 1977. Levels of processing versus transfer appropriate processing. *Journal of Verbal Learning and Verbal Behaviour* 16: I519–533.

Morton, J. 1969. Interaction of information in word recognition. *Psychological Review* 76: 165–178.

Morton, J. 1979. Word recognition. In *Psycholinguistics Series*. Vol. 2: *Structures and processes*, J. Morton & J.C. Marshall (eds), 259–268. London: Paul Elek.

Moyer, A. 2004. *Age, Accent and Experience in Second Language Acquisition: An integrated approach to critical period enquiry*. Clevedon: Multilingual Matters.

Nagy, W.E. & Anderson, R.C. 1984. How many words are there in printed school English? *Reading Research Quarterly* 19: 304–330.

Norris, D. 1994. A quantitative multiple-levels model of reading aloud. *Journal of Experimental Psychology: Human Perception and Performance* 20: 155–168.

Norris, J.M. & Ortega, L. 2000. Effectiveness of L2 instruction: A research synthesis and quantitative meta-analysis. *Language Learning* 50(3): 417–528.

Norton, E.S., Kovelman, I. & Petitto, L-A. 2007. Are there separate Neural systems for spelling? Insights into the role or rules and memory in spelling from Functional Magnetic resonance imaging. *Mind, Brain and Education*, 1, 1: 48–59.

Nunan, D. 1991. *Language Teaching Methodologies*. Englewood Cliffs NJ: Prentice-Hall.

O'Halloran, K. 2003. *Critical Discourse Analysis and Language Cognition*. Edinburgh: Edinburgh University Press.

O'Malley, M. & Chamot, A.U. 1990. *Learning Strategies in Second Language Acquisition*. Cambridge: CUP.

Ojeman, G.A. & Whitaker, H.A. 1978. The bilingual brain. *Archives of Neurology* 35: 409–412.

Oxford, R. 1990. *Language Learning Strategies: What every teacher should know*. New York NY: OUP.

Oxford, R. (ed.). 1996. *Language Learning Strategies around the World: Cross-cultural perspectives*. Honolulu HI: Second Language Teaching & Curriculum Center, University of Hawai'i at Manoa.

Oyama, S. 1976. A sensitive period for the acquisition of a nonnative phonological system. *Journal of Psycholinguistic Research* 5(3): 261–283.

Paivio, A. & Begg, I. 1981. *Psychology of Language*. Englewood Cliffs NJ: Prentice-Hall.

Palermo, D.S. & Jenkins, J.J. 1964. *Word Association Norms: Grade school through college*. Minneapolis MN: University of Minnesota Press.

Paradis, M. 1977. Bilingualism and aphasia. In *Studies in Neurolinguistics*, Vol. 3, H.A. Whitaker & H. Whitaker (eds), 65–121. New York NY: Academic Press.

Patterson, K. & Shewell, C. 1987. Speak and spell: Dissociations and word-class effects. In *The Cognitive Neuropsychology of Language*, M. Coltheart, G. Sartori & R. Job (eds), 273–294. Hillsdale NJ: Lawrence Erlbaum.

Peng, D.L., Ding, G.S., Perry, C., Xu, D., Jin, Z., Luo, Q., Zhang, L. & Deng, Y. 2004. fMRI evidence for the automatic phonological activation of briefly presented words. *Cognitive Brain Research* 20(2): 156–164.

Perret, E. 1974. The left frontal lobe of man and the suppression of habitual responses in verbal categorical behaviour. *Neuropsychologia* 12: 323–330.

Petruck, M.R.L. 1996. *Handbook of Pragmatics.* Amsterdam: John Benjamins.

Pica, T. 1994. Research on negotiation: What does it reveal about second language acquisition. *Language Learning* 44: 493–527.

Pinker, S. 1994. *The Language Instinct.* Harmondsworth: Allen Lane.

Pinker, S. 1994. *The Language Instinct: How the mind creates language.* New York NY: William Morrow.

Posner, M.I. & Raichle, M.E. 1994. *Images of Mind.* New York NY: Scientific American Library.

Prabhu, N.S. 1987. *Second Language Pedagogy.* Oxford: OUP.

Price, C.J., Green, D.W. & von Studnitz, R. 1999. A functional imaging study of translation and language switching. *Brain* 122: 2221–2235.

Pulvermüller, F. 1999. Words in the brain's mind. *Behavioral and Brain Sciences* 22: 253–279.

Randall, A.M. 1989. Recognising words in English and Arabic. PhD dissertation, University of London.

Randall, M. 1980. Word association behaviour in learners of English as a second language. *Polyglot* 2.

Randall, M. 2005. Orthographic knowledge and first language reading: Evidence from single word dictation from Chinese and Malaysian users of English as a foreign language. In *Second Language Writing Systems*, V. Cook & B. Bassetti (eds), 122–146. Clevedon: Multilingual Matters.

Randall, M. & Meara, P. 1988. How Arabs read Roman letters. *Reading in a Foreign Language* 4(2): 133–145.

Rapport, R.L., Tan, C.T. & Whitaker, H.A. 1983. Language function and dysfunction among Chinese and English-speaking polyglots: Cortical stimulation, Wada testing, and clinical studies. *Brain and Language* 18: 342–366.

Ribot, T. 1882. *The Diseases of Memory.* New York NY: Appleton.

Richards, J.C. & Rogers, T.S. *Approaches and Methods in Language Teaching.* Cambridge: CUP.

Ridgway, T. 1997. Thresholds of the background knowledge effect in foreign language reading. *Reading in a Foreign Language* 11(1): 151–168.

Ritchie, W.C. & Bhatia, T.K. (eds.) 1996. *Handbook of Second Language Acquisition.* San Diego: Academic Press.

Roach, P. 2000. *English Phonetics and Phonology (3rd Edn.).* Cambridge: Cambridge University Press.

Robinson, P. 1996. Learning simple and complex second language rules under implicit, incidental, rule-search and instructed conditions. In *Attention and Awareness in Second Language Learning*, R. Schmidt (ed.), 303–358. Honolulu HI: University of Hawaii Press.

Robinson, P. 2001a. Task complexity, cognitive resources, and syllabus design. In *Cognition and Second Language Instruction*, P. Robinson (ed.). Cambridge: CUP.

Robinson, P. (ed.). 2001b. *Cognition and Second Language Instruction.* Cambridge: CUP.

Rosch, E. & Mervis, C.B. 1975. Family resemblances: Studies in the internal structure of categories. *Cognitive Psychology* 7: 573–605.

Rosenman, M.A. & Sudweeks, F. 1995. Categorisation and prototypes in design. In *Perspectives on Cognitive Science: Theories, experiments and foundations*, P. Slezak, T. Caelli & R. Clarke (eds), 182–212. Norwood NJ: Ablex.

Rubin, G.S., Becker, C.A. & Freeman, R.H. 1979. Morphological structure and its effect on visual word recognition. *Journal of Verbal Learning and Behaviour* 18: 757–767.

Rumelhart, D.E. & McClelland. J.L. 1986. On learning the past tenses of English verbs. In *Parallel Distributed Processing*, Vol. 2, J.C. McClelland & D.E. Rumelhart (eds), 216–271. Cambridge MA: The MIT Press.

Sachs, J.S. 1967. Recognition memory for syntactic and semantic aspects of connected discourse. *Perception and Psychophysics* 2: 437–442.

Schmidt, R. 1990. The role of consciousness in second language learning. *Applied Linguistics* 11: 129–158.

Schmidt, R. & Froda, S. 1986. Developing basic conversational ability in a second language: A case-study of an adult learner. In *Talking to Learn*, R. Day (ed.). Rowley MA: Newbury House.

Scott, S., Rosen, S., Faulkner, A., Yi Yui Meng, Wise, R., Warren, J., Spitsyna, J. & Narain, C. 2003. Speech in the brain: Interactions with learning, faces and cultural differences. *Royal Society Summer Science Exhibition 2003*.

Seidenberg, M.S. & McClelland, J.L. 1989. A distributed, developmental model of word recognition and naming. *Psychological Review* 96(4): 523–568.

Seki, A., Koeda, T., Sugihara, S., Kamba, M., Hirata, Y., Ogawa, T. & Takeshita, K. 2001. A functional magnetic resonance imaging study during sentence reading in Japanese dyslexic children. *Brain and Development* 23(5): 312–316.

Shallice, T. & Warrington, E.K. 1970. Independent functioning of verbal memory stores: A neuro-psychological study. *Quarterly Journal of Experimental Psychology* 22: 261–273.

Shaywitz, S. & Shaywitz, B. 2005. Dyslexia (specific reading disability). *Biological Psychiatry* 57(11): 1301–1309.

Siok, W.T., Perfetti, C.A., Jin, Z. & Tan, L.H. 2004. Biological abnormality of impaired reading is constrained by culture. *Nature* 431: 71–76.

Skehan, P. 1996a. A framework for the implementation of task-based instruction. *Applied Linguistics* 17(1): 38–62.

Skehan, P. 1996b. Second language acquisition research and task-based learning. In *Challenge and Change in Language Teaching*, J. Willis & D. Willis (eds), 17–30. Oxford: Heineman.

Skehan, P. 1998. *A Cognitive Approach to Language Learning*. Oxford: OUP.

Skehan, P. 2003. Task based instruction. *Language Teaching* 36: 1–14.

Skinner, B.F. 1957. *Verbal Behavior*. New York NY: Appelton-Century-Crofts.

Slobin, D.I. 1971. *Psycholinguistics*. Glenville IL: Scott, Foresman.

Slobin, D.I. (ed.). 1985. *The Crosslinguistic Study of Language Acquisition*. Vol. 1: *The data*. Hillsdale NJ: Lawrence Erlbaum.

Smith, E.E., Jonides, J. & Koeppe, R.A. 1996. Dissociating verbal and spatial working memory using PET. *Cerebral Cortex* 6: 11–20.

Smith, F. 1978. *Reading*. Cambridge: CUP.

Snodgrass, J.G. & Jarvella, R.J. 1972. Some linguistic determinants of word classification times. *Psychonomic Science* 27: 220–222.

Spada, N. 1997. Form-focused instruction and second language research: A review of classroom and laboratory research. *Language Teaching* 29: 1–15.

Sperling, G. 1960. The information available in brief visual displays. *Psychological Monographs* 74: 1–29.

St. Heim, Opitz, B., Miller, K. & Friederici, A.D. 2003. Phonological processing during language production: fMRI evidence for a shared production-comprehension network. *Cognitive Brain Research Volume* 16(2): 285–296.

Strange, B.A., Fletcher, P.C., Henson, R.N.A., Friston, K.J. & Dolan, R.J. 1999. Segregating the functions of human hippocampus. *Neurobiology* 96(7): 4034–4039.

Street, B. 1984. *Literacy in Theory and Practice*. Cambridge: CUP.

Summerfield, Q. & Haggart, M. 1977. On the dissociation of spectral and temporal cues to the voicing distinction in initial stop consonants. *Journal of the Acoustical Society of America* 62: 436–445.

Swain, M. 1985. *Input in Second Language Acquisition*. New York NY: Newbury House.

Swain, M. 1998. Focus on form through conscious reflection. In *Focus on Form in Classroom Second Language Acquisition*, G. Doughty & J. Williamson (eds). Cambridge: CUP.

Swain, M. & Lapkin, S. 1995. Problems in output and the cognitive problems they generate: A step towards second language learning. *Applied Linguistics* 16: 370–391.

Taft, M. 1981. Prefix stripping revisited. *Journal of Verbal Learning and Verbal Behaviour* 20: 298–297.

Taft, M. & Foster, K.I. 1975. Lexical storage and retrieval of prefixed words. *Journal of Verbal Learning and Verbal Behaviour* 14: 638–647.

Tan, L.H., Liu, H.-L., Perfetti, C.A., Spinks, J.A., Fox, P.T. & Gao, J.-H. 2001. The neural system underlying Chinese logograph reading. *NeuroImage* 13(5): 836–846.

Vallar, G., Di Betta, A.-M. & Silveri, M.-C. 1997. The phonological short-term store-rehearsal system: Patterns of impairment and neural correlates. *Neuropsychologia* 35(6): 795–812.

Van Heuven, W.J.B. 2005. Bilingual interactive activation models of word recognition in a second language. In *Second Language Writing Systems*, V. Cook & B. Bassetti (eds). Clevedon: Multilingual Matters.

Van Patten, B. 1996. *Input Processing and Grammar Instruction*. New York NY: Ablex.

Vygotsky, L.S. 1978. *Mind in Society: The development of higher psychological processes*. Cambridge MA: Harvard University Press.

Walton, G.E., Bower, N.J.A. & Bower, T.G.R. 1992. Recognition of familiar faces by newborn children. *Infant Behavior and Development* 15: 265–269.

Wang, M. & Geva, E. 2003. Spelling performance of Chinese children using English as a second language: Lexical and visual-orthographic processes. *Applied Psycholinguistics* 24: 1–25.

Wang, M.J. 2001. The cultural characteristics of Chinese students: A study of basic attitudes and approaches to their English studies. *RELC Journal* 32(1): 16–33.

Ward, G. 2001. A critique of the working memory model. In *Working Memory in Perspective*, J. Andrade (ed.), 219–239. Hove: Psychology Press.

Warrington, E.K. & McCarthy, R. 1984. Category specific language impairments. *Brain* 107: 829–854.

Watkins, D.A. 1996. Learning theories and approaches to research: A cross-cultural perspective. In *The Chinese Learner: Cultural, psychological and contextual influences*, D.A. Watkins & J.B. Biggs (eds). Hong Kong: CERC & ACER.

Weekes, B.S., Davies, R.A. & Chen, M.-J. 2002. Picture-word interference effects on naming in Chinese. In *Cognitive Neuroscience Studies of the Chinese language*, H.S.R. Kao, C.K. Leong & D.-G. Gao (eds), 101–127. Hong Kong: Hong Kong University of Press.

Wen, G.Y. & Weekes, B. 2003. Dyslexia in Chinese: Clues from Cognitive Neuropsychology. *Annals of Dyslexia* 53: 255–279.

Werker, J.F. Gilbert, J.H. Humphrey, K. & Tees, R.C. 1981. Developmental aspects of cross-language speech perception. *Child Development* 52: 349–355.

Werker, J.F. & Tees, R.C. 1984. Cross-language speech perception: Evidence for perceptual reorganization during the first year of life. *Infant Behavior and Development*, 7: 49–63.

Whitaker, H.A. 1978. Bilingualism: A neurolinguistic perspective. In *Second Language Acquisition Research*, W.C. Ritchie (ed.). New York NY: Academic Press.

Widdowson, H.G. 1978a. *Teaching Language as Communication*. Oxford: OUP.

Widdowson, H.G. 1978b. *Learning Purpose and Language Use*. Oxford: OUP.

Wills, C. 1994. *The Runaway Brain: The evolution of human uniqueness*. London: HarperCollins.

Willis, J. 1996. *A Framework for Task-Based Learning*. London: Longman.

Willis, J. & Willis, D. (eds). 1996. *Challenge and Change in Language Teaching*. Oxford: Heineman.

Wilkins, D.A. 1976. *Notional Syllabuses: A taxonomy and its relevance to foreign language curriculum development*. London: OUP.

Wisniewski, E.J., Lamb, C.A. & Middleton, E.L. 2003. On the conceptual basis of count and mass noun distinction. *Language and Cognitive Processes* 18(5/6): 583–624.

Wood, N.L. & Cowan, N. 1995. The cocktail party phenomenon revisited: Attention and memory in the classic selective listening procedure of Cherry (1953). *Journal of Experimental Psychology: General* 124: 243–262.

Wydell, T.N. & Butterworth, B. 1999. A case study of an English–Japanese bilingual with monolingual dyslexia. *Cognition* 70(3): 273–305.

Wydell, T.N. & Kondo, T. 2003. Phonological deficit and the reliance on orthographic approximation for reading: A follow–up study on an English–Japanese bilingual with monolingual dyslexia. *Journal of Research in Reading* 26(1): 33–48.

Xue, G., Dong, O., Jin, Z. & Chen, C. 2004. Mapping of verbal working memory in nonfluent Chinese–English bilinguals with functional MRI. *NeuroImage* 22(1): 1–10.

Yoon, H.W., Cho, K.-D., Chung, J.-Y. & Park, H.W. 2005. Neural mechanisms of Korean word reading: A functional magnetic resonance imaging study. *Neuroscience Letters* 373(3): 206–211.Abu-Rabia, S. & Awwad, J.S. 2004. Morphological structures in visual word recognition: The case of Arabic. *Journal of Research in Reading* 27(3): 321–336.

Index

In the series *Language Learning & Language Teaching* the following titles have been published thus far or are scheduled for publication: